Slightly
Bad Girls
of the # Bible

LIZ CURTIS HIGGS

Slightly Bad Girls of the Bible

Flawed Women Loved by a Flawless God

WATERBROOK
PRESS

SLIGHTLY BAD GIRLS OF THE BIBLE
PUBLISHED BY WATERBROOK PRESS
12265 Oracle Boulevard, Suite 200
Colorado Springs, Colorado 80921
A division of Random House Inc.

The contemporary story in each chapter is fiction. The characters and events are fictional and are not intended to parallel exactly the biblical story.

ISBN 978-1-4000-7212-5

Library of Congress Cataloging-in-Publication Data
Higgs, Liz Curtis.
  Slightly bad girls of the Bible : flawed women loved by a flawless God / Liz Curtis Higgs.
     p. cm.
  Includes bibliographical references.
  ISBN 978-1-4000-7212-5
  1. Bible. O.T.—Biography 2. Women in the Bible—Biography. 3. Christian women—Religious life. I. Title.
  BS575.H563 2007
  221.9'22082—dc22
                                  2007025161

Printed in the United States of America
2007—First Edition

10 9 8 7 6 5 4 3 2 1

To Laura Barker,

My talented editor at WaterBrook Press
and one of the genuine Good Girls.
Your patience, kindness, and support
kept me going on many a late night
in my writing study.

Bless you for nudging without prodding,
suggesting without insisting,
and caring as much about
the finished pages as I do.
(With special emphasis on
the word *finished*.)

We did it, sis!
Thanks to you.

Contents

Controlling Interest

Let but the puppets move,
I've my desire.
CHARLES CHURCHILL

Donna gazed at the stack of mail in her husband's gloved hands as he stomped the wet snow from his shoes. "Anything interesting?" she asked, keeping her tone light.

He handed over the day's bounty from their mailbox. "See for yourself."

Donna quickly sorted through the belated Christmas cards, made thicker by family brag letters. Next year *she* might have something to crow about. If all went well, their son, Max, would be a freshman at the finest Christian college in the country. That is, *if...*

With a slight gasp she tossed the rest of the mail on the kitchen table, having found the one piece that mattered: a long, white envelope with the familiar blue logo in the corner. *Yes.* The school had promised a decision by December 31, still two days away. Surely a good sign.

She hefted the envelope in her hands, trying to judge how many pieces of paper it might contain. The letter had some weight to it. More than a kindly worded rejection, then.

Donna smiled, savoring the moment. Obviously her prayers had been answered. And months of hard work had paid off—visiting college campuses, completing online applications, gathering letters of reference, proofreading essays, forwarding transcripts. She'd drafted the cover letter herself. Made sure everything looked presentable. Max hadn't seemed terribly interested, and she had a flair for such things, didn't she?

Her husband looked over her shoulder. "So we've heard from The College of Your Choice."

Donna shrugged, pretending his gentle teasing didn't bother her. Wasn't she allowed to have an opinion about where their son spent the next four years of his life? True, he'd been accepted at other schools, but *this* was the one that counted. The admission policy was far more stringent and the list of alumni far more impressive.

And the campus…oh, the *campus*! Handsome as any Ivy League school with its stately brick buildings and manicured lawns. Last October she'd strolled along the neatly paved walkways, imagining *she* was the incoming freshman: attending classes in well-appointed lecture halls, learning from the brightest and the best thinkers, meeting students from all over the world.

On the long drive home, Max had chided her, "Why don't *you* apply, Mom?" She'd heard the hint of frustration in his voice. Had she pushed too hard, praised the school too enthusiastically? Meeting one-on-one with the admissions counselor might have been overdoing it. But the young woman had offered to answer prospective students' questions. Couldn't a mother ask them just as well while her son perused the campus bookstore?

Her husband disturbed her reverie as he slipped his damp coat over the back of a kitchen chair. "You *are* going to wait until Max gets home to open that." His firm words chafed against her conscience.

"Of course." Donna propped the envelope against the napkin holder, where it couldn't be missed. "I'm not in the habit of reading other people's mail."

When Max finally strolled in an hour later, she grabbed the envelope from the table and waved it at him. "Look what's here."

Her son opened it without comment, then sighed and handed it over. "Here you go, Mom."

Donna scanned the first three words—*Congratulations! Your application*—before letting out a huge whoop. "Max, I'm so proud of you!" Noticing her husband and daughter on the sidelines, she quickly added, "We all are."

He bobbed his head, then wandered off in the direction of his computer. Max's lack of enthusiasm didn't concern her. That was just his way. He'd warm up to the idea soon enough.

But he didn't. All through January he waffled between one school and another, finding excuses not to make a decision. At least that's how it seemed to Donna, who'd sent enrollment deposits to four schools, asking them to hold his place. "Eight hundred dollars' worth of deposits," she reminded Max whenever the subject came up.

Donna made sure it came up daily.

By February she'd run out of patience. "We'll start from the bottom. Which school *don't* you want to attend?" With some difficulty he picked one—the same one she would have chosen as least likely. "Good," she said, giving his shoulder a squeeze. "That wasn't so hard, was it? Next week we'll eliminate another one."

She helped him make that decision too, though she could tell it was harder. Why Max didn't just make a final choice, the *best* choice, was a mystery to her.

When they finally narrowed it down to two schools—her favorite one or her husband's alma mater—she breathed a sigh of relief. A nationally known, prestigious institution versus a low-profile liberal arts college close to home. No contest, really.

Max had promised to give them his decision after dinner. Donna cooked his favorite pasta dish and watched him devour it, proud of herself for not bringing up the subject of college all through the meal. As she served her son a slice of chocolate cake, she leaned down to smile at him. "You've made your decision, haven't you?"

Max met her gaze for the first time that evening. "Yes, I have, Mom."

When he blurted out the name of the school—the *wrong* school—Donna fell back a step, as if she'd been slapped. "You can't be serious."

"I *am* serious," Max assured her, exchanging glances with his dad. "They offered me a bigger scholarship—"

"Never mind the *money*." A spark of anger heated her face, sharpened her words. "You're throwing away your life, Max." *Doesn't he see? Doesn't he understand?* "If my parents had given me that kind of chance..." She choked on the words, tears tightening her throat. "If they'd been willing to pay for my education, to send me anywhere I wanted to go, that's the *last* college I would have picked."

"But, Mom—"

"I don't *care* if your father graduated from there." Donna was almost shouting now, ignoring her son's gentle protests, her daughter's shocked expression, and the hurt in her husband's eyes. "You've chosen a second-rate college in a backwater town in a state I'm ashamed to call home."

"*Donna!*"

Her husband's low voice silenced her, yet the storm inside continued to rage, even as shame and guilt began their dual attack...

A piece of work, Donna. Mistaking motherhood for puppetry, she was determined to pull everyone's strings.

Some of us have a friend like Donna.

Some of us work with a Donna.

And some of us (let's be honest) *are* Donnas. Insisting on having our way. Thinking we know what's best. Controlling whom and what we can, whenever we can. Pretending not to notice if we squash a few toes in the process.

We don't want to rule the universe—just our corner of the world. We don't mind slight delays, as long as a positive outcome is guaranteed. When God pours his blessings on us, we're truly grateful and more than willing to give him all the glory. But when he tells us "no" or "wait" or "soon but not yet," we start thinking of ways to expedite the process.

Really, Lord. I can help.

If I didn't know better, I'd think an impatient Bad Girl wrote the phrase "God helps those who help themselves." Instead, it's a line from one of Aesop's fables: "The gods help them that help themselves."[1] Maybe those man-made Greek gods required human effort, but *the* God, the Lord Almighty, doesn't need our help to accomplish his divine plan.

My definition of a Slightly Bad Girl is simply this: a woman unwilling to fully submit to God. We love him, serve him, and worship him, yet we find it difficult to trust him completely, to accept his plan for our lives, to rest in his sovereignty.

And so we quietly (or not so quietly) try to take back the reins again and again. *Let me handle things, Lord. I know what's best.* We pray, then move forward without waiting for an answer. We do all the right, Good Girl things and hope no one notices our desperate need to control every aspect of our lives. We read "She does not trust in the LORD, she does not draw near to her God"[2] and shudder at the thought, never seeing ourselves in those words.

If you've read the other books in my Bad Girls of the Bible series, you know how willing I am to open the pages of my diary, if only to encourage my sisters that God's forgiveness covers the whole of our lives, not only the years before we knew him.

And so, Donna's story is my story, and recent history at that.

What kind of Christian mother manipulates her child, belittles her husband, and throws temper tantrums at the dinner table?

This kind, I'm afraid.

As the apostle Paul said, "I know that nothing good lives in me, that is, in my sinful nature. For I have the desire to do what is good, but I cannot carry it out."[3] Amen, brother, and don't I know it.

When I finally calmed down, asked everyone's forgiveness—individually and collectively—confessed I truly *do* love my adopted state of Kentucky, and assured my dear son he'd chosen well, peace was restored in the Higgs household.

But I don't fool myself. Damage was done, and wounds were inflicted, requiring time to repair and heal.

Even two years later, when I sent these pages to my sophomore son for him to critique, he e-mailed me and admitted, "This brought tears to my eyes, Mother. I'm sorry I disappointed you so much."

Groan.

I wrote back at once. "The problem was all mine, sweet boy. You are exactly where God wanted you to be, which is wonderful. I love having you so close to home..."

That's the trouble with sin: its influence lingers. My ten-minute tirade still has the power to hurt my precious son, years after the fact. No matter what I say or do now, he will remember what I said and did then. God forgives our sins completely, yet the consequences remain. Spoken words can never be unspoken. Even so, my son closed his comments with "Please don't beat yourself up, Mom. You don't deserve it."

What I truly don't deserve is a son who extends forgiveness so generously.

Thank goodness the Lord knows what to do with Bad Girls (and Bad Boys, for that matter). He rescues us from ourselves. And showers us with grace. "He who did not spare his own Son, but gave him up for us all—how will he not also, along with him, graciously give us all things?"[4]

From the first page of his Word to the last, God reveals our badness and his goodness. Our neediness and his provision. Our brokenness and his healing touch. That's the beauty of the Bible: "It shows us life and people as they really are, not as we wish them to be."[5] It shows us the truth about God and about ourselves. I, for one, am grateful to learn our biblical ancestors were flawed. Knowing God loved this imperfect patriarchal family, we can be sure there's hope for us all.

One reader shared with me, "I'm light-years away from the Good Girls of the Bible." Here's encouraging news on that score: even the Good Girls of the Bible had their Bad Girl moments. The five females we'll be studying here are mostly good, yet slightly bad. Women of faith, but not without flaws. And all of them are seriously strong willed.

Sarah, our first Slightly Bad Girl, is touted in the New Testament as an example for us all: "For this is the way the holy women of the past who put their hope in God used to make themselves beautiful. They were submissive to their own husbands, like Sarah, who obeyed Abraham and called him her master."[6]

She did indeed call her husband lord. But, honey, that's not all she said. Wait until you hear the strident words that came out of Sarah's mouth! Even so, God blessed her, entrusted her with a son, and loved her. So did Abraham.

I'm breathing easier already. You too?

The other Slightly Bad Girls also may surprise you. Rebekah and Rachel: surely *they* were good. Well, like Sarah, they were beautiful. They were loved. And (oops) they were pushy, manipulative, willful, scheming…oh my. And while the stories of Hagar and Leah may be less familiar, they have much to teach us about the kindness and mercy God extends to women forced into bad situations. As a group, these women "grace the pages of Genesis with their laughter, their sorrows, their strength, and their power."[7] We'll also consider the men in their lives and discover they made a few Bad Boy bloopers over the years.

Each chapter begins with our Slightly Bad Girl's fictional modern counterpart to help us avoid thinking, "Things were different then." *Au contraire.* Fashions, food, and furnishings may alter over the centuries, but human nature hasn't changed since the days of our first Bad Girl, Eve. Though historically these women spanned three generations and more than two hundred years, I've chosen to place each opening scene in the present day so we can more easily relate to their stories.

Prepare to have four thousand years swept away as Sarah, Hagar, Rebekah, Leah, and Rachel walk right into your living room. So glad you're on hand to greet them, sis.

P.S. Wherever you went to college—or didn't go to college—is fine with me. Really.

A Matter of Time

I'm extraordinarily patient,
provided I get my own way in the end.
Margaret Thatcher

Two minutes? Sandi glanced at her watch, then stifled a groan. *More like ten, Alan.*

She paced outside her husband's private office, barely noticing the elegant Oriental rug beneath her feet: a gift from one of his business associates in Istanbul, woven in midnight blue and dusky rose, the colors surprisingly vibrant. Alan's interior designer dated the classic Kerman rug as late nineteenth century.

And here's another antique. Pausing at the foyer mirror, Sandi lifted a sweep of ash blond hair from her forehead, relieved not to notice any telltale silver strands, yet dismayed by the fine lines near her eyes. Alan had already crossed the half-century mark. But on a sunlit Maryland morning, he fearlessly greeted the day, sans wrinkles, while she, five years younger, hid beneath a wide-brimmed hat. Sandi took a step back, assessing her figure as well.

"Admiring the view?" Alan teased, standing in his office doorway. "I believe that's my job." He crossed the vacant foyer to stand behind her at the mirror, slipped his arms around her waist, and drew her near. When he pressed a warm kiss against the back of her neck, she felt a frisson of pleasure and watched herself blush.

Twenty-five years of marriage, and he still treated her like a princess.

She sighed, no longer irritated that he'd kept her waiting. From Alan's viewpoint, she had nothing but time. Time to shop for his designer clothes. Time to organize elaborate dinner parties. Time to travel the world at a moment's notice.

To be fair, she *did* have time; what she didn't have was children.

"You look wonderful in royal blue," Alan said, his gaze meeting hers in the mirrored glass. "Was that one of the colors our photographer suggested?"

"No, Pavla chose it."

"Ah."

Sandi heard his even tone, sensed his unspoken words. Alan thought she was too dependent on Pavla, the young housekeeper who made their lives run smoothly.

He turned Sandi around to face him, then gently kissed her. "What you need is an hour with a photographer who fawns over your beautiful self." When she protested, his features darkened into an exaggerated scowl. "None of this 'considering my age' business. The moment we step into his studio, Yafeu will insist on adding you to his roster of models."

"*Senior* models perhaps," Sandi murmured, though she held his compliments close to her heart. Few husbands were as supportive as Alan Cannon.

That evening the mingled scents of garlic and onion greeted them at the door. "Dinner at seven," Sandi reminded her husband as he headed toward his office in the back of the house. She aimed toward the kitchen, where Cossack Chicken was on the menu.

She found Pavla chopping fresh mushrooms, hands and knife moving across the cutting board with effortless precision. In a neat line along the countertop stood the other ingredients to be added: grated swiss, crumbled feta, sour cream, and nutmeg. Pavla looked up, touching the back of her hand to the mass of hair gathered into a knot on her crown. "Your photos went well, yes?"

Sandi merely shrugged. Yafeu had indeed showered her with praise. Hair, features, wardrobe, posture—his dark Egyptian eyes missed nothing. But since the appointment book noted "Family Portrait," Yafeu had asked not once but three times, "Are there no children? No grandchildren?"

"No," Alan had repeatedly answered for both of them, the resignation in his voice unmistakable. One son: that was all he prayed for, all he longed for. For her part, Sandi had felt ready to scream by session's end. Yafeu could not know the pain his innocent words inflicted. The photographer had sent them out the door with a gratis collection of sterling silver picture frames, yet his words lingered, taunting her. *No children?*

"You are tired," Pavla said simply as she added the chopped mushrooms to a saucepan. "Maybe lie down before dinner?"

"I *am* exhausted," Sandi agreed. Of late she wasn't sleeping well and had trouble staying focused. Most days her nerves were on edge, and she often snapped at Alan for no reason. At last week's visit to her ob-gyn, Sandi had recited a litany of her symptoms as Dr. Goodman nodded, then delivered a single-word diagnosis: "Perimenopausal."

No need to spell it out. At forty-six she understood too well.

Out of habit Sandi reviewed Pavla's dinner preparations once more, then retreated to the cool darkness of the master bedroom. Her housekeeper was right: a short nap would improve her perspective. After slipping off her blue dress, she snuggled under the goose-down duvet and closed her eyes, waiting for the hypnotic pull of sleep. "Bless you, Pavla," she whispered, sinking deeper into the pillow.

When Pavla Teslenko had first arrived from Ukraine seeking a new life, Alan and Sandi had ushered the girl into their home, certain they would require an au pair. As the years passed and no children came, Pavla made herself useful cleaning the house, doing laundry, running errands. Gradually she'd taken over Sandi's kitchen, specializing in Alan's favorite potato pancakes—*deruny,* she called them—and a liver pâté their dinner guests adored.

Under their guidance, the frightened, awkward teenager had grown into a self-assured and competent young woman, whose raven hair framed a round, pleasing face. Fluent in English, Pavla had become a naturalized citizen last spring, yet remained loyal to the Cannons.

More than one friend had cautioned Sandi about harboring a younger woman under the same roof as a wealthy husband. "Pavla's half your age," Lynn from their couples' class had reminded her last Sunday. "I know she's your right hand—"

"And my left as well," Sandi had told her friend, bringing the discussion to an abrupt end. She wasn't about to send away a valuable housekeeper to appease Lynn or anyone else.

Too agitated to sleep now, Sandi rolled over with a groan and squinted at the alarm clock. Did she need bifocals too?

A firm knock at the door, then Alan entered their bedroom. "Pavla said I might find you resting." He eased onto their bed and reached down to brush the hair from her eyes. "I'm sorry you've had a hard day."

She looked away, his tender expression more than she could bear. "It's worse than that."

A long silence. "Tell me again what Dr. Goodman said last week."

"He told me that…a healthy pregnancy is…unlikely." Her throat tightened. "We've done everything right, Alan. Why can't I…"

Alan bent over her and kissed each cheek. "God alone knows," he said softly, meaning to comfort her.

Sandi would never confess such a thing to her saintly husband, but she wasn't convinced God cared enough to intervene. He'd created the world and all it contained. Could he not bless her womb with one healthy son? Was it too much to ask? She and Alan had endured years of fertility tests and medical procedures, each failure crushing their hopes yet again.

Dr. Goodman had ruled out in vitro fertilization. And adoption was out of the question since Alan insisted their child be biologically his. "Not because adoption isn't a wonderful thing," he assured her each time she raised the possibility. "But God has assured me that if I'll trust him, he'll give us a son of our own someday. I know that's what you want too."

Sandi just wanted a child in her arms. *Soon. Tomorrow. Now.*

When Alan stood, he pulled her up with him. "Come to dinner, sweetheart. There's no heartache Pavla can't mend with her cooking."

Dear, thoughtful Alan. The man was determined to make her happy.

Minutes later, freshly dressed and perfumed, Sandi joined her husband in their oversize dining room, designed with entertaining in mind. They sat at one end of the long table, a spray of red gladioli creating a more intimate space. Pavla served the meal as usual, placing each course before them with quiet assurance.

Sandi watched her closely, noticing as if for the first time how mature

Pavla had become. A healthy, twenty-something woman. Full of energy, brimming with life. The perfect age for conceiving a child, for giving birth...

Sandi's eyes widened. *There's no heartache Pavla can't mend.*

Alan's words, but with a very different meaning.

Pavla. Bearing my husband's child. For me.

Sandi blanched at the outrageous notion. Had anyone she'd ever known done such a thing? Yet if the law allowed surrogate motherhood and if both parties were willing, might it not be the very best solution?

Distracted by her thoughts, she let Alan carry their dinner conversation until Pavla arrived with dessert...

Sarai: Princess Bride

A lovely name, Sarah. All soft consonants and airy vowels. Not so much spoken as released, like a sigh. Among popular biblical names, *Sarah* reigns and rightly so: her name means "princess."[1]

You'll find her mentioned by name in Scripture more than any other woman—an impressive fifty-three times in the NIV translation, beginning here:

> The name of Abram's wife was Sarai... *Genesis 11:29*

No, not a typo; for most of her life she was known as "Sarai." Scholars say, even with the *i*, the meaning of her name is "princess," but one source offers an intriguing alternative definition for *Sarai:* "argumentative."[2] Keep that feisty notion in mind as our story unfolds. *Sarai* was also a popular name among devotees of Ningal, consort of the moon god, worshiped in her native Assyria.[3] No wonder the Lord was eager to change the spelling of *Sarai* to *Sarah*!

Ah, but we're getting ahead of ourselves. We can assume that, with such a royal name, Sarai was born at the top of the social ladder and "lived a privileged life in one of the ancient world's great cities."[4] That is to say, Ur.

Reminds me of that sound people make when they're stalling for time. "Where's home?"

"Uh...er..."

However plain the name, Ur in its day was a commercial and cultural hub, a gathering place for philosophers and astronomers.[5] Thanks to the nightly news, we can point to the region on a world map, between the head of the Persian Gulf and Baghdad.

That's right: southeastern Iraq.

Twelve thousand people crowded the streets of Ur when the place was really hopping, around 2100 BC.[6] Archaeologists have unearthed a treasure trove of objects where Ur once stood: gold, silver, precious stones, musical instruments, weapons, even game boards.[7] (I haven't a Clue whether they played Monopoly, Scrabble, Candy Land...oh, Sorry!)

When my husband read this part of the manuscript, he piped up, "The Royal Game of Ur." *The what?* Turns out, it's a wooden board game still on the market, a replica of the ancient gaming board found in the Royal Cemetery of Ur by Sir Leonard Woolley in the 1920s.[8]

Just think: Abram and Sarai might have been gamers!

But they weren't playing games when it came to marriage. Their 'til-death-do-us-part relationship lasted a *century* or more, depending on Sarai's age the day they wed. Though the ancients said she was a beauty—"All the maidens and all the brides that go beneath the wedding canopy are not more fair than she"[9]—a dark cloud shadowed Sarai's tent.

Now Sarai was barren; she had no children. *Genesis 11:30*

Oh dear. Whether phrased as a singular "child" (NASB) or plural "children," the sad truth is made doubly clear in one stark verse. By describing Sarai as barren *and* without children, Scripture "emphasizes the seriousness of her plight by the repetition."[10]

Listen, we got it the first time. We're already grieving for this beautiful but infertile woman, imagining the hope that blossomed in her heart each month, only to be crushed by despair when she found a spot of blood on her tunic. *Not this month. Not any month.*

Four thousand years ago barrenness was "the ultimate disgrace, understood as a sign of divine disfavor."[11] A woman who couldn't conceive would have been considered a Bad Girl indeed. Furthermore, a barren woman "suffered not only lack of esteem, but also threat of divorce."[12] Talk about adding insult to injury: she was ridiculed by others, believed to be shunned by God, *and* considered disposable by her husband.

Thank goodness we no longer use the word *barren* to describe a woman unable to bear children. *Sterile* or *infertile* sounds more clinical and less judgmental, though for a woman who longs to give birth, the unfortunate outcome is the same: an empty womb.

Some of us understand Sarai's heartache at a deeply personal level. Is that you, dear sister? Then a word of comfort before we go any further: you are safe here. I'll not prod at your pain. And you can be very sure it wasn't Sarai's inability to conceive that made her a Slightly Bad Girl. Not for one minute. In fact, her childless state made room for a miracle. God was not displeased with her; he intended to be glorified in her. Think of that! Barrenness became "the arena of God's life-giving action."[13]

Though Ur is where Sarai's story began, that's not where it ended. This family was on the move.

> Terah took his son Abram, his grandson Lot son of Haran, and his
> daughter-in-law Sarai, the wife of his son Abram, and together they
> set out from Ur of the Chaldeans to go to Canaan. *Genesis 11:31*

The centuries have reduced prosperous Ur to ruins, with one prominent object left standing: a "pyramid-like brick tower, or ziggurat, built in tribute to Sin, the moon god."[14] Naturally, Abram and Sarai had to turn their backs on Sin to follow God (sorry, couldn't resist), and so this determined couple directed their camels northward, skirting the vast Arabian Desert.

Sarai exchanged "certainty for uncertainty, possession for chance, acquaintances for strangers...the amenities of the city for the hardships of the desert."[15] She displayed strength, bravery, and a willingness to take risks. I like her already.

But when they came to Haran, they settled there. *Genesis 11:31*

Not for long. Though some family members remained in Haran, Abram and Sarai knew their journey had only begun.

> The LORD had said to Abram, "Leave your country, your people and your father's household and go to the land I will show you."
> *Genesis 12:1*

No question, God was asking a great deal of Abram, including "giving up his inheritance and his right to family property."[16] You and I know courageous friends who've left behind loved ones and all their earthly possessions, headed for a distant mission field. I stand in awe of such commitment.

But God expected even more of Abram and Sarai. The Land I Will Show You doesn't appear on any map. God didn't explain the location of this unnamed land or how many years he intended Abram and company to stay there. God just said, "Go and I will show you." Period. As callings go, this one was "dangerously open-ended."[17]

I travel easier with a return ticket in my purse, don't you?

That's precisely why Abram and Sarai are celebrated for their faith: *they went.* And put their trust in the Lord—in Yahweh—a very different deity than the gods of Ur, tied to their ziggurats and statues. "Yahweh stands alone."[18] And moves around. And bids his people follow.

Two thousand years later God's Son offered the same imperative: "Whoever serves me must follow me."[19] He neither drags us nor pushes us. Rather, the Lord Jesus walks ahead of us, planting footsteps in the sand so we'll never lose sight of him. All of history affirms the wisdom of following God; Abram and Sarai were our pioneers. We'll discover their imperfections soon enough. When we do, keep in mind the courage required to take that first step.

An Iron Will

Though the Lord spoke only to Abram, I feel certain the man shared every word with his wife. Who could keep quiet about astounding promises like these?

"I will make you into a great nation and I will bless you; I will make your name great, and you will be a blessing." *Genesis 12:2*

If Sarai was present, you know she raised her hand on that first one. "A great nation? From a barren wife? Never happen." We're quick to see our limitations, yet God even more swiftly offers guarantees. Look at all these "I wills"!

"I will bless those who bless you, and whoever curses you I will curse;…" *Genesis 12:3*

Tuck that in your memory bank for a certain scene not far down the pike when a whole household suffered under a curse because of this man. Finally God stated the most important point again.

"…and all peoples on earth will be blessed through you." *Genesis 12:3*

Abram and Sarai couldn't have guessed what that would look like down the ages. Paul called it "the gospel in advance,"[20] preparing the way for the good news of God's grace. "It was all laid out beforehand in Scripture that God would set things right with non-Jews by faith. Scripture anticipated this in the promise to Abraham: 'All nations will be blessed in you.' "[21]

That blessing would come through Abram, yes, and also through the womb of a woman. Sarai was part of God's plan for Abram from the beginning, though she didn't know it yet—a detail that will soon become a major sticking point in our story. For the moment, "Sarai had nothing but Abram's word on which to base the most radical move of her life."[22]

Abram was seventy-five years old when he set out from Haran.
Genesis 12:4

Back then, seventy-five was the new forty, since the life span of a patriarch was nearly double our own.[23] Abram had another century ahead of him, and Sarai, ten years his junior, still had plenty of get-up-and-go. Good thing, since she got up and went.

He took his wife Sarai… *Genesis 12:5*

No protest, no complaining, no demands—at least not recorded in Scripture. So far Sarai gets a gold star for accepting God's call on her husband's life. If you've followed a spouse to a foreign mission field or a new job far from home, you, too, deserve an attagirl for your willingness to follow God *and* your mate.

We can picture these ancient travelers "in heavy leather sandals and loose woolen robes dyed in brilliant combinations of yellow, red, and blue"[24] as they made their way south. Unlike Lot's wife in a later scene,[25] Sarai apparently didn't look back, pining for the life and luxury she once knew. She pressed on, trusting her husband and the God who'd called them to a nomadic life.

Let's face it: Abram "needed a plucky wife, and he got one."[26]

> …and they set out for the land of Canaan, and they arrived there.
> *Genesis 12:5*

The weather in this part of the world is all about extremes, with torrential downpours quickly followed by bright blue skies. The landscape is varied as well: hills and deep valleys, fertile plains and stretches of wilderness.[27]

Awandering Abram and Sarai went, past "the great tree of Moreh at Shechem,"[28] where the Lord appeared to Abram and promised the land to his offspring. No real estate for Abe, mind you, but at least the grandkids would have property to call their own. Marking the spot, Abram built an altar, then moved on to the hills east of Bethel, where he built another altar—"the first in the Holy Land"[29]—and "called on the name of the LORD."[30]

Unfortunately, the couple's joy in the land of promise was short lived. The ground beneath their feet soon became as barren as…well, you know.

> Now there was a famine in the land, and Abram went down to Egypt
> to live there for a while because the famine was severe. *Genesis 12:10*

Famine plays a starring role in the Bible. Of some one hundred references, this is the first. According to geologists and archaeologists, during Abram's lifetime a "massive three-hundred-year drought"[31] ravaged the Canaanite countryside. No rain, no crops, no food.

Had I been Sarai, I'd have been seriously whining by this point. "Are you sure God wanted us in Canaan? Maybe he meant Canada. I told you we should have stopped and asked for directions…"

Desperate and hungry, Abram made tracks for the fertile land of the Pharaohs. We have no record that he checked with God or prayed for help when he headed west with his famished bride. Sister, you *know* trouble was on the horizon.

> As he was about to enter Egypt, he said to his wife Sarai, "I know
> what a beautiful woman you are." *Genesis 12:11*

The Hebrew makes it clear she was "a fair woman to look upon" (KJV) and "beautiful in appearance" (NRSV). Even the Dead Sea Scrolls include a flattering description of Sarai: "how fine is the hair of her head, how pleasing her nose and all the radiance of her face."[32]

Wait. Her *nose* was pleasing?

Historians say Cleopatra sported a distinctively large nose; maybe Egyptians fancied a prominent schnoz. Whatever Sarai's features, "her dignity, her bearing, her countenance"[33] all added up to an attractive female certain to catch Pharaoh's eye. And that was the problem.

> "When the Egyptians see you, they will say, 'This is his wife.' Then
> they will kill me but will let you live." *Genesis 12:12*

In this culture "adultery was considered a very grievous offense,"[34] but there was no law against Pharaoh killing a man. Apparently, with the husband conveniently dispatched, his widow became fair game for this decadent ruler, who possessed "one of the largest harems in all the world."[35]

Easy to forgive Abram for panicking. Not so easy to forgive his shameless request.

> "Say you are my sister…" *Genesis 12:13*

Adding "I pray thee" (KJV) or "please" (NASB) didn't improve things. He was still asking his wife to lie. Okay, *half* lie. Since Sarai was his father's daughter by a different mother, she was his half sister.[36] But it still seems like the coward's way out. More to the point, we have no record of God instructing Abram to head for Egypt. Looks like Abram acted on his own.

"...so that I will be treated well for your sake..." *Genesis 12:13*

"Because of their interest in you" (NLT), Abram told Sarai, "it may go well with me" (NASB). Humph. It would have been nicer if he'd said, "it may go well with *us*."

"...and my life will be spared because of you." *Genesis 12:13*

What about *her* life?

I realize Abram was Papa Patriarch, but I can't let his shoddy behavior slip by without comment. What kind of husband subjects his wife to moral and physical danger? "Faced with the threat of death, he surrenders what he ought not surrender."[37] Boy howdy.

Some commentators chalk up Abram's actions to "unbelief and distrust,"[38] seeing him as "an anxious man, a man of unfaith,"[39] whose "prime fault and folly...consisted in not waiting for the divine direction."[40] Others defend him, remarking that he hadn't traveled much and lived in "a rough and perilous time."[41] Especially perilous for Sarai, I'd say.

When a scene like this unfolds, one does begin to wonder: Did Sarai's barrenness make her less valuable to him? Or was her love for Abram so powerful her husband knew she would do anything to spare his life?

Whatever the case, nascent Israel was "in danger of losing its ancestress."[42]

Harem Scare 'Em

When Abram came to Egypt, the Egyptians saw that she was a very beautiful woman. *Genesis 12:14*

Just as Abram feared, "everyone spoke of her beauty" (NLT). All well and good to have a trophy wife—until someone wants your prize for his display case.

Back in 1963 Jimmy Soul crooned, "If you wanna be happy for the rest of your life, never make a pretty woman your wife."[43] Bet Abram was whistling that one under his breath as they neared the palace. In Scripture the mention of a woman's beauty often portends disaster, since "beauty sets up the beautiful to be desired and taken."[44] Ask Bathsheba or Dinah or Tamar, the sister of Absalom, how beauty can lead to tragedy.

Please talk to us, Sarai. Were you frightened when the Egyptians "took one look" and declared you "stunningly beautiful" (MSG)? Were you disgusted by their interest? Or secretly flattered? (We won't tell.)

Alas, we'll never know what she was thinking because Sarai remains maddeningly silent in this biblical scene, "a testimony to her powerlessness."[45] At this juncture in our story, I can't decide if she was Mostly Good because she obeyed her husband or Slightly Bad because she "consented to a deception."[46]

Here's another possibility: maybe Sarai trusted God more than her husband did. Maybe she prayed to Yahweh to protect her or to provide a means of escape. Maybe she strolled into Pharaoh's presence with her elegant nose held high, confident of God's deliverance, knowing a lie on her part would not be necessary.

> And when Pharaoh's officials saw her, they praised her to Pharaoh,
> and she was taken into his palace. *Genesis 12:15*

More specifically, "she was taken into his harem" (NLT). Since it was a supermarket-sized one, a few weeks may have gone by before Pharaoh noticed the comely addition. Sarai was a bit past her prime for those skimpy Egyptian costumes, but "Pharaoh would not hesitate to add a striking older woman to his harem to give variety."[47] Think Meryl Streep in *The Devil Wears Prada* or Helen Mirren in *Calendar Girls*.

As to Pharaoh's officials, revered commentator Matthew Henry described them as "Pharaoh's princes (his pimps rather)."[48] His *what*? Indeed, that centuries-old word suits the situation perfectly. According to Rev. Henry, these officials commended Sarai "not for that which was really her praise—her virtue and modesty, her faith and piety," but for her beauty.[49]

The more things change, the more they... Well, you know the rest.

It *is* encouraging to realize the Bible mentions a woman's appearance only when her story hinges on that fact. What the Lord applauds in his Word is a woman's character. In the whole of Proverbs 31—that litmus test for godly women—nothing is said of an ideal woman's physical appearance. No, not even the size of her nose. Instead, we learn she was dressed in dignity and feared God, for, after all, "beauty is fleeting."[50]

Speaking of which, Pharaoh clearly got a gander at Sarai and liked what he saw.

> He treated Abram well for her sake… *Genesis 12:16*

Very well. Pharaoh didn't just spare the man's life; he showered him with goodies.

> …and Abram acquired sheep and cattle, male and female donkeys, menservants and maidservants, and camels. *Genesis 12:16*

No small outpouring. Obviously, "Pharaoh viewed Abram as nobility" and may have intended these gifts to serve "as an elaborate dowry for Sarai."[51]

Dowry, as in a *wedding*? Didn't Abram see where this was going? Or was he too busy counting sheep?

Somebody please yell, "Stop!"

> But the LORD inflicted serious diseases on Pharaoh and his household because of Abram's wife Sarai. *Genesis 12:17*

When it comes to timing, no chronometer on earth is the equal of God's stopwatch. At the perfect moment, in the nick of time, "Yahweh entered the scene."[52] And what a scene it was. "The LORD plagued Pharaoh and his house with great plagues" (KJV), and "everybody in the palace got seriously sick" (MSG). *Ick.*

Don't blame the lettuce. Or spinach. Or contaminated irrigation water.

In the ancient world, "disease was considered the direct result of sin or some violation of custom."[53] Pharaoh was no fool. He understood "a powerful deity was cursing him because of Sarai's presence in his household."[54]

And how did Pharaoh know that? Only two persons in the palace remained disease free: Abram and Sarai, who were surely avoiding Pharaoh like the plague.

> So Pharaoh summoned Abram. "What have you done to me?" he said. "Why didn't you tell me she was your wife?" *Genesis 12:18*

He didn't summon beautiful Sarai. Ohhh no. Pharaoh made sure the Hebrew head of the household took the heat on this one. The terseness of Pharaoh's words and his rapid-fire questions make his anger apparent.

> "Why did you say, 'She is my sister,'..." *Genesis 12:19*

Now that's interesting. I thought Abram asked Sarai to lie. Apparently he went first.

> "...so that I took her to be my wife?" *Genesis 12:19*

I'm getting nervous here. What does Pharaoh mean by he "took her"? Some translations—"I made her my wife" (ICB) or "Now I've married her" (CEV)—give cause for concern. "Sarah seems to have had sexual relations with Pharaoh."[55]

Say it isn't so! Not our silent Sarai, who trusted God to protect her.

Other translations offer a more hopeful view. "I might have taken her to me to wife" (KJV) or "Why were you willing to let me marry her?" (NLT) suggests their union was contemplated but not consummated. *Whew.*

Since God, with his flawless timing, acted here "not to punish Abraham for lying, but to protect Sarah from assault,"[56] he apparently intervened before Sarai's virtue was compromised.

Pharaoh, as a gesture of respect, didn't use Sarai's name when he sent them packing.

> "Now then, here is your wife. Take her and go!" *Genesis 12:19*

Having scolded Abram for lying, Pharaoh evicted him from the country. The Egyptian couldn't have made his wishes plainer: "be gone" (NRSV), "go thy way" (KJV), "take her and get out!" (MSG). Okay, okay, they're leaving already.

> Then Pharaoh gave orders about Abram to his men, and they sent
> him on his way, with his wife and everything he had. *Genesis 12:20*

"Everything" included servants. The sages of old believed that Pharaoh gave "his own daughter to Sarai, one that had been born to one of his concubines" to serve as Sarai's handmaiden and that "her name was Hagar, and she was very young and strong."[57] Though we have no biblical proof, I find it a credible story. More on that when we meet Hagar, who would one day serve this couple in ways they never could have predicted.

Still not a peep from Abe as the twosome were "whisked out of Egypt under military escort"[58] with their gifts in tow but their pride duly trampled. The nomadic followers of Yahweh, loaded down with gold and silver, flocks and herds, slowly moved "from place to place,"[59] "traveling by stages."[60] When Abram and his nephew Lot began to cramp each other's style, they went their separate ways.

Counting the Stars

Some time later Abram experienced his "first actual dialogue with God."[61] The Lord began by putting him at ease.

> …the word of the LORD came to Abram in a vision: "Do not
> be afraid, Abram. I am your shield, your very great reward."
> *Genesis 15:1*

In his Word, God says, "Fear not" (KJV) about seventy-five times, yet we can't seem to hear it enough. I confess, fear nags at me constantly, as it does at many take-charge chicks. *Am I good enough? Have I done enough? Are others pleased with me?* Grabbing for control is our attempt to hold such fears at bay. Only when we realize God is in control can we truly let go of our apprehensions.

"Do not be afraid," God says. To Abram, to Sarai, to us.

Fretful Abram didn't distinguish himself with his response, missing completely God's promise to guard him and crying out a lament that "implies a reproach."[62]

> But Abram said, "O Sovereign LORD, what can you give me since I remain childless and the one who will inherit my estate is Eliezer of Damascus?" *Genesis 15:2*

Eliezer was Abram's chief servant. According to the law of the land, if Abram died without sons, his servant would become his heir. Once again the discussion centered on Sarai's barrenness, and Abram put the blame squarely on God: "you have given me everything I could ask for, except children" (CEV).

The Lord quickly quashed any notion of Abram's bestowing his inheritance on a servant.

> "This man will not be your heir, but a son coming from your own body will be your heir." *Genesis 15:4*

No question about it: Abram would father a son. And from that son would come countless more.

> "Look up at the heavens and count the stars—if indeed you can count them." Then he said to him, "So shall your offspring be." *Genesis 15:5*

We can hear Abram's mental wheels turning. *But I'm getting older. Sarai is barren.* How could such a seemingly impossible promise be fulfilled? By faith alone. And so our flawed but willing hero took that sacred leap.

> Abram believed the LORD… *Genesis 15:6*

Don't let those words slip past you: "And he believed! Believed GOD!" (MSG).

Heavenly Father, help us see the enormity of this truth: a man filled with fear, filled with doubt, laid aside his limitations and was filled with faith. He simply *believed* in your spoken word. Without evidence or proof, without knowing the details of how, when, or where, Abram "believed in (trusted in, relied on, remained steadfast to) the Lord" (AMP).

A perfect man? Pharaoh knew better, and so do we.

But God's man? Absolutely.

> ...and he credited it to him as righteousness. *Genesis 15:6*

The word "credited" here is also translated "counted" (KJV) and "reckoned" (NASB). Simply put, a sizable deposit was made in Abram's spiritual bank account. Riches not borrowed, but bestowed. Not earned, but inherited. Not a debit, but a credit.

"Righteousness" doesn't refer to Abram's good behavior or ours; it means "right standing with God" (AMP). Only the Lord can determine where we stand with him. Truth is, "Abram had no righteousness," not of his own making. "And if he had not, no man had."[63] No woman either. Not *this* woman, for sure!

When the prophet Isaiah moans, "All our righteous acts are like filthy rags,"[64] we moan right along with him, knowing how many times we've done good works for all the wrong reasons. But Isaiah didn't quit there, beloved, nor should we: "Yet, O LORD, you are our Father."[65] Even dressed in filthy rags, we are his. Even after lying to Pharaohs, we are his. Even while pushing and prodding our college-bound children, *we are his.*

"God declared him 'Set-Right-with-God' " (MSG), and so he was. The gift the Lord gave Abram is the same gift he presents to us: a paid-in-full account of righteousness.

Considering that Sarai was barren and soon would be past the age of childbearing, Abram's ability to believe in the promise of countless offspring required an enormous leap of faith—a leap only God could empower, a faith defined as "being sure of what we hope for and certain of what we do not see."[66]

Did Sarai share her husband's over-the-top faith? Let's press on with her story and find out. You'll see that the next chapter of Genesis opens with the word *now,* which is meant to "interrupt the flow of the story—that is, it marks the beginning of a new episode."[67] And what an episode it is...

Sarai Takes Charge

Now Sarai, Abram's wife, had borne him no children. Genesis 16:1

The poor woman. How many times have we gone over this? The fact that she "hadn't yet produced a child" (MSG) continued to trouble her because "there was no other way for a woman to be a member of society."[68] Sarai had to be getting desperate.

She was seventy-five and her husband, eighty-five.

Too late, too late, too late.

Sister, when we stare anxiously at calendars and clocks rather than turn to God, we're looking in the wrong direction. Weary of numbering the wrinkles reflected in her polished brass mirror, Sarai cast her gaze toward a young servant.

But she had an Egyptian maidservant named Hagar... Genesis 16:1

"But..." When I think of the times I've justified my rebellious behavior by tossing out that innocent word! If I've pegged her right, Sarai lined up excuses like tin cans on a fence, daring God to shoot them down.

"But my husband must have a son."

"But I'm too old to be a mother."

"But I have this slave girl..."

The young woman was a "handmaid, an Egyptian, whose name was Hagar" (KJV). Just the word "Egyptian" reminds us of the incident with Pharaoh, of foreign people worshiping foreign gods, of *other.* "Hagar was on the outside looking in."[69]

Sarai and Hagar couldn't have been more different: one Hebrew, one Gentile; one married, one single; one wealthy, one poor; one a mistress, one a slave. Concerning the matter at hand, one woman was "brittle, aging, and barren," while the other was "resilient, young, and fertile."[70] I wonder if Sarai resented Hagar's youthful energy or if Hagar coveted Sarai's wealth and comfort. Whatever their relationship, Hagar was the property of her mistress. Hagar could not even call her womb her own, as we'll discover shortly.

Silent in the biblical account until this moment, Sarai finally spoke up.

> ...so she said to Abram, "The LORD has kept me from having
> children." *Genesis 16:2*

Despite how inflammatory her words sound, Sarai was not blaming God per se, merely acknowledging what all believed to be true in her day: the Lord "restrained" (KJV) or "prevented" (NASB) women from bearing children for reasons known only to him. "GOD has not seen fit to let me have a child" (MSG), Sarai told Abram. Do you hear in her voice bitterness or sorrow? Was she angry or merely resigned? Any of those emotions would be valid, yet none of them are recorded in Scripture.

One scholar insisted her words bespoke "the usual impatience of unbelief,"[71] but I'll stand up for Sarai on this one. She'd been exceedingly patient—with her husband, with her God, with her barrenness—from the day she married, as much as *sixty years* earlier. If her patience was running thin, no wonder. If her faith was waning, who could fault her?

At this crucial point, if she'd called out to God for strength, prayed to God for direction, or pleaded with God to open her womb, we would defend her without question. "Had Sarah said, Nature has failed me, but God is my resource, how different it would have been!"[72]

But Sarai did not call on God. Instead, she came up with a ready remedy for the hubby-needs-an-heir problem. With her next words, our aging Princess tilted her crown at a defiant angle and a Slightly Bad Girl stepped forward.

> "Go, sleep with my maidservant..." *Genesis 16:2*

No matter the translation, those words hit us like a slap. "Go *what*?!"

Remember how Abram added "I pray thee" when he asked Sarai to lie to the Egyptians? We find the same wheedling "I pray thee" (KJV) in this verse—except here we have an altogether different form of lying. Sarai didn't ask her man to catch forty winks with Hagar; she demanded that he "have sexual relations" (NCV), "have intercourse" (AMP), indeed "go in to my maid" (NASB).

Heavens! What was Sarai thinking?

Perhaps she decided that if she didn't do something, her husband might take another wife and leave her in disgrace. Or that her family's destiny rested solely in her hands and she needed to act. Or that if she waited much longer, Abram might be as incapable of fathering a child as she was of conceiving one. Whatever her reasoning, Sarai believed her infertility "forced her to find a way out of this embarrassment to her husband."[73]

Hence, her forthright words to Abram: "Sleep with my maid" (MSG).

Scandalous as her plan appears, Sarai didn't come up with this on her own. An Assyrian marriage contract, dating from around 1900 BC, stipulated "if the wife does not give birth in two years, she will purchase a slave woman for the husband."[74] Still, no matter how common that solution was in her culture, *Sarai was not of that culture.* God had set apart Abram and Sarai. His promises were extended to no other man or woman on earth.

Tempting as it is to wag my finger at Sarai, I see in my own life the same willingness to follow the law of the land rather than God's command. "Give to Caesar what is Caesar's," Jesus said.[75] Yet when April 15 draws near and Caesar demands his due, I find myself staring at the figures on the 1040 form, wondering if there isn't *some* legal loophole we could slip part of our income through.

The Word tells us, "Commit to the LORD whatever you do, and your plans will succeed."[76] But Sarai had a better plan, or so she thought.

"…perhaps I can build a family through her." *Genesis 16:2*

By law Sarai could claim any child born to Hagar as her own. What would Hagar get out of the deal? A very wealthy husband.

"Liz, do you mean…"

I do.

"We have here the marriage of Abram to Hagar, who was his secondary wife."[77] Not a concubine or a mistress or a surrogate mother for his child. A *wife* in every sense of the word. Unbelievable as it sounds, Sarai was agreeing to "share her husband with another woman."[78]

Swallow a Tums to calm your churning stomach and imagine for one awful moment that you were Sarai. What sort of woman would you choose to play Hagar's role? Beautiful, for your husband's sake? Or unattractive, for yours? One writer thought Sarai selected "the most physically appealing, intelligent, spiritually evolved woman in her household."[79] If the goal was solely to produce a healthy, bright child, that approach sounds prudent. But if I were choosing a secondary wife for my husband, she'd be the plainest, dullest woman in five states!

This much we do know: Sarai "was guilty of no light sin."[80] Without seeking God's direction in the matter, she chose "a Gentile idolater from a pagan country…to bear the promised seed."[81]

All was not lost, however. Abram still had to comply with his wife's audacious plan. A man who had spoken with God, who had faith in God's word, and who'd been declared righteous by a grace-giving God—surely this man would refuse to sin so egregiously.

Abram the Cave Man

Abram agreed to what Sarai said. *Genesis 16:2*

No resistance? No discussion? No seeking God's blessing before proceeding with this no-no? Uh…no. Abram "listened to the voice of Sarai" (NASB) and "heeded what Sarai said" (AMP).

We've heard this before: "Here, honey. Try this tasty fruit." From the beginning, women have gently but firmly bent their husbands to their will, sometimes without saying a word. Abram offered "no more protest to his wife's plan than Adam had to Eve's picnic in paradise."[82]

Admit it: we women often get what we want through not-so-subtle persuasion, verbal agility, and emotional expression. At least, that's how it works in our family. We live in the old farmhouse I fell in love with and drive the Toyota I picked out. Does my dear husband have an opinion? Of course. My husband, Bill, is also a peacemaker, and granting my wishes gives him what *he* wants: harmony at the Higgs house.

I can see Abram nodding (and Sarai glaring at me for giving away our time-honored tactics) as her husband sought "to buy conjugal peace at almost any price."[83] How else to explain why Abram, after attaining such spiritual heights, caved "to domestic pressure, pliant under his wife's planning and scolding"?[84]

Sarai was a Slightly Bad Girl, all right, married to a Slightly Bad Boy who didn't hesitate to follow her advice, "guided by reason and *the voice of Sarai...* not of the Lord."[85]

> So after Abram had been living in Canaan ten years, Sarai his wife
> took her Egyptian maidservant Hagar and gave her to her husband
> to be his wife. *Genesis 16:3*

The date stamp—ten years in Canaan—helps us keep track of things. And note who was in charge. "Sarai gave Hagar to her husband Abram" (NCV). Sarai was no innocent bystander, simply making suggestions. She "took" and "gave," just like Eve, who "took some and...gave some to her husband."[86]

Hagar's foreign nationality is emphasized here for good reason: hers was not the womb God intended for Abram's seed. Could the Lord have made Hagar barren as well? Easy answer: of course. Then why didn't he? Tricky answer, soon to follow.

The Egyptian maid's new role was clear: "to be his wife" (KJV), the same Hebrew word used to describe Abram's relationship with Sarai, who "voluntarily granted to Hagar all the rights and privileges of a full-fledged wife."[87] I can't fathom how difficult that must have been for Sarai, and yet by law these rights were necessary for Hagar's offspring to qualify as Abram's legitimate heir.[88]

What Sarai went through to be a mother!

Had she and Abram sought God's help, surely the Lord would have responded. Instead, they pressed on with a desperate human solution rather than seek divine intervention. With little fanfare, Abram "married without God's consent."[89]

> He slept with Hagar... *Genesis 16:4*

Naturally, much more than sleeping was involved. Poor Sarai, waiting alone in her tent, trying not to imagine Abram and Hagar together. (Frankly,

I'd rather not picture it either. An octogenarian sharing a bed with a woman young enough to be his great-granddaughter? Draw the tent curtains, please.)

Poor Hagar, too, with no choice whatsoever in the matter—both women victimized by a social system that "valued women only for their reproductive capacity."[90]

> …and she conceived. *Genesis 16:4*

The rabbis of old insist Hagar conceived "after the first intimacy with Abram,"[91] proving beyond any doubt Abram's virility. How the news of Hagar's pregnancy must have confounded our Sarai! A flutter of joy, knowing she would soon hold her husband's heir on her knees, followed by sorrow, realizing her empty womb was indeed to blame all along.

Here's my question: if Sarai wanted an heir for Abram, why didn't she choose someone from her own tribe? By pairing her Hebrew husband with an Egyptian wife, "she originated a rivalry which has run in the keenest animosity through the ages, and which oceans of blood have not quenched."[92]

We're about to see the seeds of that rivalry—planted in the proud heart of Hagar and fertilized by Sarai's jealousy—take root in a scene "so true to human nature that it is difficult to understand how any one could ever imagine that this story was fiction."[93]

Like a Woman Scorned

> When [Hagar] knew she was pregnant, she began to despise her mistress. *Genesis 16:4*

"Despise." One word gives us the whole ugly picture: a pregnant, haughty servant looking down her nose at a barren, miserable wife.

"Humiliated in the very core of her heart,"[94] Sarai prepared to reveal "the less pleasant side of her character."[95] I'll say! The woman unleashed a diatribe filled with "tempestuous wrath"[96] and "righteous rage"[97] meant to knock Abram back on his heels.

Honey, she was *livid.*

> Then Sarai said to Abram, "You are responsible for the wrong I am
> suffering." *Genesis 16:5*

Before you jump to conclusions (as I did at first blush), Sarai was not placing all the blame on Abram for Hagar's presumptuous behavior. While other translations read, "May the wrong done to me be on you!" (NRSV) and "It's all your fault!" (NLT), the Hebrew text indicates Sarai was merely reminding her husband that, as the head of the household, he alone had the power to fix things. And she wanted them fixed, pronto.

This whole scene constitutes "a judicial, legal proceeding."[98] Wives had certain rights, and Sarai was about to assert hers. To me, the text reads like a *Law & Order* script—one of those episodes when a female attorney doesn't let Assistant D.A. Jack McCoy get a word in edgewise. We can imagine Sarai pacing the courtroom floor, her dark eyes flashing, her Near Eastern complexion burnished to a high color by the heat of her words.

> "I put my servant in your arms…" *Genesis 16:5*

Sarai gets points for honesty. No hedging here. "I myself gave her the privilege of sleeping with you" (NLT). This, too, was "recognized legal phraseology"[99] but also "pointedly sexual."[100]

> "…and now that she knows she is pregnant, she despises me."
> *Genesis 16:5*

Here's what Sarai was so steamed about: she expected her husband to speak up for her rather than meekly stand by while an uppity servant-turned-wife usurped her authority. Hagar turned out to be "the unforeseen wild card"[101] in this Royal Game of Err.

As mistress of the household, Sarai held the oldest and first rights,[102] and she knew the law of the land was on her side: "If a slave promoted to be a wife could not hold the new position with proper decorum, she was to return to her former state."[103] Nebraska maybe. Or Texas. Somewhere far away from Canaan.

With all eyes fixed on her, Sarai offered her closing argument.

"May the LORD judge between you and me." *Genesis 16:5*

How disheartening to hear Sarai speak to Abram in so harsh a manner: "The LORD will make you pay for doing this to me!" (NLT). When Sarai cried, "Let the LORD decide who is right—you or me" (NCV), commentators suggest she was alluding to the time in Egypt when Abram asked her to lie on his behalf, a "morally repugnant" request.[104]

Oh, *that.* Some married people keep a detailed account of their partners' wrongdoings, using them like sharply tipped arrows when skirmishes arise. But Abram chose not to engage in battle and instead let Sarai win without releasing a single shaft.

"Your servant is in your hands," Abram said. *Genesis 16:6*

With those words—a legal pronouncement—Hagar was reduced to her former role as a mere maidservant under Sarai's authority.[105] "Your slave-girl is in your power" (NRSV), Abram told her. "Your maid is your business" (MSG).

Boy, that was quick. Maybe he'd sensed God's displeasure long before Sarai expressed hers. Maybe he'd grown weary of watching these two women snap at each other like Nile crocodiles. Or maybe he'd realized what a mess he and Sarai had made of things and so "voluntarily dismissed the wife who had been given to him."[106]

Whatever Abram's reasoning, his next words send a chill down my spine.

"Do with her whatever you think best." *Genesis 16:6*

Dangerous, to give a wronged wife that sort of license. "Do anything you want to her" (NCV), Abram said. "Deal with her as you see fit" (NLT). See why I'm nervous?

Sarai had asked Abram to take responsibility as head of the household. Instead, he avoided it. More troubling still, we sense "no compassion, affection, or even concern for Hagar's welfare"[107] on Abram's part even though he'd embraced her and filled her with his seed. Now he was "abandoning the woman carrying his child to the fury of her jealous rival"[108] without doing anything to protect Hagar *or* his future heir.

Boggles the mind, doesn't it? Abram, "the father of us all,"[109] behaving like a deadbeat dad.

As for Sarai, she grabbed that "power and freedom, and she became relentless."[110]

Mean Girls

Then Sarai mistreated Hagar;... *Genesis 16:6*

"Mistreated" can mean a lot of things. Did Sarai make Hagar work harder than ever, despite her pregnancy, assigning "excessively numerous menial tasks"?[111] Or by dealing "harshly with her" (NRSV), does the Bible mean Sarai threw cruel words at her maid like stones, hard and sharp, meant to inflict pain? If she "dealt severely with her, humbling and afflicting her" (AMP), we have a clearer picture of how difficult this must have been for Hagar.

But the closest translation to the original Hebrew is this: "Sarai was abusive to Hagar" (MSG). That is, she literally "applied force to her, treated her with violence."[112]

Oh, Sarai. How could you? Hagar did only what you asked her to do.

Yes, Hagar was boastful, and her attitude was vexing. Yes, she was a servant, and you were her mistress. Correct her in some proper way if you must. But to hurt her, to strike her, to treat her as something less than human—that was hardly the behavior of a godly woman. To think "our revered foremother, a woman of deep spirituality" could be so abusive! "What a cautionary message for all of us."[113]

Yes, *all* of us, beloved. I'm not tempted to lift my hand against friend or foe, but I can strike with words as sharp as flint, especially when I feel wronged, slighted, or ignored. Instead of just biting my tongue, maybe I should glue it to the roof of my mouth with peanut butter—anything to keep from hurting others with my words, or worse, as Sarai apparently did.

You'll be relieved to know this wasn't the end of Sarai's story. Happier days awaited our fallen princess, including a new name, a personal encounter with the God of Abraham, and a long-anticipated answer to her prayers. We'll examine the next season of Sarai's life in chapter 3. Yet our time spent in this barren stretch has been fruitful, if only to reveal our own flawed natures.

Have I ever lambasted my husband, as Sarai did? Sorry to say, I have.

Did I make those who once worked for me feel less than appreciated on occasion? To my discredit, I did.

Are there times I should have prayed rather than plotted? Trusted God instead of crafting my own foolish plans? Waited rather than acted? A thousand times, yes.

If you'd rather think of Sarai as a saintly role model who never stumbled, "that would rob Sarah of her human dimension—and deprive us of the lessons we can learn."[114] She was human, just as we are, and, as such, her story gives us hope.

The Lord wasn't finished with Sarai of Ur, and he isn't finished with you and me. He loves us far too much to let us soak in our sinfulness or drown in our guilt. Slightly Bad Girls we may be, but what a truly good God is he.

Let's spend a moment reflecting on the truths we've gleaned thus far from Sarai's life. Then we'll catch up with Hagar, a woman whose story is about to take a dramatic turn.

What Lessons Can We Learn from Sarai?

For those who love God, there are no white lies.

When Abram begged Sarai, "Say you are my sister," he was asking her to tell a white lie—a supposedly harmless untruth meant to serve a useful purpose. But there's nothing harmless about lying. God doesn't want us to fib to save our necks or anyone else's. If even those we love and trust ask us to speak deceitfully—"When so-and-so calls, say I'm not here" or "Tell our accountant that trip was a business expense"—we can respectfully decline and seek a better solution that meets their needs yet honors God.

Therefore each of you must put off falsehood and speak truthfully
to his neighbor. *Ephesians 4:25*

Know when it's time for a new wardrobe.

In the early years of Sarai's married life, she was "clothed…with joy"[115]—
following Abram on his God-led journey without question or complaint,
tramping across the desert, doing all that her husband asked. But when the
years of barrenness took their toll, her patience wore as thin as an old woolen
robe, and her treatment of those closest to her grew as rough as the leather
straps on her worn-out sandals. *What Not to Wear,* circa 1800 BC. We can
learn from Sarai's fashion faux pas and choose instead to dress in spiritual
garments that never go out of style.

> Therefore, as God's chosen people, holy and dearly loved, clothe
> yourselves with compassion, kindness, humility, gentleness and
> patience. *Colossians 3:12*

Trusting in the Lord is the best plan.

The psalmist sang out, "Trust in the LORD,"[116] calling on God's people to let
the sovereign Lord be their guide. But when our patience runs out, trust
often goes along with it. We give up on God ever answering our prayers and
start looking for quick fixes. We stop listening to the advice of others and
make hasty, often regrettable decisions. Sarai exhibited many admirable
traits, but her take-charge-rather-than-trust-God plan was not one of them.
Let's lift a page from her life and turn it upside down: depending on God
rather than seeking easy solutions, and heeding wise counsel rather than
charging ahead without counting the cost.

> Trust in the LORD with all your heart and lean not on your own
> understanding. *Proverbs 3:5*

Tempers are safest when tempered.

Tempered steel is heated, then cooled to make the metal become stronger.
When our tempers flare, as Sarai's did with both Hagar and Abram, we can

try dousing our anger with cold truth. What are we *really* so hot about? Are we too focused on the weaknesses of others to see our own failings? Is some deep-seated disappointment from the past interfering with our ability to act fairly now? Is our anger righteous or sparked by nothing more than pride and envy? In the heat of the moment, let's pause long enough for our tempers to cool, knowing we'll be stronger for the effort…and won't send others running for safety.

> Anger is cruel and fury overwhelming, but who can stand before jealousy? *Proverbs 27:4*

Good Girl Thoughts Worth Considering

1. What was your opinion of Sarai *before* you studied her story in Genesis 11–16? And what do you think of her now? Based on your personal experience or observation, what are the blessings of being married to a man uniquely called by God? And what are the challenges?

2. Sarai is the first woman in Scripture described as barren. Since "children are a gift from the LORD,"[117] to what end might God have closed Sarai's womb for a long season? Is childbearing still a source of esteem for women? What are some ways modern society measures the worth of a woman? How do you measure your own worth?

3. Abram and Sarai left everything—family and friends, houses and lands, and all their worldly goods that wouldn't fit on a camel—to follow God's leading. If the Lord asked you to leave everything and follow his lead, how would you respond? The Lord made several "I will" statements to Abram, promising to bless him and to make him famous. How might such promises increase your faith?

4. When you learned that Sarai was a beautiful woman, in what way did that alter your perception of her? Did you fear for her in Pharaoh's court or

assume her pleasing appearance would protect her? In our culture how is beauty an advantage? A disadvantage?

5. In Genesis 15, God told Abram he would father a son from his own seed but did not mention the mother's name. How might the story have unfolded differently if God had said, "And Sarai will bear this son"? Since we know "his way is perfect,"[118] why do you think God withheld this vital fact? Ten years passed before Sarai took steps to secure an heir for Abram. What do you suppose finally prompted her to act?

6. When Sarai gave Hagar to her husband, how had she "opened the door to spiritual catastrophe"?[119] In what ways did Hagar's quick conception make matters worse for Sarai? In your own life, when have you taken your future into your own impatient hands without seeking God's guidance? And what was the outcome?

7. According to her tersely presented prosecution, Sarai wanted Abram to rectify the situation. Describe the "wrong" she was suffering (Genesis 16:5). Once again, Sarai did not turn to the Lord for help. What reason would you offer? This chapter of Sarai's life ended on a distressing note. Have you lost respect for her, or are you willing to give her another chance? Explain why.

8. What's the most important lesson you learned from Sarai, a princess bride who ran out of patience?

Flight Plan

Hiding places there are innumerable,
escape is only one.
F R A N Z   K A F K A

P avla couldn't run from the pain; she could only endure it, crying out for mercy.

"Not much longer," Sandi said with certainty. As if she knew, as if she were in control.

But of course Sandi Cannon had been in control from the very start. *Pavla, I have a great favor to ask of you...* Too great a favor Pavla had soon realized. Far too great even with all Sandi had promised in return.

Exhausted from a long night of labor, Pavla faded into a stupor between contractions, staring through bleary eyes at her surroundings: beige tile, bright lights, silver trays, nurses in teal-colored scrubs.

Her mistress stood at her bedside, looking anxious: Sandi, the woman responsible for her pain. "No drugs," she'd told the anesthesiologist earlier, brandishing a legal form bearing Pavla's signature. "We can't risk even the slightest complication."

We. Sandi's favorite word. At monthly doctor visits, in the children's department at Lord & Taylor, at Lamaze classes. Always *we. We're looking for... We need to have... We mustn't be kept waiting...*

After one particularly stressful day, Pavla had lashed out at her in Dr. Goodman's crowded waiting room. *"We* are not pregnant. *I* am," she told her. "Your back does not hurt, your legs do not cramp, and your hands do not swell. *I* am carrying this baby. Not you."

Pavla never apologized. And Sandi never forgave her.

"Pavla?" Dr. Goodman's voice floated toward her from the end of the bed.

She couldn't see past the sheet draped across her knees, but she felt his gloved hands probing. Sensed her abdomen tightening again.

"Almost there, Pavla. Everything's proceeding on schedule."

"Whose schedule?" she ground out as a fresh contraction gripped her, nearly lifting her off the bed. Pavla tried to breathe. Couldn't. Tried to scream. Couldn't. She could only push.

Moments later, when she heard Sandi's exclamation followed by an infant's plaintive cry, Pavla smiled in spite of the agonizing pain. *My son. Alan's son.* All around her a flurry of activity ensued as she sank into the bed, barely conscious.

"Well done!" Dr. Goodman leaned over her, beaming. "A fine way to start the morning, I'd say."

Pavla nodded faintly, watching the nurses attend the wriggling infant while Sandi hovered over them, asking questions. Was his color good? Did he have a healthy pulse? Was his breathing normal? Pavla wanted to know those things too.

Another nurse changed her sheets and helped her into a new hospital gown, then gave Pavla the drink of water she'd been longing for all through labor. Sandi held her son now. *Her son.* Pavla wanted to look away but couldn't. He was so tiny and pink, his head covered with swirls of wet dark hair. *Like mine.*

Instinctively Pavla reached toward him. *Please?*

Sandi gasped slightly and drew him closer still. "Pavla, we agreed..."

Her empty arms fell to her side. *We did.* The attorney had repeated each phrase until he was certain she'd understood. *Voluntary Termination of Parental Rights. Consent to Adoption.*

Relinquishment. Pavla turned her head to hide her tears while two nurses wheeled her into the recovery room, Sandi not far behind with the baby in her arms.

"A perfectly natural response when you give birth," one of the nurses said softly, dabbing Pavla's cheeks with a tissue. "All those fluctuating hormones, you know."

Pavla didn't correct her. Most surrogate mothers, she'd learned, were married women with children of their own. They were happy to carry another couple's child for the satisfaction of bringing joy to an eager family even more than for the sizable financial reward. But Pavla had no such incentive.

"Alan and I prefer not to pay you cash," Sandi had explained at the outset, not quite making eye contact as she outlined her unconventional plan. Apparently money was too coarse an offering for something so sacred. "Suppose we move the rest of your family here from Ukraine. Provide housing. Help them get settled and find work. Would that please you?"

How could Pavla ever have refused? To have her mother and two brothers with her in the United States. To be together again as a family. She'd never dared to hope for such an opportunity.

But her elation faded when the doctor visits began. Artificial insemination was just that: artificial, clinical, medical. When she conceived in the first month, the Cannons were jubilant, convinced that God had blessed their plans. Sandi practically took credit, as if she were responsible instead of God.

Pavla knew the truth. From the moment she discovered a child growing inside her, God had revealed himself to her in new ways. When she prayed, she sensed him listening. When she listened, she sensed him speaking. When her child bucked and kicked like a mule the last few weeks, as if demanding his freedom, God assured her all was well.

Looking at her son now, peacefully nestled in Sandi's arms, he hardly seemed like the same baby. "Ivan?" Pavla called softly, hoping he might recognize her voice. Did he turn toward her, even a little? She'd insisted on the legal right to name him. A small concession, Sandi had decided, though she didn't care for *Ivan*. When Pavla explained the name meant "God's gift," Sandi had offered no further complaint.

Pavla didn't tell her the real reason: *Ivan* was her father's name. Ivan Teslenko of Berdychiv. She intended to honor his memory even though *Teslenko* would not appear on the birth certificate. "Ivan," she said again, comforted by the sound. And secretly pleased when a look of distaste crossed Sandi's features.

"Alan will be here shortly," Sandi announced. "I had one of the nurses phone him."

Pavla said nothing. She'd felt awkward around Alan from the moment she signed the stack of legal documents that tied her womb to his seed. However removed he was from the process, she could not deny that carrying his son had created a bond between them. More than once he'd splayed his hand across her expanding middle to pray for his son. She'd felt the warmth of his palm through her maternity dress and saw the flicker of compassion in his eyes. "God bless you," he'd said each time. His touch had felt like the touch of God, holy and good.

While various machines monitored her vital signs, Pavla watched the gap in the privacy curtain, ashamed of her eagerness. Alan was coming to see his son, not her. Yet he might say a kind word, even take her hand in gratitude.

A nurse appeared instead, wearing a stern look. "The pediatrician is here for morning rounds. Your son belongs in his bassinet."

Sandi showed the nurse the back of her designer sweater as she cradled the babe protectively. "But I'm expecting my husband any second now."

"Send him to the nursery," the woman said curtly, lifting the small bundle from Sandi's arms despite her indignant protests. The nurse left in a hurry with Sandi close on her heels.

Pavla pressed her lips together lest Sandi return and catch her smiling, then patted her damp forehead with the corner of her pillowcase. What a mess she must look with her hair gathered beneath a blue paper cap and her face bathed in sweat. Better that Alan not find her this way.

But her heart quickened a minute later at the sound of his voice in the hall.

"Is a gentleman welcome?" He pulled aside the curtain a little, then awaited her response.

"Y-yes," she said, smoothing the sheets around her, willing her legs not to tremble. A normal postdelivery reaction, the nurses had assured her.

One of those angels of mercy brushed past Alan, bringing Pavla a welcome cup of juice. "No visitors in the recovery room, sir."

Alan's cheeks turned ruddy. "I'm the...father of the baby."

"I see." The nurse shot him a look that would peel paint. "All right with you, Pavla?"

She nodded, then said in Ukrainian, *"Tak,"* hoping to make Alan smile, perhaps even relax a bit.

"Thank you for saying yes," he responded, stepping into the small area ringed in white curtains. "I mean, for saying yes to...everything." He was indeed smiling; more warmly than usual, she thought.

When the nurse disappeared, he moved closer. "Pavla, you have blessed me more than I can ever tell you." His gaze met hers; his hand rested on hers as well. "You've blessed *us,* that is. Blessed our family."

Alan's eyes watered when he spoke the word. *Family.* Pavla understood. Love for her own family had compelled her to make this sacrifice for his happiness. "I am glad you have a healthy son," she said, and meant it. "Have you seen him?"

"Not yet."

He'd come to see her first, then.

Pavla moistened her lips, which felt like paper. "Ivan has handsome features," she said. *Like yours.* "His head is covered with black wavy hair."

"Like yours." Alan touched a stray wisp that had escaped from her cap.

The curtains parted with a sudden *whoosh.* "There you are." Sandi didn't sound relieved; she sounded angry.

Alan stepped back, shoving both hands into his pockets like a guilty schoolboy. "Where else would I be? Pavla deserves our thanks—"

"So she does," Sandi retorted, "and the fortune you've spent immigrating her family should be thanks enough."

Her words hung in the air like bits of glass, sharpening the silence.

Pavla finally spoke. "You have your family. And I have mine. It is enough." She gestured toward the hall. "Go see your son. Ivan is all that matters now..."

Hagar: Catfight in Canaan

All through Hagar's ordeal, we heard nary a peep from her. Did she feel used and abused by master and mistress alike? Certainly our twenty-first-century sensibilities are offended by such a marital arrangement. But in that time and place, a wealthy wife stepping aside and inviting another woman to bear her son was considered an honor. Well, in theory anyway. The reality might have felt less like honor for the expectant mother and more like shame. Especially once the abuse began.

Since Hagar lived a shadowy existence until this point in the biblical narrative, suppose we back up a few steps and consider what we *do* know about her and what brought her to this desperate point.

For Sarai to select Hagar as her personal maidservant, "a position of some importance in the household,"[1] Hagar had clearly proven herself a trustworthy young woman, who "served her mistress with devotion."[2] She must have been smart as well, ingratiating herself to Abram and Sarai, "making herself so valuable, that they would not sell her into a worse existence."[3] What a tightrope this Egyptian maid walked, trying to maintain her sense of self while living in bondage to her Hebrew owners.

On the day she became Abram's secondary wife, everything changed—for better and for worse. Hagar gained a powerful new husband and a more powerful enemy in his first wife. Now she held a child in her womb yet faint hope for a happy future.

Was Hagar a Slightly Bad Girl for agreeing to Sarai's surrogate plan? Not from where I'm sitting. If anything, Hagar was "the only innocent one, a slave with little power to resist."[4] But her innocence was short lived.

> When [Hagar] knew she was pregnant, she began to despise her
> mistress. *Genesis 16:4*

We get a fuller sense of the situation when we toss together the various translations like a bowl of mixed greens: "she began to treat...Sarai badly" (NCV), "she looked down on her mistress" (MSG), and "was hateful to Sarai" (CEV). Compared to a pregnant wife, barren Sarai sank lower in stature, so Hagar "began to gloat."[5]

If, as legend tells it, "Hagar was once a princess in her father's house,"[6] the pampered daughter of a Pharaoh and his concubine, then we can more easily understand her haughty attitude. Most servants did as they were told without complaint and certainly without challenging their masters. Princess or pauper, Hagar's mean-spirited behavior merits a Slightly Bad Girl ribbon pinned to her maternity dress.

Scripture records neither Hagar's words nor her actions, but we know how it came down. She tipped up her chin in Sarai's presence and did not bother to meet her mistress's gaze. Her tone was insolent, and her body language disdainful, filled with exaggerated shrugs and dismissive hand gestures. As the child grew inside her, Hagar pushed her abdomen out as far as she could, rubbing her belly or pressing a hand to the small of her back, emphasizing her condition. This servant, "in many little ways understood by women, ventured to show her contempt for her childless mistress,"[7] giving us a glimpse of her "passionate and uncontrolled"[8] nature.

I wonder if Hagar always expressed her emotions so freely or if hormones had something to do with it. Maybe she was entering her last trimester, when anything can set a woman off. As Nora Ephron said, "If pregnancy were a book, they would cut the last two chapters."[9] Perhaps Hagar envied Sarai's obvious command of her husband's affections and so struck her mistress with the lowest of blows: "I'm carrying his child, and you're not." Apparently Hagar thought herself "a better woman than Sarai, more favored by Heaven, and likely to be better beloved by Abram."[10] A foolhardy assumption on Hagar's part. Her mistress may not have given Abram a child, but Sarai had given the man her undivided loyalty and affection for nigh unto sixty years so far.

Unfortunately, as we saw in the previous chapter, Sarai proved anything but loyal to the woman bearing her husband's child. In fact, she "chose to mistreat the servant so severely that Hagar ran away."[11] Demoted from secondary wife to unwed mother and ill treated by her mistress, Hagar ignored the law of the land and broke free from Sarai's clutches.

...she fled from her. *Genesis 16:6*

Some might say the patriarchal couple got what they deserved. "Instead of securing the fulfillment of their wishes, Sarai and Abram had reaped nothing but grief and vexation,"[12] losing both a useful maidservant and Abram's unborn child.

Was Hagar's escape premeditated or a sudden act of desperation? Did she cautiously slip away after sundown, hoping no one would see her, or run from Sarai's presence in broad daylight, tears streaming down her face? Her very name, Hagar, means "flight"[13] or "wanderer," from the Arabic word *hajara*.[14] Our Slightly Bad Girl was on the go, all right. Running from Sarai's anger and Abram's neglect. Punishing them by taking their precious heir in her womb. Escaping toward Egypt, toward home.

Though we might applaud her bid for freedom, "to flee was a thing forbidden to a bondwoman."[15] Much as she wins our sympathy, legally she was in the wrong. Unfair, I know. The words *justice* and *slavery* can hardly be used in the same sentence.

Taking flight as she did—"pregnant, afflicted, humiliated, frightened, and alone"[16]—Hagar was unprepared for the long journey south across the wilderness. We can feel the heat of the noonday sun draining her energy. Imagine the coarse sand burning the soles of her feet. Hear the groan of her empty stomach. Beneath the vast canopy of the desert sky, Hagar must have sensed "her own insignificance as she had never felt it before."[17]

She was not insignificant to God, though.

So he came looking for her.

Touched by an Angel

The angel of the LORD found Hagar near a spring in the desert;...
Genesis 16:7

Sister, I could write an entire book about this one incredible statement. A heavenly visitor, a spring of living water, and a woman trying to break free from bondage—the symbolism alone sends my heart spinning!

For starters, we have the first appearance of an angel in Scripture. Not just any angel, but *the* angel of the Lord. This divine messenger, this "temporary manifestation of God,"[18] looked "just like a human being"—never mind all that business with "wings, halos, and glorious raiment."[19]

Go ahead, check any translation you like: God didn't show up in angelic attire when he spoke with Adam or Noah or even Abram. But with Hagar— "a woman, an Egyptian woman, and a slave at that"[20]—God came down and met her "by a fountain of water in the wilderness" (KJV).

> …it was the spring that is beside the road to Shur. *Genesis 16:7*

Shur, eh? Just as we suspected, Hagar was returning to Egypt. The angel of the Lord knew that as well, but still he asked her to put her plan into words.

> "Hagar, servant of Sarai, where have you come from, and where are you going?" *Genesis 16:8*

Did she gasp when he spoke her name? Frown at the reminder of her lowly station in life and her abandoned duties, perhaps intended by the angel to serve as "a check to her pride"?[21] Hagar was well aware she had no resources and no refuge. Hearing the words "slave-girl of Sarai" (NRSV) no doubt stirred inside her a jumble of emotions: "anger, abandonment, betrayal, and fear."[22]

Then the angel asked two questions that would sum up Hagar's existence: "whence camest thou? and whither wilt thou go?" (KJV). Or, as translated in the LRV (Lizzie Revised Version), "Wassup, girl?"

> "I'm running away from my mistress Sarai," she answered. *Genesis 16:8*

Gotta give the woman points for honesty. No prevaricating here. Maybe Hagar spoke so "openly and defiantly"[23] in hopes the angel wouldn't notice she'd skipped his second question about where she was headed.

Turns out, her travel plans didn't matter. God had a different destination in mind.

> Then the angel of the LORD told her, "Go back to your mistress and submit to her." *Genesis 16:9*

Not much room for discussion there. "Go" and "submit" are strong, imperative verbs—not suggestions, but commands. The first part, "Return to thy mistress" (KJV), was for Hagar's own benefit: she and her child would be cared for. An ideal situation? Far from it. But better than wandering in the wilderness without food, clothing, shelter, or protection.

The second part, "submit yourself to her authority" (NASB), was undeniably tougher: Hagar would have to endure Sarai's mistreatment. As the apostle Peter later wrote, "Slaves, submit yourselves to your masters with all respect, not only to those who are good and considerate, but also to those who are harsh."[24] Before we complain or demand an explanation, the next verse reminds us that submission to a higher authority honors the One we truly serve: "What counts is that you put up with it for God's sake."[25]

But did Hagar—a Gentile—see the value in obeying Yahweh?

In all her years among the tents of Abram, she'd no doubt heard about his God. And the angel's "knowing words"[26] had surely given away his heavenly identity. Still, accepting God's existence is one thing; honoring his command is another matter entirely, especially if we're required to go back when we'd rather go forward.

Before I met my Bill, he worked at a local Christian radio station to support himself while earning his doctorate at seminary. Once he had his PhD (and me) firmly in hand, Bill waved farewell to his broadcasting buddies and began a one-year teaching position at a college, certain his radio days were over. But when the academic year ended and a full-time position elsewhere didn't materialize—despite his valiant efforts—Bill resumed his old radio job to support his new family.

Believe me, the humility and godly obedience required to "go back" and "submit" is something to behold. Let's see how Hagar handled things.

And Now for Some Good News

Any protest on Hagar's part evaporated when our holy messenger, in language "proper only to the Lord himself,"[27] offered her a brighter future than she could ever imagine.

> The angel added, "I will so increase your descendants that they will
> be too numerous to count." *Genesis 16:10*

You mean the first woman in Scripture to be given a divine promise of descendants was Hagar, the headstrong slave? You betcha. She was also the only woman in Genesis who received such a promise "directly from God."[28]

Yes, but…

Lord, did you think you were speaking with Sarai? Oh. So you *knew* this was Hagar, her bondservant. And you promised to "greatly multiply" Hagar's offspring (NRSV), fully aware she would "become the mother of another religion."[29]

Yes.

This is God being God, dear sister. "How unsearchable his judgments, and his paths beyond tracing out!"[30] He honored his earlier promise to Abram by blessing the seed that grew inside Hagar. Not because Abram was worthy or Sarai was worthy or Hagar was worthy, but because of the vastness of God's grace perfectly expressed in the words we know well: "For God so loved the world…"[31] Not just the part of the world that looks and sounds and thinks and lives like we do, but the *whole* world.

His love saw beyond everything that humanly defined Hagar—gender, race, nationality, class, religion—and gave her a new identity.

There's no other word for it: God *saved* Hagar in the desert. Saved her from starving to death and saved her unborn child as well. Saved her from her prideful spirit and the misery her attitude had produced. Saved her from herself, which God alone can do.

Again, Hagar did nothing to merit the Lord's favor. God honored the seed of Abram *because he said he would.* Write this on the tablet of your heart, beloved: God keeps his word.

> The angel of the LORD also said to her: "You are now with child and
> you will have a son." *Genesis 16:11*

Hmm. Sound familiar? Mary, the mother of Jesus, heard similar words from the angel Gabriel: "You will be with child and give birth to a son."[32]

And both women were "addressed personally, not through their husbands."[33] The comparison ends there, but we can't ignore the truth: God
attended to Hagar's needs just as he did Mary's.

And look what glad tidings the angel of the Lord revealed to Hagar! She
already knew about the child growing inside her, but she hadn't known he
was a *he*. As to buying a book of baby names, no worries. God had that covered too.

"You shall name him Ishmael…" *Genesis 16:11*

Even people who haven't read *Moby-Dick* recognize Herman Melville's
famous opening line, "Call me Ishmael." But centuries earlier Hagar's baby
boy bore that name, chosen not by his mother or father or Melville but by
his Creator. Though Ishmael was the first person named before birth by God,
he was not the last; God also ordained the names of Isaac, Josiah, Jedidiah
(also known as Solomon), John the Baptist, and his own Son, Jesus. An
impressive lineup of patriarchs, prophets, kings, and one glorious Savior.

But first, Ishmael.

"…for the LORD has heard of your misery." *Genesis 16:11*

Ishmael means "God hears." The misery or "affliction" (NASB) refers to
Sarai's harsh treatment of her maidservant. Perhaps this was God's gentle way
of acknowledging the sacrifice he asked of Hagar. *Go back.*

It's reassuring to know our suffering never escapes his notice. God sees
and God hears. Hears our muffled sobs late at night. Hears our whispered
pleas in doctors' waiting rooms. Hears our unspoken words when we struggle to pray. What comfort, knowing we're loved by a God who listens.

He again spoke to expectant Hagar, describing Ishmael in terms well
suited to this "rebellious and proud mother."[34]

"He will be a wild donkey of a man;…" *Genesis 16:12*

Maybe you, too, have mothered "a bucking bronco" (MSG). Some young
men just can't sit still and aren't happy unless they're climbing onto a motor-
cycle, a skateboard, a horse, *something*. (We don't have anybody who fits that

description at the Higgs house, but I dated a few broncos in my youth!) A true Bedouin of the desert, Ishmael would be "wild, free, untamable,"[35] much like a wild donkey or onager, a sturdy desert animal that cannot be domesticated.

On the heels of God's naming her son, Hagar did something no other biblical character dared do: *she named God.*

> She gave this name to the LORD who spoke to her: "You are the God who sees me." *Genesis 16:13*

My mind is duly blown. Once God saw Hagar, in the fullness of the word *saw*—looked at, recognized, called by name, understood, visited with, provided for her—she had the chutzpah to name him "God who sees me" (NCV). Some think Hagar assigned this all-seeing deity a name so she might "invoke him in the future."[36] An amusing concept, since she hadn't summoned him in the first place: "the angel came of his own accord."[37]

Not only did God see Hagar; *she saw God.*

> "I have now seen the One who sees me." *Genesis 16:13*

We hear a sense of wonder, even a hint of disbelief in her voice. Eugene Peterson captures her amazement with "Yes! He saw me; and then I saw him!" (MSG), though many translations pose this verse as a question, perhaps whispered in awe: "Have I really seen God and remained alive after seeing him?" (NRSV). After all, Egyptian and Canaanite gods were not to be trifled with. Even this God later said, "You cannot see my face, for no one may see me and live."[38] Yet Hagar saw the angel of the Lord and lived to talk about it. Imagine that!

The name she gave the Lord became attached to the place where they met, a spot where both water and mercy flowed in abundance.

> That is why the well was called Beer Lahai Roi. *Genesis 16:14*

Literally, "a well to the Living One Who sees me" (AMP), one of the many wells described in Genesis. Did Hagar take a long drink before she turned back toward Abram's tents? Search for her reflection in the stream bubbling up from the ground, curious to see if her countenance had been altered by her encounter with *El Roi*, with God Who Sees Me? Or did she splash her face with water, like one trying to wake from a dream?

We aren't told what Hagar did next, but it's clear what she *didn't* do: refuse to go back to her mistress. Instead, she "turned right around and retraced her steps,"[39] undoubtedly with her head held high, her shoulders squared, and her footing sure. She'd fled Abram's tents feeling unseen, unheard, unloved. Now she walked back, having been seen, heard, and loved by One far greater than Abram or Sarai. She'd left with no other identity than slave and found her true calling through the eyes of El Roi, the One who'd blessed her womb, the One who'd made her a mother.

Happy Birth Day

> So Hagar bore Abram a son, and Abram gave the name Ishmael to the son she had borne. *Genesis 16:15*

Abram may have spoken the name of Ishmael, but he didn't choose it. Hagar obviously had told Abram of her encounter with the angel of the Lord—every word of it, knowing our spunky sister. Bet that changed in a hurry how he viewed Hagar.

"You saw an *angel*? And he said *what*?"

I suspect this future mother of multitudes received a softer pallet to sleep on, better food to eat, and kinder treatment from her mistress. Especially if the man of the household "accepted Ishmael as the child of promise,"[40] as I feel certain Hagar did when she realized Abram's God and her El Roi were one and the same. Think about it: since the Lord told Abram he'd have many descendants and the angel of the Lord told Hagar the same thing, the two naturally (but erroneously) concluded their long line of offspring would begin with this firstborn son.

> Abram was eighty-six years old when Hagar bore him Ishmael. *Genesis 16:16*

Someone has disappeared from our story: Sarai. What did she think when this maidservant came strolling back into her life? Was she relieved to see Hagar or furious? Eager to attend Ishmael's birth or loath to gaze upon him? Did she cradle the boy in her arms and claim him as her son or turn away when he cried for attention? As the months went by, did Sarai oversee Ishmael's upbringing or leave everything to Hagar?

Since the biblical record is silent about such details, I can't in good conscience fill them in. (I'm reminded of that scene in *My Big Fat Greek Wedding* when Gus slumps on his plastic-covered couch, muttering in frustration, "I don't know, I don't know, I don't know!")

We'll get a better grip on the situation if we fast-forward sixteen years or so and see how things stand between Hagar, her mistress, and the firstborn son of Abram. Because by that point, a *second* son had joined the family: Isaac, born to Sarah. (Long story there, and we'll cover it all in the next chapter, I promise.)

Meanwhile, forgive the leap in time (and the name changes for Abraham and Sarah). Once we've finished our visit with an older Hagar, we'll step back and rejoin Sarai on a far happier day than the one before us.

A risky business, children's parties. Maybe if they'd hired a clown…

On the day Isaac was weaned Abraham held a great feast. *Genesis 21:8*

When a wealthy man like Abraham hosted "a big party" (NLT), everybody came. On this occasion they were celebrating a rite of passage—the weaning of a child who'd "survived this first and particularly dangerous stage of his life."[41] In ancient times mothers nursed their children for about three years,[42] though one commentator suggested that, because of Sarah's advanced age, "Isaac was probably weaned earlier."[43] Are you kidding? The woman waited *ninety years* to have a baby! No way would she give up nursing her son one day sooner than absolutely necessary.

When I weaned my dear baby girl one September eve, it was a bittersweet moment; throwing a party for the neighborhood was the last thing on my mind. Sarah no doubt struggled with fluctuating hormones, separation anxiety, and a healthy concern for Isaac's future, especially with his older half brother, Ishmael, hanging around.

> But Sarah saw that the son whom Hagar the Egyptian had borne to Abraham was mocking… *Genesis 21:9*

Uh-oh. Not "Sarah's son" but *"the* son." Not good. And the emphasis on Hagar's foreignness gives us another clue to the strained relationship between the two women. "Borne to Abraham" and not "borne for Sarah" provides a possible answer to our question about Sarah's involvement in Ishmael's up-bringing. Zilch, I'd say.

If Sarah had embraced her husband's firstborn and the child's mother as well, "all future history might have been different, tribe might have learned to love tribe."[44] But that wasn't how it happened. From the moment Hagar became pregnant, these two women were at odds.

Maybe that's where it all started: the problem of women sabotaging women.

It's subtle, but insidious. Women who choose natural childbirth at home believe they're more maternal, while women who have epidurals in the hospital think their approach is more practical. Breast-feeding mothers criticize women who bottle-feed their babies, while bottle users think nursing mothers are fanatics. Stay-at-home moms disparage mothers who work outside the home, while working mothers dismiss stay-at-home mothers as kept women. Mothers who give birth view women with adopted or stepchildren as something less than *real* mothers. And women without children feel utterly left out in the company of any of the above.

We rarely say this stuff aloud, not even to our close friends, not even in jest.

But we've thought it, sis. We have. And those are just the domestic issues; female rivalry can get even uglier in the workplace.

Maybe Sarah saw red when she spied Ishmael mocking Isaac because it reminded her of a season in her life when Hagar had behaved the same way toward her. Mocking. Deriding. Taunting.

Now Ishmael was following in his mother's footsteps.

We can visualize the scene: a strong-limbed, agile teenager teasing a round-faced toddler still clinging to his mother's skirts. Commentators can't agree on precisely what Ishmael was doing with Isaac—"perhaps playing, perhaps mocking, perhaps imitating."[45] But whether Ishmael offered his little brother a "laugh of derision,"[46] a "sneer,"[47] or a "malignant expression of scorn,"[48] we get the idea: he was "making fun of Isaac" (NCV).

Did Hagar chastise Ishmael for his inappropriate behavior? Or did she egg him on? Maybe she looked the other way, her Slightly Bad Girl heart warming at the thought of marring the day's festivities for Sarah. Could be Hagar felt envious of Isaac's big party. Chances are, when she stopped nursing Ishmael, no confetti was tossed, no canapés were passed around the women's tents.

As for Sarah, she'd had quite enough of this high-handed servant and her insolent son. Ishmael could easily harm Isaac, even kill him. Abraham was more than a century old, and she wasn't far behind; they might both be gone in a year's time. Better not to have this pretender to the throne hanging around while Isaac was too young to defend himself.

Clearly, the two brothers could not coexist, not with "murder in the wind."[49] So Sarah lashed out at her husband, though it was Hagar who truly felt the sting of her whip.

> ...and she said to Abraham, "Get rid of that slave woman and her
> son..." *Genesis 21:10*

Ouch, ouch, ouch. Sarah "turned to Abraham and demanded" (NLT) that he "cast out" (KJV), "drive out" (NASB), "throw out" (NCV)... We get it. No names were spoken, only "this maid and her son" (NASB). Whatever bond once existed between mistress and servant had disintegrated to ashes. Hagar no longer had a relationship, legal or otherwise, with Sarah; by this point "only Abraham has authority over her."[50] At least we can relax about one thing: the abuse surely ended after Hagar returned home; the father of her child would have seen to that.

But her mistress's words cut deep enough to wound.

"...for that slave woman's son will never share in the inheritance
with my son Isaac." *Genesis 21:10*

Sarah couldn't bring herself to speak their names: just "the son of this
bondwoman" (KJV). So demeaning, so dismissive. Her language alone "reflects
the increasing distance between the two women."[51] Forget using a yardstick;
even a steel tape measure wouldn't be long enough to gauge the widening gap.

As for Hagar, her problems were quickly mounting: Sarah's insistence
that mother and son be cast out of their home amounted to "a death sentence"[52] since only an inhospitable desert awaited them. What must Hagar
have thought? She'd lived among Abraham's tents for many years; Canaan
wasn't Egypt, but it was home. The first time she'd fled the camp of her own
volition, and when El Roi had commanded her to return, she'd obeyed. Now
she was being banished by her harsh mistress with no hope of being welcomed back. Might her master intervene?

Listen, Abraham

The matter distressed Abraham greatly because it concerned his son.
Genesis 21:11

I love biblical understatement. The word "distressed" is a bit soft; "troubled" (NCV) and "upset" (NLT) don't add much volume; "the thing was very
grievous (serious, evil) in Abraham's sight" (AMP) strikes a more resonant
chord. Abraham was definitely worried about Ishmael and Hagar—though
not sufficiently worried to risk opposing his first wife.

But God said to him, "Do not be so distressed about the boy and
your maidservant." *Genesis 21:12*

How interesting that God should appear at this juncture. I wonder if
Abraham heard the Lord's voice as some of us do, deep inside our hearts. Or
if God spoke to him aloud with words only Abraham could hear. Otherwise
the whole rite-of-passage party got an earful when they heard what God said
next.

"Listen to whatever Sarah tells you..." *Genesis 21:12*

I confess, I'm scratching my head. Wasn't Abraham the master of his household? "God's siding with her was quite unexpected."[53] You're telling me! Listen to *Sarah,* who'd made a career out of mistreating Hagar? God nonetheless encouraged Abraham to "hearken unto her voice" (KJV) and "do whatever Sarah tells you" (NCV).

Before we embroider "Listen to Whatever Your Wife Tells You" on throw pillows, ready to toss at our men as needed, it's important to view this scene from God's perspective. He was helping Abraham, a "reluctant, ambiguous father,"[54] handle an unfortunate situation. Rather like "two men coping with a cantankerous woman."[55]

"...because it is through Isaac that your offspring will be reckoned."
Genesis 21:12

I'll bet Sarah was relieved to hear that! No doubt she took credit for it down the pike: "If I hadn't kicked out that no-good Egyptian slave and her son..." Like many strong-willed women, Sarah believed she alone made things happen instead of seeing the hand of the Almighty. Before the beginning of time, God had drafted a blueprint for humankind, including this patriarchal addition. God told Abraham to listen to his wife, not because he "approved her disposition, but because God wanted the work that he authored accomplished."[56]

Before Abraham could protest, "But what will happen to Ishmael?" God unveiled his specific plan for Hagar's son.

"I will make the son of the maidservant into a nation also, because
he is your offspring." *Genesis 21:13*

Could God have destroyed Hagar and Ishmael? Of course. Instead God guarded the seed of Abraham, just as he'd promised. And the fruit of the seed Abraham first sowed—at Sarah's insistence—was about to travel south to Egypt.

In that climate journeys began at sunrise to avoid the midday heat. A short night for Hagar, then, and no doubt a sleepless one. Hagar knew she would not return; her mistress had spoken.

> Early the next morning Abraham took some food and a skin of
> water and gave them to Hagar. *Genesis 21:14*

Dawn had barely broken. Not many among the tents were busy about their work. Abraham assumed the role of servant to Hagar, providing food and a kidskin bottle of water—hardly enough to meet her needs in the desert, yet all she could carry on her back.

Was this send-off gruff or tender? For many years Hagar had been the mother of his only son. Even though she was both a foreigner and a slave in his household, Abraham must have felt something toward her and even more affection for Ishmael. Did the three of them tarry at the edge of Abraham's vast circle of tents, struggling to express their sorrow? Hagar wouldn't miss Sarah, but perhaps she regretted leaving her child's aging father.

His vision no doubt clouded by tears, Abraham bid his one-time secondary wife and firstborn son farewell, sending them on their way with the most meager of provisions.

> He set them on her shoulders and then sent her off with the boy.
> *Genesis 21:14*

John Calvin fumed, "Why did he not at least load up a donkey with more food? Why did he not assign one of his servants to them?"[57] Yes, why *didn't* you, Abraham? Maybe he was too distraught to think of such practicalities. Or maybe he counted on Hagar's traveling only a short distance and then returning home as she had before. Or maybe—just maybe—Abraham trusted God to meet Hagar's needs.

Wandering in the Wilderness

> She went on her way and wandered in the desert of Beersheba.
> *Genesis 21:14*

Sixteen years earlier Hagar had fled to the desert alone, seeking refuge from Sarah's cruelty. This time, son in tow, she was "wandering aimlessly" (NLT). Life as she knew it was over: Sarah had won; Ishmael would not be Abraham's heir after all. Her husband's refusal to oppose his first wife's heartless demands left Hagar reeling.

For the single mothers among us, Hagar's anguish may feel painfully familiar. She raised her son in Isaac's shadow, with little support from Ishmael's father. When she went to the well to draw water, she had to endure the easy laughter of women with husbands who loved them. At night she lay alone on her bed, her future no more certain than when she'd lifted her head that morning. Centuries later single mothers still long for their children to have a father figure, still struggle with envy when surrounded by all those perfect-looking families at church, still suffer from loneliness and uncertainty. No wonder the story of Hagar—the first single mom mentioned in the Bible[58]—rings true.

With so little food and water on her back, Hagar knew her Egyptian homeland was beyond reach. Did she call out to El Roi, to God Who Sees Me, hoping he might appear at her bidding and provide divine assistance? In the intervening years, had Hagar worshiped El Roi, prayed to him, or sought his counsel? The biblical record doesn't tell us, though I imagine she'd whispered his promise like a mantra through many a troubled hour, picturing those descendants "too numerous to count."[59]

How hollow the angel's promise must have sounded as Hagar offered the last drop of water to her precious son.

> When the water in the skin was gone, she put the boy under one of the bushes. *Genesis 21:15*

Not much grew in this inhospitable desert other than low brush and dwarf bushes,[60] the only shelter Hagar could offer her son. The teenage Ishmael was "thoroughly humbled as well as wearied, and therefore passive under his mother's guidance."[61] When my own son was seventeen and had his wisdom teeth removed, he was helpless that first day: too woozy to walk, he sat propped up on the couch, waiting for me to feed him spoonfuls of Jell-O. That's the image I have of Ishmael, though in far worse condition: fainting from the heat and delirious with thirst.

As for our outcast sister, Hagar had lost hope. Her water was gone and so, apparently, was her faith in El Roi. Some Slightly Bad Girls take control when God doesn't act quickly enough to suit them. This Slightly Bad Girl slumped to the ground in defeat.

> Then she went off and sat down nearby, about a bowshot away...
> *Genesis 21:16*

How close is "nearby," and how far is a "bowshot"? Depends on the talent of the archer, though here the phrase was nothing more than a common Hebrew simile.[62] Whether Hagar was "a good way off" (KJV), "fifty yards or so" (MSG), or "about a hundred yards away" (NLT), she'd distanced herself from Ishmael by intent.

> ...for she thought, "I cannot watch the boy die."
> *Genesis 21:16*

Though I would hold my son until his last breath, pleading with God to be merciful, Hagar was so undone she couldn't bear to see Ishmael suffer. Across the centuries our hearts go out to her. We envision her grieving like a mother with a gravely ill child in the hospital, sitting by his bedside hour after hour, then stepping into the hall for a moment to lean against the cold tile wall and weep.

> And as she sat there nearby, she began to sob. *Genesis 21:16*

If this were a Shakespearean tragedy, we could avert our gaze from the stage or quietly close the script. But this is a real chapter in Hebrew history, and we cannot escape the painful scene before us: a mother in despair, collapsed in the dirt, unable to help her child, unwilling to face his death. No wonder she "lifted up her voice and wept" (NASB).

Hagar was not the only one.

God heard the boy crying… *Genesis 21:17*

Why did the Lord not hear Hagar weeping rather than "the voice of the lad" (KJV)? Since Ishmael was of Abraham's seed, perhaps God hearkened to him first. But not to worry: he heard Hagar too. Even if she did not cry out his name, God listened and God spoke.

> …and the angel of God called to Hagar from heaven and said to
> her, "What is the matter, Hagar?" *Genesis 21:17*

Did the Lord know "what aileth thee?" (KJV)? We can be sure of it; the Bible declares, "for the Lord God omnipotent reigneth."[63] He knew Hagar's hurts just as he knows ours. Yet he asked her to confess her failures, her fears, her faithlessness for her own good, all the while intending to help her.

Even before Hagar could respond, the angel of the Lord offered a word of comfort.

> "Do not be afraid; God has heard the boy crying as he lies there."
> *Genesis 21:17*

We learned this first from our Genesis narrator and now from the angel of the Lord. Such repetition is for our benefit so we don't miss the message: *God hears.*

> "Lift the boy up and take him by the hand…" *Genesis 21:18*

God was saying more than "pick up your son." He instructed Hagar to "go to him and comfort him" (NLT), literally "make your hand firm upon him," both emotionally and physically, "lending support and encouragement."[64] After all, without his father to guide him, Ishmael would need Hagar's constant care. His future rested in his mother's hands.

Last time he came to her in the desert, God promised Hagar her son would have countless descendants. This time God expanded that vision.

> "…for I will make him into a great nation." *Genesis 21:18*

Not only would Sarah's son produce the twelve tribes of Israel, but Hagar's son would be the father of twelve tribes as well: "These were the sons of Ishmael, and these are the names of the twelve tribal rulers according to their settlements and camps."[65]

Whole *tribes* of men from one Ishmael? Only God could make such a bold claim while looking down on a dying child. Out of hopelessness came hope. Out of death, life!

An Eye-Opening Experience

Then God opened her eyes... *Genesis 21:19*

Interesting phrasing: not "Hagar opened her eyes," but "God opened Hagar's eyes" (NLT). One scholar insisted such wording merely indicated "the cheering of her mind and the sharpening of her attention,"[66] but I think it means exactly what it says. "God then opened her eyes, and she saw what she had not seen before."[67]

...and she saw a well of water. *Genesis 21:19*

Rather, "God showed Hagar a well of water" (NCV).

Now, that's odd. She had stopped because her skin of water was empty, yet there was a well not a stone's throw away. Had Hagar missed this life-giving source because she was so wrapped up in her troubles? If so, we'll not condemn her for it; God doesn't. When we're in pain, we're often unaware of our surroundings. Our gaze is unfocused, our attention turned inward. Faces and voices are fuzzy, muted. If Hagar needed help seeing the obvious, her dire circumstances earn her a measure of grace.

Or did God make the well miraculously appear? Nothing is too difficult for him, especially not providing for so basic a human need. Scripture is brimming with water: springs of water, living water, jars of water, parting water, floods of water. At the first hour of creation, "the Spirit of God was hovering over the waters."[68] Then, as his Word draws to a close, we're reminded, "Whoever is thirsty, let him come; and whoever wishes, let him take the free gift of the water of life."[69] Like a master artist with a favorite medium, God loves to work in water.

So was this an eye-opening revelation for Hagar or a well-timed act of divine provision? I appreciate the ambiguity, the unanswered question, because either way, we see that God met the needs of this mother and child. Either way, it was miraculous.

Hagar wasted no time in partaking of that spring in the desert.

> So she went and filled the skin with water and gave the boy a drink.
> *Genesis 21:19*

Ooh, just imagine that refreshing liquid running over his parched tongue! And catch the look of relief on Ishmael's face when Hagar "gave the boy a long, cool drink" (MSG). Thirsty as she must have been, Hagar selflessly gave Ishmael a drink first. How like a mother.

Unlike Abraham's short-term supply, God provided Hagar "with a source of water that will endure."[70] Not a mere skin of water, but a flowing stream in the desert. We see the pattern repeated all through Scripture: our efforts are temporal; the Lord's provision is eternal.

> God was with the boy as he grew up. *Genesis 21:20*

Don't hurry past this one, dear sister. *God was with Ishmael.* In the years to come, God would also be with Jacob, Joseph, and Joshua, Samson, Samuel, and Solomon—men of God whose praises are sung throughout Scripture. But here in the desert of Beersheba and on through their travels, God was with the son of an Egyptian woman. We dare not call Ishmael illegitimate! Yes, Abraham's offspring would be reckoned through Isaac, but God did not turn his back on this son and his heirs.

If God was with Ishmael—and he was—then God was near the young man's mother as well. "Christians tend to forget about Hagar and her story. We forget her pain, her courage, her resistance to mistreatment."[71] We seldom mention her in the same breath with Hannah and Hadassah, yet God paid close attention to Hagar and blessed her son.

He lived in the desert and became an archer. *Genesis 21:20*

You'll recall Hagar just a few verses ago tucked Ishmael beneath some bushes, then sat down "a bowshot away."[72] Who but God knew he would turn to archery and become "an expert with the bow" (NRSV)? Her bucking bronco took on the world with bow and arrow in hand—"a leader, an archer, a fighter."[73] And, eventually, an Egyptian maid's husband.

> While he was living in the Desert of Paran, his mother got a wife
> for him from Egypt. *Genesis 21:21*

We're not surprised he married "a young woman from Egypt" (NLT). What *was* unusual was that Hagar handled the betrothal herself. For the record, she's "the only woman in the Hebrew Bible to select a wife for her son."[74] Yet another historical first that landed on Hagar's lengthy résumé.

Her tenacity and her audacity ring through the ages. Though the "strength of Islam…is said to be bound up with the name of Hagar,"[75] more than two millennia passed before that new religion emerged in Arabia in the seventh century AD, guided by the prophet Muhammad. "Ishmael's pedigree lent legitimacy to the new faith, but the Koran never mentions Hagar's name."[76]

The Bible, however, includes the name of Hagar fifteen times, and today Hagar has become a "symbol of downtrodden women who persevere."[77] A quick perusal on the Internet reveals outreach efforts named "Hagar's House" and "El Roi"—ministries to single parents, to battered women, to those who feel estranged, pushed out, discounted.

Hagar has also been immortalized by dozens of artists through the centuries—Pencz, Rembrandt, Verhaghen, Corot, Chagall[78]—all drawn to the story of a woman cast into the wilderness, only to be found by God, heard by God, seen by God, loved by God.

What an unexpected role model our Slightly Bad Girl turned out to be!

As to her mistress, Sarah, we'll soon discover how much God loved this take-charge woman despite her obvious flaws.

What Lessons Can We Learn from Hagar?

Running can be a sign of strength.

A woman trapped in an abusive relationship may long to flee from her home, as Hagar did, yet fear for her life if she leaves. Great courage is required to gather a few belongings and run for the safety of a shelter—and great humility as well, to admit needing such a refuge. In my youth I tried to evict an abusive man from my life and found it far easier said than done. Friends lost patience with me, and the authorities weren't particularly supportive (no wonder, when I kept taking him back!). In the end, for Hagar and her sisters in suffering, the decision to run (or, in my case, to walk very fast to a locksmith) marks the beginning of a new life.

> When you are persecuted in one place, flee to another.
> *Matthew 10:23*

We have a Hero who hears.

In movies, characters facing life-or-death dilemmas invariably call out God's name—not because they have a relationship with him, but because they're desperate—only to be promptly rescued by Spider-Man, Wolverine, or Bruce Willis. During Hagar's two crises in the wilderness, she learned that God is the best of heroes, clearing the path of obstacles and deflecting unseen dangers. Indeed, God sees our needs before we speak them and does not wait to be summoned, though if we call out his name, he is sure to listen.

> Let them give thanks to the LORD for his unfailing love and his
> wonderful deeds for men, for he satisfies the thirsty and fills the
> hungry with good things. *Psalm 107:8–9*

Lord, open our eyes that we may see.

When Hagar and her son were dying of thirst, God opened her eyes and showed her a well. Opened eyes, opened ground—who can say which was the greater miracle? When we're mired in misery, we often can't see farther than the tissue pressed against our runny noses. It's natural to plead for our circumstances to change, but let's also pray that the Lord will open our eyes to the wondrous possibilities right in front of us and the everyday miracles bestowed by his generous hand.

> Ah, Sovereign LORD, you have made the heavens and the earth by your great power and outstretched arm. Nothing is too hard for you. *Jeremiah 32:17*

True freedom is found only in God.

When Sarah insisted her husband cast Hagar and Ishmael into the wilderness, she unwittingly gave mother and son their freedom. Sarah intended to harm them, but God intended it for good to accomplish his perfect will: Hagar and Ishmael would be far happier in Egypt, and Isaac would be safer once they exited Canaan. Sarah emancipated Hagar from slavery, yet God freed Hagar and her son from imminent death and gave them new lives in their home-land. The Lord stands ready to set us free as well: from past mistakes that have a stranglehold on us, from present burdens too heavy to bear, from a future that appears murky and uncertain. When we embrace that freedom with our whole hearts and trust him to guide us, our feet will have wings.

> I run in the path of your commands, for you have set my heart free. *Psalm 119:32*

Good Girl Thoughts Worth Considering

1. How acquainted were you with Hagar's story before reading this study? Did you expect to like or dislike her, and why? Now that you've spent time with Hagar, list her Slightly Bad Girl qualities as well as her Mostly Good Girl attributes. Which of her negative traits landed her in the most trouble? And which of her positive traits do you most admire?

2. Do you think Hagar was a Slightly Bad Girl for agreeing to sleep with Abram? What other choices would a slave have had in her time and place?

Can you think of a recent situation in your life when you felt compelled to do something you didn't agree with simply because that particular behavior is deemed acceptable in our culture? If so, how did you handle things? When God's Word says one thing and society says another, how can we find the strength to stand up for what we believe?

3. When the angel commanded Hagar to go back to Sarai, she didn't protest, despite the pain that might await her. How would you explain Hagar's willingness to obey his angelic order? As you review Genesis 16:9–12, you'll notice Hagar fell silent for a bit. What might have stilled her tongue? If the Lord has ever compelled you to return to a trying situation, what was the outcome? And how did you grow as a result of your obedience?

4. Hagar showed great confidence in naming him God Who Sees Me. What would you name God, and why? Do you believe God also sees you? Hears you? Loves you? On what do you base your beliefs?

5. Describe Abraham's feast on the day Isaac was weaned, as you picture it. What were the guests talking about? What foods do you suppose were served? When teenage Ishmael mocked toddler Isaac, what words might Ishmael have said? Do you think Hagar tried to prevent Ishmael's insubordinate behavior? Or might she have encouraged it, and if so, to what end?

6. Twice Hagar found herself in "a land of deserts and rifts, a land of drought and darkness, a land where no one travels and no one lives."[79] What's the significance of Hagar's wandering in a desert rather than through a forest or a meadow? If you've ever spent time in a spiritual wilderness, describe your experience. In what ways have you experienced God as a spring of living water that quenches your thirst?

7. In what ways do you think God was "with the boy" Ishmael as he matured (Genesis 21:20)? How do you explain God's loving care of Hagar

and her son when Ishmael was not the one through whom Abraham's bless-ing would flow? Is it necessary to fully understand God's ways before you put your faith in him? What *must* you know about God to trust him as Hagar did?

8. What's the most important lesson you learned from Hagar, who beat a path to the desert twice and found God waiting for her both times?

The Last Laugh

I should prefer to die laughing,
and, on more than one occasion,
thought I might.
JOSEPH EPSTEIN

M rs. Cannon?" The salon receptionist approached with eyebrows lifted. "Your husband is on the phone. He said your cellular was—"

"Turned off, of course." Sandra held up her freshly manicured hands, the red polish gleaming wet. "Can't you take a message?"

"I'm sorry, but he said it was urgent." The young woman pulled a cordless phone from the pocket of her rose-colored smock. "I'll gladly hold it for you."

"Fine, fine." Sandra motioned her closer, then inclined her head as the receiver touched her ear. "Alan?"

"Sandi, I'm sorry to bother you…"

She winced at hearing her old nickname. No one called her Sandi anymore, not since the year she'd turned fifty and insisted on *Sandra*. Most people remembered; Alan wasn't one of them.

When his words began tumbling over themselves, she cut him off. "Wait. *How* many people are joining us for dinner?"

"Three ministers from the West Coast, here for the denominational conference. Pastor Davidson just found out they're coming a day earlier than planned, and he won't return home until tomorrow. We're to expect the men about seven o'clock."

Sandra glanced at her watch, careful not to smudge her polish. Even on her housekeeper's day off, three dinner guests were of no concern. But three hours to plan a menu, shop for fresh ingredients, and prepare each dish to her usual high standards posed a minor emergency. She barely heard Alan's suggestions—veal, asparagus, couscous—until the last item.

"And you'll make *paska*, yes?"

Pavla's recipe.

Sandra kept her voice even. "It's a very long process, I'm afraid. The dough has to rise three times. And anyway, it's meant to be served at Easter."

"But surely the Lord's resurrection merits celebration any day."

"Oh, Alan…" She rolled her eyes, glad he couldn't see her. After thirty years of marriage, he knew exactly which buttons to push. "I'll see what I can do."

An hour later she stood in her kitchen, covered with flour. Pavla had always turned her nose up at bread machines, insisting the best dough was hand-kneaded. If Pavla could manage, so could she. Sandra tipped her bifocals, trying to read Pavla's old recipe scrawled on an index card. "Dough should be stiff," Sandra muttered, thrusting her fists into the yeasty mixture. That much she'd accomplished.

She should have called her caterer. Henri always had something delicious on hand. Or an ethnic bakery, though they'd hardly offer Ukrainian paska in June. Stubborn pride kept her from phoning the one person who could truly help her: Pavla Teslenko, her next-door neighbor. Living in the house that Alan had built for Pavla's mother and brothers. Living with the son that wasn't Sandra's after all.

With a lengthy sigh, she focused on the task at hand. Even if it did ruin her manicure, kneading the dough proved to be therapeutic. Pushing and pulling the sticky mass across a floured board released some of her lingering frustration. With Pavla. With Alan. With herself.

At first Sandra had tried to care for newborn Ivan on her own, but she quickly discovered how ill-prepared she was for late-night feedings and round-the-clock diaper changes. Struggles with colic came a few weeks later, then teething, then ear infections. Pavla always hurried to her rescue at a moment's notice, eager to help her son and no doubt pleased to see Sandra so inept. The girl positively *glowed* every time she walked through the door. And Alan seemed entirely too glad to see her.

The situation came to a head on Ivan's first birthday. Pavla took him next door to be with her family, then returned alone to face the Cannons. "Ivan is happier with me," she'd said calmly. "My mother is younger than you and can help raise him as well."

Her cruel words cut Sandra to the quick, though she couldn't deny the truth: Ivan *was* happier with his biological mother, and it was Sandra's own fault. Three days after his birth, when Pavla's breasts were swollen with milk, she'd begged Sandra to let her nurse him. Knowing the benefits, Sandra couldn't refuse. Hadn't she once hoped to breast-feed a child?

From that hour the bond between mother and son had strengthened. Ivan brightened at the sound of Pavla's voice, not hers. He always smiled for Pavla but rarely for her. As the months passed, Ivan looked less like Alan and more—much more—like Pavla. In the end, all the court documents in the world couldn't force a mother to stop loving her child nor a child to stop loving his mother.

Ivan belonged to Pavla now. Even the law said so.

Sandra slowed her kneading long enough to gaze through the Palladian window at the Teslenkos' brick home, an acre away. She pictured five-year-old Ivan the way she'd seen him last: at the dinner table, sitting on a proper chair, eating meat cut into bite-size pieces, drinking from a glass.

He should have been mine, Lord. Mine and Alan's. But her husband had not stood up for her when she and Pavla exchanged volleys. "This was your idea," Alan reminded her. "I'll trust you and God to handle it." She had done her part. If only God had done the same…

"Enough," Sandra said firmly. Nothing could be done to change the past, and little could be done to alter the future. At her age conception was no longer possible. She eased the smooth mound of dough into a buttered bowl and covered it with a cloth, wishing her heartache could be dispensed with so easily.

"Here's my lovely bride." Alan smiled at her across the dining room. "And bearing bread, I see."

Sandra joined her guests at the table, the fragrant aroma of paska wafting up from the sterling silver basket lined with French linens. "Forgive me, gentlemen. Our maid is off on Tuesdays, leaving me to fend for myself."

One of their guests, the tall and imposing Rev. Finney, assured her, "You're fending very well, Mrs. Cannon."

He seemed to serve as the unofficial spokesman for the three. Perhaps because his voice was more commanding or his reputation more established. Sandra had heard of Rev. Theo Finney. He reputedly had the gift of prophecy, though Sandra had her doubts.

Their meal progressed smoothly with the usual compliments on the cuisine. The inevitable question of family arose near dinner's end. "Does your son live nearby?" Rev. Finney wanted to know.

A fleeting thought of Ivan skipped through Sandra's mind, though she said nothing except what must be said. "Alan and I have no children."

"Really?" The minister looked taken aback. "I imagined…that is to say, I was quite certain you were…a mother."

Heat rushed to her face. Surely no one had told him about Ivan. About Pavla.

She and Alan exchanged uneasy glances. "No…," her husband said, though he hardly sounded convincing.

"If you'll pardon me." Sandra abruptly stood, with the men hurrying to follow suit. "Dessert won't be a moment."

She removed their plates, vaguely resentful of the menial task. Could they not have come on any other night of the week? Once the table was cleared, she made quick work of assembling their dessert—sweet berries, fresh cream, delicate ladyfingers—while bits and pieces of dinner conversation floated through the open doorway.

When Rev. Finney circled around to the topic of children again, her hands stilled as she strained to listen.

"Mature couples make fine parents." His voice exuded confidence. "Truly, Alan, it's not too late for you to have children of your own."

Sandra's mouth fell open. Did the man think she was twenty years younger?

She heard Alan respectfully protest, "Pastor, what you're suggesting—"

"Is well within God's power."

Oh, really? A laugh slipped out before she could stop herself. Mortified, she pressed a hand to her mouth but not before she laughed again. *Sandra!*

Had they heard her? Surely not from the kitchen. The dining room had fallen quiet, though, and her laugh *was* rather loud. Nothing to be done but serve dessert and pray her amusement had gone undetected.

As she approached the table, Alan was shaking his head as Rev. Finney said, "Yes, I distinctly heard Mrs. Cannon laugh."

"So I did." She placed a dessert plate in front of him with a decided bang. "You must admit, the idea *is* laughable at my age."

He looked at her so intently that one of the desserts nearly slipped from her grasp. "Your age, madam, is of no concern to God."

She stiffened. "My doctor would beg to differ."

"Then perhaps it's time for another Physician," the minister said smoothly, taking up his spoon. "You won't mind if I stop by when we're in town next year just so I might see your infant son with my own eyes?"

"How *dare* he!" Sandra fumed, punching numbers into the telephone in Alan's home office. Morning had dawned, and she was still angry. The *nerve* of that man suggesting she would give birth by next spring. Had she been thirty-two, even forty-two, his comments would have been merely in poor taste. But at fifty-two she had every right to be offended.

Rev. Finney did not realize how close he'd come to having ladyfingers sticking out of his hair and cream dripping from his ears.

"Dr. Goodman, please." Sandra impatiently tapped her pen on Alan's leather desk top. Her ob-gyn would set the record straight. A pregnancy when she was menopausal? The very idea.

"Mrs. Cannon, what a pleasant surprise." They hadn't spoken since her last exam nearly a year ago. "How may I help you today?"

"I need you to tell me that a woman my age cannot conceive by natural means." When he didn't answer right away, she pressed on. "Surely such a thing isn't even remotely possible."

"Well, it's been a few years, but"—he cleared his throat—"a woman in Washington State conceived naturally and gave birth to triplets at the age of fifty-four."

Sandra slumped against her chair. "You're kidding."

"After all you've been through, Sandra? I would never joke about such a thing…"

Sarah: No Laughing Matter

After Hagar's many trials, you might consider a second visit with Sarai anything but amusing. You may even think she belongs with the Really, *Really* Bad Girls of the Bible.

Aye, but here's the rub: God didn't give up on Sarai. Despite her ruthless banishment of Hagar and Ishmael, Sarai was still cherished by God. Because she improved her attitude or behavior? No, because God never changes. From the beginning, he chose her as the Main Mom.

Did Sarai do anything to deserve the title? Not that we've seen. Her actions so far point to an impatient woman who thought she had a better plan for bringing God's promise of offspring to fruition and a vindictive woman who got what she asked for, then didn't want it.

Good thing our grace-giving God calls the shots, or we'd have sent Sarai marching back to Ur, proud of ourselves for helping Canaan have one less Bad Girl. Unfortunately, the world would've had one less Isaac. And Jacob. And Judah. And the Lion of Judah. See why God's in charge and we're not?

Now we'll move our biblical calendar back a few years to the time when Ishmael was thirteen, Hagar was still in residence, and Sarai was still barren. Free-floating angst must have filled their tents like sand in a windstorm. No doubt when the Lord stopped by, Abram was glad for his company.

> When Abram was ninety-nine years old, the LORD appeared to him and said, "I am God Almighty;…" *Genesis 17:1*

Isn't it grand when God identifies himself? In any translation or paraphrase the words leap off the page: "I am God All-Powerful" (ICB). Think how it must have been for Abram to hear Yahweh speak the words aloud!

"…walk before me and be blameless." *Genesis 17:1*

Don't take "walk before me" too literally. God wasn't urging Abram to take up aerobic exercise but to "live entirely before me" (MSG). No hidden sins, no secret acts, no shameful deeds. As God later told Solomon, and asks of us as well, "Walk before me in integrity of heart and uprightness,"[1] a feat we can manage only through the strength of our powerful God.

When God confirmed his previous covenant with Abram, promising to greatly increase the number of his descendants, "Abram fell face down in the dust."[2] Then God promptly changed the man's name.

> "No longer will you be called Abram; your name will be
> Abraham…" *Genesis 17:5*

What a difference a *ha* makes! That simple addition "represented Jehovah."[3] The Lord made it clear that Abraham belonged to him and that their relationship would be mutual and everlasting.

> God also said to Abraham, "As for Sarai your wife, you are no
> longer to call her Sarai; her name will be Sarah." *Genesis 17:15*

With this subtle change—only an *h*—Sarah's name became sacramental, covenantal. Though *Sarah* still meant "princess," the Talmud expands the shift in meaning: "a princess to all the world."[4] Her influence would extend far past the boundaries of Canaan.

Here's the *truly* exciting part: God irrevocably included Sarah in his promises to Abraham.

> "I will bless her and will surely give you a son by her. I will bless her
> so that she will be the mother of nations; kings of peoples will come
> from her." *Genesis 17:16*

Can anyone say, "Finally!"?

"I'll bless her…. Oh, how I'll bless her!" (MSG). Promised twice, for emphasis. And "moreover I will give you a son by her" (RSV). Not only a child but also an heir. God made his covenant, then, with all those "who can call Sarah mother."[5] Talk about a ton of people! Nations upon nations, kings upon kings—all because God was about to bless Sarah's womb.

I wish I could tell you Abraham was beside himself with joy. That he wept with gratitude, then wiped his tears away, gazing in the direction of Sarah's tent, longing to tell her the news.

Instead, he fell down laughing. No, really.

> Abraham fell facedown; he laughed... *Genesis 17:17*

Okay, maybe he "bowed down to the ground," but he still "laughed to himself in disbelief" (NLT). I think Abraham was hiding his amusement under the guise of reverence, hoping God wouldn't notice the big grin on his face, let alone read his thoughts.

> ...and said to himself, "Will a son be born to a man a hundred years
> old? Will Sarah bear a child at the age of ninety?" *Genesis 17:17*

He still had a full year to go, but already Abraham was rehearsing that daunting century mark. (I did the same thing the year I turned fifty.) Hard to say which possibility stymied the patriarch more: fathering a child at his advanced age or pacing the ground outside Sarah's tent while she gave birth. The whole idea was...well, inconceivable.

"Sarah is ninety; how could she have a baby?" (NLT). Wisely, Abraham kept his thoughts to himself and pointed the Almighty toward the son he'd already fathered.

> And Abraham said to God, "If only Ishmael might live under your
> blessing!" *Genesis 17:18*

I can't decide (and neither can the translators) whether Abraham was disagreeing with God's plan—"Why not let Ishmael inherit what you have promised me?" (CEV)—or if he was genuinely concerned his beloved first son might be done away with. "Oh, keep Ishmael alive and well before you!" (MSG).

The Lord wasn't about to be thrown off topic.

> Then God said, "Yes, but your wife Sarah will bear you a son, and
> you will call him Isaac." *Genesis 17:19*

Ancient Hebrew doesn't include precise words for *yes* and *no.* That's why a few modern translations have God saying, "Yes," and many more of them have God saying, "No." The word that matters more is the next one: "but." As in, "That's not what I mean" (MSG).

Sarah's son ranked as God's primary concern. As he did with Ishmael before his birth, God chose the lad's name: "Isaac [laughter]" (AMP). *Laughter?* What kind of name was that for an heir? Abraham might have thought the Lord was kidding—until he made a very serious promise.

> "I will establish my covenant with him as an everlasting covenant
> for his descendants after him." *Genesis 17:19*

If Abraham didn't believe God at first, he must have been convinced by then. God doesn't make "To-Do" lists; God makes "Done" lists.

Sarah, the mother. Check.

Isaac, the son. Check.

Covenant: The Next Generation. Check.

Mercifully, God didn't cross Abraham's first son off his list.

> "And as for Ishmael, I have heard you." *Genesis 17:20*

The Lord assured this concerned father, "Yes, I heard your prayer for him" (MSG), then described his plan to make Ishmael the father of twelve rulers. One last time, just in case Abraham had missed it, God reminded him through which son the great promise would flow.

> "But my covenant I will establish with Isaac, whom Sarah will bear
> to you by this time next year." *Genesis 17:21*

Note that one detail, added almost as an afterthought: "at this season next year" (NASB). If Sarah was going to deliver a baby twelve months hence, Abraham had to...um, get busy.

When he had finished speaking with Abraham, God went up from him. *Genesis 17:22*

I giggled when I read this translation: "That ended the conversation" (NLT). I'll just bet it did! "Your ninety-year-old wife will give birth a year from now" would bring most chitchat to a screeching halt.

One question still nags at me: after God told Abraham what he had in mind for Sarah, did Abraham tell his wife? I personally think he treasured up all these things and pondered them in his heart rather than tell his post-menopausal wife what God had in store. Let's see if the next scene provides an answer.

Unexpected Guests

The LORD appeared to Abraham near the great trees of Mamre... *Genesis 18:1*

The great trees were "terebinths" (AMP), long-lived trees, much like oaks, prized for the shade beneath their spreading branches. Such renowned trees also hinted at fertility—appropriate, considering what was about to transpire.

...while [Abraham] was sitting at the entrance to his tent in the heat of the day. *Genesis 18:1*

A fine place to greet visitors, handle family disputes, and guard the contents of the tent while the dark goatskin walls were thrown open, allowing the desert breezes to pass through.

Curtains separated the commodious space into various areas for sleeping and eating, while woven mats served as rugs, seats, and beds.[6] Perhaps Abraham leaned back into the entranceway to avoid the worst of the sun, not quite escaping the noonday heat as he shaded his eyes from the airborne sand.

Abraham looked up and saw three men standing nearby. *Genesis 18:2*

We've already been told "the LORD appeared," so one of these three men was God in the guise of a man—a theophany—while the two accompanying him were angels. The phrase "behold, three men" (NASB) tells us they didn't stroll up; they made a "sudden appearance."[7]

No wonder Abraham scrambled to his feet to make them welcome.

> "Let a little water be brought, and then you may all wash your feet
> and rest under this tree." *Genesis 18:4*

Wasn't Abe the perfect host? In a dry and dusty climate, open leather sandals were de rigueur, and washing the feet of guests was the first lesson in Hospitality 101.[8] The second lesson? Promise little, deliver much. Bragging about what you had in your pantry was considered tacky.

> "Let me get you something to eat, so you can be refreshed…"
> *Genesis 18:5*

Why did desert folk bend over backward to make strangers feel welcome? So they could "transform potential enemies into at least temporary friends."[9] With a nod from his guests, Abraham dashed into the tent to find Sarah and breathlessly ordered their meal.

> "Quick," he said, "get three seahs of fine flour and knead it and
> bake some bread." *Genesis 18:6*

If a man spoke so brusquely with his wife today, he might find that flour poured over his head. But Sarah understood the need for haste and went about her business, turning their best flour—"a kind of semolina"[10]—into loaves of bread, while Abraham selected a choice, tender calf and ordered a servant to prepare it.

Like a maître d' at the ready, Abraham stood while the three visitors enjoyed their food, his heart beating with anticipation. A shared meal signified that he and his guests were "at peace, in union" and that God was about to bless him.[11]

> "Where is your wife Sarah?" they asked him. *Genesis 18:9*

A curious question: the Lord and his messengers surely knew Sarah's whereabouts. They also knew the custom of the day: women were not welcome in the company of male visitors.[12] The fact that they spoke Sarah's name and inquired about her location proved "these men were not ordinary travelers."[13]

Maybe they wanted to be certain Sarah was listening. Hearing her name spoken by strangers would certainly draw her attention. Abraham pointed in Sarah's direction, though he didn't invite her to join them. Was he leery of their intentions? Wishing he'd told her, "Say you are my sister"? Or was the air alive with prophetic energy? Whatever his concerns, Abraham trusted the men enough to reveal Sarah's whereabouts.

"There, in the tent," he said. *Genesis 18:9*

Apparently that was close enough for the men. No problem if Sarah remained out of sight, "but she must not be out of hearing."[14] During the Lord's previous visits with Abraham, Sarah had not been present. Now, with her new name, her new identity, her new calling, she would have the new privilege of listening to the Lord directly. Because of her barrenness, what God was about to ask of her would require great faith. And since "faith comes from hearing,"[15] Sarah needed to hear this promise with her own ears.

Then the LORD said, "I will surely return to you about this time
next year…" *Genesis 18:10*

Fascinating how the Lord began with the same words he'd used at the end of the last scene: "this time next year." That could suggest "the time when it is reviving,"[16] meaning spring. Or "according to the time of life" (KJV), meaning the nine months of pregnancy. How about we stick with "this time next year"? That was already more than this elderly couple could grasp: *soon.*

"…and Sarah your wife will have a son." *Genesis 18:10*

Sarah your wife. Not some other Sarah and not some other wife. This woman you've been married to forever. *This* Sarah.

No question Abraham's heir would soon be born. Not *may,* but *will.*

We've been wondering if Abraham ever told Sarah about the prophecy first described in Genesis 17:16. I vote no for three reasons:

(1) We have no biblical record of Abraham's informing Sarah of the news.

(2) God showed up to tell her personally.

(3) Sarah's reaction suggests a woman caught off guard.

Look what happened and judge for yourself...

> Now Sarah was listening at the entrance to the tent, which was behind him. *Genesis 18:10*

Women had their own tents, so I suspect that's where Sarah stood—out of sight but well within earshot. Listening, just as the Lord intended. Seemingly out of nowhere came this timely reminder, like the words of an offstage announcer narrating the scene.

> Abraham and Sarah were already old and well advanced in years, and Sarah was past the age of childbearing. *Genesis 18:11*

Resist the urge to roll your eyes. I *know* you know this, and so did Sarah. But there's one new bit of information: "it had ceased to be with Sarah after the manner of women" (NRSV). Even allowing for longer life spans in the Old Testament, she'd been through what my mother demurely called the Change. Once a woman no longer had a monthly cycle, conception would not be merely difficult; it would be "a biological impossibility."[17]

You Gotta Be Kidding

Abraham fathering a child at ninety-nine was not really an issue. He went on to father more sons after Sarah's death three decades later: six sons with his second wife, Keturah, and several more by his concubines.[18] Sarah's retired womb presented the challenge. No healthy eggs, no nutrient-rich lining, and no chance of conception—short of a flat-out miracle.

Sarah your wife will have a son?

What a joke.

So Sarah laughed to herself... *Genesis 18:12*

I think Sarah showed great restraint in not bursting into tears. Easy enough for Abraham to sire a son at an advanced age; quite another matter for an old woman to carry a child for nine months and live through childbirth!

She didn't laugh aloud, only "silently" (NLT), "within herself" (KJV). Maybe if she'd fallen on her face, like Abraham, and concealed her bemused expression, she would have gotten away with it.

Instead, her soundless chuckle became the laugh heard 'round the world. Oh, the ink scholars have spilled over Sarah laughing up her sleeve!

As Inigo says in *The Princess Bride,* "Let me explain. No, there is too much. Let me sum up." Depending on which resource you turn to, Sarah's stifled laugh expressed "disbelief," "postmenopausal irony," "derision," "incredulous surprise," or a "hysterical" reaction.[19] While Abraham's response was considered a "joyous outburst of astonishment," Sarah's laugh smacked of "doubt and unbelief."[20] His was "a pleasing laughter of faith," but her reaction suggested "mistrust."[21]

You get the picture: Mostly Good Abraham, Slightly Bad Sarah.

True, she did laugh at God's words. But I wonder if she even knew this was the Lord speaking? After all, she'd not heard his voice before, as Abraham had. And he'd come in the guise of a man.

As a perimenopausal woman, my own laugh at such a moment would be loud and long, covering all the suggested emotions and then some—hysteria, in particular. A *baby*? At *that* age?

"Complicated"[22] describes Sarah's laugh best. After ninety years her hopes had simmered so long they'd finally evaporated. Think how many times Abraham must have told her, "Don't lose heart. Just trust God." So she'd trusted. She'd waited. She'd made every effort she could—not all of them virtuous—to provide a son for her husband.

When the God of Abraham finally spoke her name, he said everything she longed to hear. But he'd come too late.

We know that for all things "the LORD set a time"[23] and that his timing is perfect. We know his Word says, "My righteousness will never fail,"[24] and so we have reason to trust him. We know we're called to "wait in hope for the LORD,"[25] and so we do. But when we've trusted and waited and hoped and trusted and waited and hoped, yet God has not answered our prayers, it's hard to keep trusting and even harder to keep waiting and nearly impossible to keep hoping.

If that's you, beloved, take heart. Sarah also thought God was too late: another Slightly Bad Girl moment of doubt. But just as God knew how to deal with Sarah's doubt, he can handle ours.

As she stood at the entranceway to her tent, a bittersweet smile played at the corners of Sarah's mouth.

> …as she thought, "After I am worn out and my master is old, will I now have this pleasure?" *Genesis 18:12*

Picture a tattered cotton shirt with frayed cuffs and a torn hem. Or a pair of old sandals with leather soles so thin that daylight seeps through. That's what this phrase "worn out" means in Hebrew: something that "cannot be worn again."[26]

As to Sarah's "pleasure" (NRSV), "delight" (AMP), "happiness" (CEV), we're not talking about the joy of having a baby; the word suggests "sexual pleasure."[27] Sarah was frankly amused at the thought of two old people trying to conceive a baby. The whole thing sounded illogical. Ridiculous. And so she "bluntly dismisses the matter as absurd."[28]

I mean, really. "Pablum and Pampers at ninety?"[29]

Bill and I were in our thirties—not Sarah's age, but older than most of our peers—when we discovered we were going to be parents. On that November morning when my queasy stomach refused to calm down, we made a quick trip to the drugstore, put an E.P.T. through its paces, and watched in amazement as our lives changed before our eyes. We laughed *and* cried on that memorable day.

But when Sarah heard the news, she simply laughed, dismissing God's promise as impossible, unaware he was listening.

Then the LORD said to Abraham, "Why did Sarah laugh and say,
'Will I really have a child, now that I am old?'" *Genesis 18:13*

Sarah's heart must have lodged in her throat. Had she spoken aloud…or had he read her thoughts? It seemed their unnamed visitor "knew her own heart."[30] He openly questioned her laugh and her disparagement of her worn-out body, though he didn't repeat her thoughts about Abraham's advancing years. Indeed, only Sarah's age presented a stumbling block.

But not for God.

"Is anything too hard for the LORD?" *Genesis 18:14*

A rhetorical question, much quoted. Indeed, *is* anything "too difficult" (NASB), "too wonderful for the LORD?" (NRSV). A rebuke from God, some say, though I read this as a gentle but firm reminder of his limitless power, not a biting chastisement for her lack of faith.

God fully intended to bless Sarah no matter how much she laughed.

Why then the delayed conception, long past her childbearing years? So the birth of Isaac might be seen for what it was: "a divine gift of grace."[31]

"I will return to you at the appointed time next year and Sarah will
have a son." *Genesis 18:14*

An echo of God's promise four verses earlier, except here Sarah is not identified as "your wife." God now included Sarah in the conversation by name, beckoning her closer. At that moment, I believe she realized who was speaking. And who'd been listening.

Sarah was afraid… *Genesis 18:15*

I'm trembling right along with her. Whether she meant to or not, she'd laughed at the Lord. Mocked his promises, dismissed his power. No getting around it: her attitude "was displeasing to God."[32]

The time had come for Sarah to step forward and confess her flagging faith. Instead, she took a spiritual step backward.

...so she lied and said, "I did not laugh." *Genesis 18:15*

A Slightly Bad Girl for laughing? Maybe, but Abraham had laughed too. A Slightly Bad Girl for lying? 'Fraid so.

What's not clear is whether she spoke these words aloud to the Lord or simply *thought* them, whether she walked out to address him face to face or tarried near her tent door. It was as if the two angelic men and Abraham were no longer present, so direct was Sarah's brief conversation with God.

Though he didn't punish her for laughing *or* for lying, God also didn't let her get away with either one.

But he said, "Yes, you did laugh." *Genesis 18:15*

It's only fitting that God have the last word, spoken to her directly: "thou didst laugh" (KJV). Not an accusation, just "a friendly reprehension."[33] A heavenly gotcha, if you will. A reminder from the Lord that he knows everything we think, say, and do, yet abides with us still. And blesses us in spite of ourselves. Remarkable, isn't it?

Sarah Laughs Again

Sarah, who'd learned the prudence of silencing one's mouth *and* one's thoughts in God's presence, did not offer a second response. Nor did she dispute his promise. Nor did she deny the truth about her sin.

I consider this Sarah's big moment, when she truly believed, and it was reckoned unto her as righteousness. Though God exposed her sin, he did not punish Sarah, nor did he retract his promise. In fact, as far as the record shows, God never again brought up her disbelief or her denial.

Wow, sis. What an amazing example of grace, right here in the Old Testament. She acted rashly without seeking his will, she acted unkindly without seeking his forgiveness, and she acted foolishly without believing his promises—yet God showered Sarah with mercy again and again. Will he do the same for you? Absolutely. "His mercy extends to those who fear him, from generation to generation."[34] God's compassion for Slightly Bad Girls like Sarah—like us—knows no bounds.

> Now the LORD was gracious to Sarah as he had said, and the LORD did for Sarah what he had promised. *Genesis 21:1*

How I love this verse! Yes, God kept his promise to Abraham, but he also kept his promise to Sarah, showing us the personal nature of his grace. Such tender words: he "visited" (KJV), "took note of" (NASB), and "cared for Sarah" (NCV). Not because of her goodness, but because of his graciousness, God turned a loving eye on our aging sister and honored his word.

> Sarah became pregnant and bore a son to Abraham in his old age, at the very time God had promised him. *Genesis 21:2*

How like the Lord to simply state the glorious fulfillment of a promise made long ago. "Everything happened at the time God had said it would" (NCV). Had Sarah authored the account of her conception, pregnancy, and delivery, Genesis would contain ten extra chapters. But the Bible is God's journal, not ours; his Word is sufficient.

The rabbis of old believed that when Sarah conceived "so did all the barren women on earth."[35] As if the miracle were too great not to be shared. As if one woman's womb could not contain all the blessings God wanted to bestow.

> Abraham gave the name Isaac to the son Sarah bore him.
> *Genesis 21:3*

As with Ishmael, the Lord—not Abraham—ordained the name *Isaac*. A perfect choice, considering all the laughter this child had brought his parents before his conception. In Hebrew "*yitzchak* actually sounds like a little guffaw."[36] Or a little sneeze.

Obedient as ever, Abraham circumcised his son on the eighth day while Sarah summed up her lifelong journey toward motherhood with the broadest of smiles on her weathered face.

Sarah said, "God has brought me laughter…" *Genesis 21:6*

Our sister's words were doubly true: her son was named Laughter, and joy was restored to her weary soul. If that silent laugh back in the tent indicated derision, this one rang with elation, with celebration, with faith. Sarah had learned to embrace "this God of surprises."[37] She could laugh at death, having borne a new life. She could laugh at barrenness, knowing those years were behind her. And she could laugh at herself, at her foolishness, at her impatience, now that she understood God's unfailing love.

Sarah's laughter was carried on the wind, like a joyous contagion.

"…and everyone who hears about this will laugh with me."
Genesis 21:6

The Hebrew suggests that "all who get the news" (MSG) might laugh *at* her as well.[38] We can only imagine the cruel glances and sharp barbs of her neighbors through her Sarai years. Sarah no longer cared one whit. She had the last laugh; that was all that mattered to her.

And she added, "Who would have said to Abraham that Sarah would nurse children?" *Genesis 21:7*

The answer to "Who would have said…" was "No one" (NCV). All but God had written off Sarah's chances of having a son. The birth of Isaac wasn't just the talk of Abraham's camp; such astounding news would have traveled from Haran to Beersheba, from Bethel to Ur. "The woman was *how* old?"

By the way, our fictional Dr. Goodman was right: Arcelia Garcia of Sunnyside, Washington, *did* give birth to naturally conceived female triplets in 1999 at the age of fifty-four. She was already the mother of eight and the grandmother of fifteen.[39] Oh babies!

Sarah had her arthritic hands full with one newborn. According to this verse, Sarah nursed Isaac herself, if only to marvel at God's provision through her sagging breasts. Women of her station usually entrusted their children to a wet nurse, but in this verse I hear the triumphant note of a lactating mother.

"Yet I have borne him a son in his old age." *Genesis 21:7*

She began the scene praising God for his gift of laughter and concluded it sharing that happy gift with her husband. "I've given the old man a son!" (MSG). Who knew that calling the patriarch of the house "old man" started with Abraham?! Sarah practically crowed, her heart was so full.

Unfortunately, we know what comes next in Scripture, having already studied the incident when Ishmael mocked Isaac and Sarah drove Hagar into the wilderness. I confess, I'd rather picture Sarah as she was here: honoring God and her husband, embracing life with joyous abandon, waving her AARP card in one hand and her son's pacifier in the other.

Yes, we've seen her at her Slightly Bad Girl worst. But what Sarah's story most often calls to mind, millennia later, is her faith. Legend says a cloud hovered above Sarah's tent while she lived, a "sign of the divine presence over her home."[40] She may have laughed at God's promise, but she was the first to praise him when that promise was fulfilled. She lied out of fear and shame yet later spoke the truth loud and clear: "God has made me laugh."[41]

Once Hagar was given her freedom and peace was restored in Sarah's household, we hear no more of our matriarch until her death.

Sarah lived to be a hundred and twenty-seven years old. *Genesis 23:1*

She's the only woman in Scripture whose age is noted—not once, but several times. Since God kept a careful chronology of Abraham's life—he was seventy-five years old when he set out from Haran,[42] eighty-six when Hagar bore him Ishmael,[43] and a hundred years old when Isaac was born[44]—we always know Sarah's age, too, because she was a decade younger than her husband. I suspect she teased him about that every time he had a milestone birthday. (My husband is only two years older, and I never fail to remind him of his seniority when he blows out the candles on his cake.)

When those milestones turned to millstones for Sarah and the onset of menopause seemingly ended her dream of giving Abraham a son, God filled her womb with life and her mouth with laughter. Not only did God bless Sarah; so did her husband to the very end.

> She died at Kiriath Arba (that is, Hebron) in the land of Canaan,
> and Abraham went to mourn for Sarah and to weep over her.
> *Genesis 23:2*

Mourning was a social expectation, but the tears came from his heart. Abraham purchased a cave in the field of Machpelah, and there he buried his beloved wife, no doubt with Isaac standing by his side, bereft at the loss of a mother who'd doted on him from the hour of his birth.

Neither man could know that a beautiful young woman from Paddan Aram would one day enter Sarah's tent and fill the air afresh with laughter, as we'll discover in our next chapter.

What Lessons Can We Learn from Sarah?

Miracles never cease.

Abraham and Sarah doubted God's ability to do the miraculous—to nurture an old man's seed in an old woman's womb—and expressed their incredulity with similar words, both citing Sarah's age as the impediment. "Is anything too hard for the LORD?"[45] was God's way of reminding this couple that miracles are his stock in trade. For the Creator of the universe and all it contains, bringing a sleeping womb to life was child's play. Consider this, dear sister: "If God could do this impossible thing for Sarah at the age of ninety…what will he do for you and me?"[46]

> Who among the gods is like you, O LORD? Who is like you—
> majestic in holiness, awesome in glory, working wonders?
> *Exodus 15:11*

Let's show more than a little respect.

If you're over forty, you may recall the Chiffon margarine commercial that ended with the line "It's not nice to fool Mother Nature." And it's downright dangerous to try fooling Father God. Ask Sarah. On what should have been the happiest day of her life, she was too wrapped up in fear, too stuck in her sin to rejoice over the good news God had brought her. Instead, she mocked his promise, questioned his abilities, then lied about laughing—only to be pulled up short by God, who'd heard it all. I'm guessing Sarah didn't make that mistake again. In the television spot, Mother Nature's words were followed by a thunderous lightning strike. The Lord is far more gracious, but we should never doubt his power.

Do not be deceived: God cannot be mocked. *Galatians 6:7*

There *is* a time to laugh.

One of my dear friends often says, "God makes me laugh," before describing the unusual ways God is working in her life. Imagine her delight when I pointed out Sarah's words: "God hath made me to laugh"![47] Sarah showed us why laughing *at* God isn't wise but laughing *with* God honors his gift of joy. Sarah's first laugh was provoked by disbelief and covered with a lie. But her second laugh rang out openly and unashamedly, inviting all to laugh with her. And then, to top it all off, God named her son "Laughter"! Truly, the Lord does have a sense of humor, even as he "makes the laughable believable."[48]

You turned my wailing into dancing; you removed my sackcloth
and clothed me with joy. *Psalm 30:11*

A eulogy says more than a birth announcement.

When our daughter was born, we had announcements printed and dropped in the mail within hours of her birth, featuring only her name and vital statistics. Compare that to a heartfelt eulogy spoken at the funeral of a loved one. Recollections, both funny and tender, pour forth. The unique personality of the deceased is celebrated. However exuberant Abraham might have been at the birth of his son, his response to the death of his wife—complete with mourning and tears—was what found its way into Scripture. Sarah is memorialized not only for the son she bore but also for the life she lived: "a matriarch of the first order, respected by rulers and husbands alike, a spirited woman and bold companion."[49]

A wife of noble character is her husband's crown. *Proverbs 12:4*

Good Girl Thoughts Worth Considering

1. Though we see little difference between the names *Sarai* and *Sarah,* the distinction mattered to God. He marked her new identity just as he marked Abraham's body through circumcision. What role did God give Sarah in his everlasting covenant? In what ways will the life you live today affect the future of your family? Of our society? Of God's creation? Of God's kingdom?

2. Abraham laughed to himself when God promised to give him a son by Sarah, yet God did not ask him, "Why did you laugh?" What explanation might you offer for God accepting Abraham's amusement but not Sarah's? What does our laughter reveal about us? And what did Sarah's laugh that day indicate about her?

3. One writer suggested, "Instead of Sarah the Faithful, she could as easily be called Sarah the Scornful or Sarah the Spiteful."[50] Taking into account the whole of her life, what descriptive word(s) would you assign to Sarah, and why? How has your own attitude about life, about others, about God changed in the last decade? If your friends were to assign you a telling title that reflects your faith—Susan the Brave or Kathy the Timid—what words might they choose, and why?

4. The question was raised, did Abraham tell Sarah about God's promise concerning her bearing his heir, or did she hear it first from the Lord when he appeared at their tents in Mamre? I offered three reasons why I think her husband didn't tell her. Which of those ring true to you, and why? What other option(s) can you suggest? Why might Sarah have benefited from hearing the news directly from God rather than from her husband?

5. A promise or prophecy fulfilled in Scripture builds our faith in a God who keeps his word. When Sarah bore a son to Abraham "at the very time God had promised him" (Genesis 21:2), how do you suppose that changed

her relationship with her husband? And with her God? Perhaps the greatest promise in God's Word is this: "If you confess with your mouth, 'Jesus is Lord,' and believe in your heart that God raised him from the dead, you will be saved."[51] How have you embraced that truth for yourself?

6. We didn't study Abraham's later willingness to sacrifice Isaac on Mount Moriah (see Genesis 22:1–19) because it fell outside the parameters of Sarah's story. But she was very much alive when it happened. Do you imagine Sarah knew about Abraham's intentions when he left with Isaac that day? What makes you say that? How might a mother handle such a request from God differently than a father would? And how can we trust a God who would require such a sacrifice?

7. How would you characterize Abraham and Sarah's marriage relationship? Which one seemed to have the stronger personality? Explain your answer. What did you respect about Abraham as a husband? And what did you find difficult to accept about him? What does Abraham's grieving tell us about their years together?

8. What's the most important lesson you learned from Sarah, a woman who laughed at God and (almost) got away with it?

A Willful Bride

A virtuous wife
when she obeys her husband
obtains the command over him.
Publilius Syrus

I hope Eric Seaver knows what a blessed man he is."

Rosalind tugged on her white silk gloves, blushing like the bride she was. Though her older brother, Ben, had a glib tongue, his comment still pleased her since he was the one giving her away.

"I'm also blessed to have Eric Seaver for a husband," she reminded him, brushing a wisp of lint from Ben's rented tuxedo. "He's a gentleman in every sense of the word."

"And rich." Ben's laugh was low, conspiratorial. "You'll live very comfortably in that palace of his. Is he letting you drive his Jag or the Bentley Eight?"

"Shh." Rosalind frowned, glancing over his shoulder toward the sanctuary. They had the secluded alcove to themselves but not for long. Her wedding coordinator would soon come looking for her. "You know very well I'm not marrying Eric because he's wealthy."

"Oh, right." Her brother snorted. "And he's not marrying you because you're beautiful."

"Ben!"

"Don't be naive, little sister." Any trace of humor had vanished. "The way I see it, it's a sugar daddy for you, arm candy for him. You both stand to benefit from your match made in heaven."

"That's exactly what this is," she said firmly. Sometimes her brother could be so crass. "Eric believes the Lord brought us together, and so does his father."

Ben held up his hands. "Who am I to argue with God?"

"Enough scheming, you two." Maryanne, the wedding coordinator, hurried toward them, her taffeta dress rustling. "Rosalind, we need you in the bride's dressing room for your last set of photos." She gave Ben a pointed look. "And *you* belong in the vestibule, waiting to escort your lovely sister down the aisle."

"I am yours to command," he said with a slight bow, then disappeared through a side door.

"Come." Maryanne's gloved hand touched Rosalind's elbow. "We've only a few minutes before the music starts." A Sacramento native, Maryanne knew the city, knew the country club where they were having the reception, and knew the church. From the moment Rosalind had stepped off the plane, she'd put the woman's expertise to good use.

Rosalind lifted her hem as she walked, trying to move faster. Her form-fitting, ivory gown—a gift from her future husband—complemented her pale skin and russet hair. Her bridesmaids were dressed in creamy yellow sheaths with matching hats, like elegant, long-stemmed roses. Annalise, Chelsea, and Paige, her childhood friends from Portland, had traveled south with her in a private jet, quietly paid for by Eric's father.

Mr. Seaver insisted on handling all the wedding expenses. Perhaps because her own father was no longer living. Or because the man was exceedingly generous. "When it comes to my son," he'd told Rosalind last week, clasping her hands in his, "no cost is too high, no sacrifice too great. Eric must have the perfect bride, chosen by God…"

"Here I am," Rosalind sang out, sweeping into the bride's room with Maryanne in her wake. "Mr. Lewis, we've barely five minutes."

The photographer arranged the other women in natural poses and strategically positioned Rosalind in the most flattering light. "You'll spoil me," she cautioned him, then smiled demurely for the camera. "I'm not used to being the center of attention."

"Rosalind Dalton, you've never been anything else," Paige teased. "Half the photos in our senior yearbook featured you front and center."

"Maybe because she was the editor," Chelsea said.

Rosalind stepped on her toe, prompting a yelp.

"Ladies!" Maryanne motioned aside the photographer. "It's time."

The muffled sound of a pipe organ sent the bridal party flying into the hall. Maryanne led the way, while Annalise carried Rosalind's flowers, Paige adjusted her veil en route, and Chelsea lifted her train, all of them breathless with excitement. Rosalind simply walked, head held high, relishing the spectacle.

When they turned the corner, the women found several latecomers milling about, so they tarried in the shadows while the last of the guests were escorted to their seats. Rosalind admired the vestibule, pleased with her efforts. Yellow and ivory roses brightened the dim corners and filled the air with a sweet fragrance, just as she'd planned.

All was quiet at last. Her brother stepped forward, offering his arm. "Mrs. Seaver?"

"Almost." She slipped her hand through the crook of his elbow. "Consider this a rehearsal, Ben. Someday you'll give your own daughter away."

"So I will." He grinned, his dark eyes twinkling. "But first my sister."

The two stood out of view while the center doors opened, then each groomsman in turn ushered a bridesmaid down the aisle. "Not too close together," Rosalind quietly advised each couple. A lengthier procession heightened anticipation. When a musical flourish from the organist cued the wedding guests to stand, Ben slowly guided her through the arched entrance and into the candlelit sanctuary.

Rosalind paused, savoring the moment. Every eye was on her.

"Behold, the queen," Ben murmured, broadening her smile.

Brother and sister moved forward at a stately pace, keeping their steps in time with Wagner's "Bridal Chorus" from *Lohengrin*. Rosalind looked straight ahead, preferring not to be distracted by the blur of happy faces. Very few were familiar—the downside of marrying in Eric's hometown instead of hers. Still, she'd selected each song, designed the bouquets, and chosen the dinner menu from soup to nuts. Even with Mr. Seaver picking up the tab, this was *her* wedding.

And Eric's, of course.

Rosalind aimed her gaze toward the altar where her fiancé waited patiently, resplendent in his black formalwear. Older than her by a decade and more settled in his ways, Eric had loved her from the hour they met. Proposed before their first date. Promised her the world, then gave her his heart. What woman could resist such an offer?

He touched his jacket pocket as she drew near, no doubt wanting to be sure their vows were in hand. She shook her head ever so slightly. *You won't need them. You'll remember.* Hadn't she coached him a dozen times at last night's rehearsal?

The music swelled to a crescendo as she and Ben finally reached the altar, surrounded by candelabras and a profusion of roses. When the minister greeted them, then asked, "Who gives this woman in marriage?" Ben's answer was swift, certain. "I do."

She released him with a heartfelt smile, then took Eric's arm, surprised to feel him trembling.

Eric drew her closer, as if for strength, then nodded at the minister.

Robed in white, Rev. Elroy cast a benevolent gaze on the congregation, then spoke the timeless words: "Dearly beloved, we are gathered here in the sight of God and in the presence of these witnesses to join together this man and this woman in holy matrimony…"

Rebekah the Wife: Becky Does Well

Rebekah's love story began well—and *at* a well—but oh the drama that followed!

As usual I'm getting ahead of myself. Our last chapter ended with Abraham at Sarah's graveside, mourning his wife. How aware of his own mortality he must have been at that sad hour and more so as the seasons passed.

> Abraham was now old and well advanced in years, and the LORD had blessed him in every way. *Genesis 24:1*

His son Isaac was nearing the Big 4-0. Abraham knew the time had come to establish the next generation. Rather than sending Isaac off to find a wife on his own, Abraham dispatched the "eldest servant of his house"[1] to handle the betrothal. Some writers assume he was Eliezer of Damascus, the man named in Genesis 15:2. But that was *fifty years* earlier, a long stint for a servant. (Come to think of it, the same dear woman has cut my hair for more than two decades; maybe Eliezer *did* serve Abraham that long.) Whatever the case, all through the twenty-fourth chapter of Genesis, Abraham's servant remains unnamed, and so we'll follow suit.

> He said to the chief servant in his household, the one in charge of
> all that he had, "Put your hand under my thigh." *Genesis 24:2*

Hmmm. That sounds uncomfortable. And a tad too personal.

So it was. In ancient times an oath taker rested his hand on the most vital part of a man's body as a pledge of allegiance. Let's make this quick, shall we?

> "I want you to swear by the LORD, the God of heaven and the God
> of earth, that you will not get a wife for my son from the daughters
> of the Canaanites, among whom I am living…" *Genesis 24:3*

No local cultic princess for Isaac, then. His father wanted a God-fearing, mail-order bride personally delivered by his trustworthy servant.

> "…go to my country and my own relatives and get a wife for my
> son Isaac." *Genesis 24:4*

The two men volleyed back and forth, with the servant worried about the young woman not wanting to leave her homeland and Abraham more concerned about Isaac departing for a distant country. "Beware lest you take my son back there!"[2] he warned. The Lord had promised to give Abraham's offspring *this* land, not Paddan Aram, so the elderly patriarch wanted to be very sure Isaac stayed put.

As to selecting his future daughter-in-law and convincing her to come, Abraham told his servant, "Chilleth out," knowing God would do the choosing.

"The LORD, the God of heaven…he will send his angel before you
so that you can get a wife for my son from there." *Genesis 24:7*

Assured of heavenly guidance, the servant hit the road without delay.

The servant took ten of his master's camels and left. *Genesis 24:10*

Ten camels for one bride? My, they were traveling in style. These hump-backed quadrupeds were built for the desert, capable of carting supplies across harsh terrain, then bearing home a bride and her maidservants. Camels were also the Rolls-Royce of the ancient Near East: an extravagant display of wealth.

The journey itself is not described in Scripture, though about five hundred miles stretch between Canaan and Haran. We know only what happened when the servant and the men traveling with him (those ten camels didn't steer themselves) arrived at Abraham's old stomping ground.

He had the camels kneel down near the well outside the town; it
was toward evening, the time the women go out to draw water.
Genesis 24:11

Since carrying water was women's work, our road-weary servant parked his camels near the well, then prayed for God's favor, pleading for a distinctive sign to identify Isaac's bride-to-be.

"May it be that when I say to a girl, 'Please let down your jar that
I may have a drink,' and she says, 'Drink, and I'll water your camels
too'—let her be the one you have chosen for your servant Isaac."
Genesis 24:14

A young woman pouring a drink for a traveler would have been commonplace; the rules of hospitality required such service. But offering to water ten thirsty camels? That would take a miracle of God and one very benevolent young woman.

Before he had finished praying, Rebekah came out with her jar
on her shoulder. *Genesis 24:15*

How about that? God answered his request midprayer. David said it best: "Before a word is on my tongue you know it completely, O LORD."[3] And here came the future bride of Isaac on cue, bearing an earthen water jar upon her shoulder, just as women in Palestine do today.

> The girl was very beautiful... *Genesis 24:16*

To his credit, the servant didn't pray for a young woman of surpassing beauty; he was seeking God's will, not man's pleasure. Nonetheless, Rebekah was "very fair to look upon" (NRSV). We imagine her as artists have depicted her over the centuries: a cascade of dark hair, luminous eyes, and pleasing features aglow with the innocence of a maiden.

> ...a virgin; no man had ever lain with her. *Genesis 24:16*

How could he know that just by looking at her? Perhaps unmarried women wore their clothes or hair a certain way to indicate their marital status, though the Bible contains little description of how people dressed in the patriarchal years. Or this may be our biblical narrator at work, filling in the details for us.

The girl's purity wasn't simply a moral issue: she *had* to be a virgin to ensure that the first child she bore came from the seed of Isaac and no other.

So far, so good: beautiful, "modest, and unmarried" (AMP), Rebekah headed for the well.

> She went down to the spring, filled her jar and came up again.
> *Genesis 24:16*

Toss out any notions of circular brick wishing wells fitted with pulleys and buckets. A spring-fed well "could be reached only by descending a flight of broad stone steps circling deep below ground"[4]—sometimes as deep as 140 feet.[5] Then, after filling her clay jar with about three gallons of water, a woman climbed back up those steps, being careful not to spill a precious drop. Water was too hard to come by in the desert.

The minute Rebekah emerged from her subterranean errand, our man made his move.

The servant hurried to meet her and said, "Please give me a little water from your jar." *Genesis 24:17*

He wasn't asking for much. Just a "sip" (NRSV).

"Drink, my lord," she said, and quickly lowered the jar to her hands and gave him a drink. *Genesis 24:18*

We can picture Rebekah easing her clay jar off her shoulder in a single, graceful movement, then pouring a bit of water into her tightly cupped hand and holding it up for him to drink.

All the while he had to be smiling. Hoping she'd noticed his noisy, smelly, thirsty camels. Praying she'd make an offer only the Lord could prompt.

After she had given him a drink, she said, "I'll draw water for your camels too, until they have finished drinking." *Genesis 24:19*

Well done, Rebekah.

Though he was patently a man of means—or in service to one—Rebekah knew neither his identity nor his mission. Her offer seems borne of a generous heart. She would water his beasts "until they have had enough" (NLT).

How much water would that be? About twenty-five gallons per camel.[6] Do the math: eighty-four trips up and down those stone steps. Girl, she deserved a *big* diamond.

So she quickly emptied her jar into the trough, ran back to the well to draw more water, and drew enough for all his camels. *Genesis 24:20*

Like Abraham hurriedly caring for his visitors' needs, Rebekah moved at a swift pace, running back and forth from well to trough in "a nonstop blur of motion."[7] Her good health and physical strength, both important for motherhood, were on full display. Still, the servant dared not introduce himself or disclose his intentions quite yet.

Without saying a word, the man watched her closely to learn whether or not the LORD had made his journey successful. *Genesis 24:21*

He stood there, "gazing at her in silence" (NASB) and "wondering whether or not she was the one" (NLT). That's odd. Wasn't "I'll water your camels" the affirmation he was waiting for? Maybe he wanted to observe her mannerisms, her way of speaking to see if she was worthy of his young master. Or perhaps he wanted to see if she would finish what she had started, if she was a young woman of her word: "until they've drunk their fill" (MSG).

By the time the camels were satisfied, so was Abraham's servant.

> When the camels had finished drinking, the man took out a gold nose ring... *Genesis 24:22*

Oh baby. Can a diamond be far away?

The gold ring weighed a *beka,* or about "one-fifth of an ounce" (NCV). A beka for Rebekah...love it! Nose rings were a popular adornment in those days, sometimes featuring a tiny pendant.[8] Women of all ages wore them delicately dangling from one nostril.

While she pinched her nose ring in place, Abraham's servant pulled out even more impressive jewelry.

> ...two gold bracelets weighing ten shekels. *Genesis 24:22*

Since a laborer earned at most ten shekels annually,[9] we're talking a whole year's wages circling her wrists. Scholars caution us not to jump to conclusions: these were merely gifts of thanks, "not some sort of bride price!"[10] Come to think of it, the servant could hardly have proposed on Isaac's behalf without her parents' consent.

Time to find Mum and Dad.

> Then he asked, "Whose daughter are you?" *Genesis 24:23*

Things couldn't progress further "without first ascertaining her pedigree."[11] Before she answered, he pressed on with an inquiry about lodging. Cheeky as his request might sound to us, Motel 6 wasn't leaving the light on for anyone in those days. Travelers depended on the kindness of strangers.

"Please tell me, is there room in your father's house for us to spend
the night?" *Genesis 24:23*

Rebekah answered his questions in order, starting with her all-important
family connections.

"I am the daughter of Bethuel, the son that Milcah bore to Nahor."
Genesis 24:24

The mention of her father and grandfather—Bethuel and Nahor—
followed standard "Who's your daddy?" procedure. But the mention of
Rebekah's grandmother, Milcah, brings a welcome drop of estrogen to this
patriarchal saga.

And she added, "We have plenty of straw and fodder, as well as
room for you to spend the night." *Genesis 24:25*

He'd only requested lodging for himself and his traveling companions.
Yet Rebekah generously offered to shelter his beasts as well. We've not seen
even a hint of her Slightly Bad Girl nature yet, though her eagerness to please
others may stem from a tendency toward manipulation. *I'll give you what you
need now in exchange for what I'll want later.*

After all those steps and all those clay jars full of water, Rebekah still had
enough energy to dash home, jingling her bling for all to see.

A Decent Proposal

The girl ran and told her mother's household about these things.
Genesis 24:28

A few verses earlier the servant had asked about her father's house, yet
here we have "her mother's household," a phrase commonly used by young
unmarried women.[12] Another reason Mom was mentioned? Most scholars
believe Rebekah's father was dead[13] since her brother came out to greet the
esteemed visitor on behalf of their family.

Now Rebekah had a brother named Laban... *Genesis 24:29*

That heads-up word "now" alerts us to a pivotal shift in the story with the introduction of this new character. Though his name means "white,"[14] suggesting innocence, you can trust me on this: Laban is the sort of person you'll find "easy to resent later on."[15]

...and he hurried out to the man at the spring. *Genesis 24:29*

Another example of hurry-up hospitality. Unless it was prompted by the new jewelry adorning his sister.

As soon as he had seen the nose ring, and the bracelets on his sister's arms... *Genesis 24:30*

Yup. The jewelry.

...and had heard Rebekah tell what the man said to her...
Genesis 24:30

Brother Laban kept a "sharp eye on the precious gifts"[16] while he listened to his sister's story, then hustled out to meet the servant.

...he went out to the man and found him standing by the camels near the spring. *Genesis 24:30*

Remember how the ancient rule of hospitality meant understating one's stores and extending a low-key welcome? Laban's magnanimous greeting "leaves the unmistakable impression that his hospitality was motivated by self-interest."[17]

"Come, you who are blessed by the LORD," he said. "Why are you standing out here?" *Genesis 24:31*

We can hear Laban gushing, "Come on in, blessed of GOD!" (MSG). Over the top and then some. "I've got the house ready for you" (MSG) suggests his coffers were yawning, waiting to be filled with gold.

The camels were unloaded and fed while the visitors were provided water to wash their feet. (The fretful mother in me hopes they washed their hands and faces too.) No sooner was a meal served than our mission-minded servant held up his hand to bring things to a temporary halt. Although famished from traveling, he insisted on attending to his master's business first.

So he said, "I am Abraham's servant." *Genesis 24:34*

We can imagine smiles and nods around the table at the mention of this esteemed relative.

> "The LORD has blessed my master abundantly, and he has become
> wealthy. He has given him sheep and cattle, silver and gold, men-
> servants and maidservants, and camels and donkeys." *Genesis 24:35*

We've read that list before: Pharaoh endowed Abraham with such treasures, yet we know that "every good and perfect gift is from above."[18] Laban must have been calculating his uncle's wealth, wondering how much of it might land in *his* tent. Was Rebekah doing the same, we wonder, following her brother's avaricious lead?

> "My master's wife Sarah has borne him a son in her old age, and he
> has given him everything he owns." *Genesis 24:36*

Ah, even better news: only one son to inherit his father's wealth. Laban must have been beside himself. Hadn't he always said this beautiful sister was going to make them all rich?

The servant went on (and on and on) relating his conversation with his master, his oath to find a wife from Abraham's clan, and his prayer for God's leading at the well.

> "Before I finished praying in my heart, Rebekah came out, with her
> jar on her shoulder." *Genesis 24:45*

That's how it happened, all right. We have no record of Rebekah (or anyone else) mentioning her name to the servant. Perhaps by then he had heard it spoken in the household and so used her name freely. "Rebekah" suited her, since it means "loop" or "tie"[19] or, more often, "ensnarer,"[20] though my favorite definition is "captivating."[21]

At the moment the servant was hoping to lasso a bride for Isaac. And look how quickly Laban jumped at the chance to marry his sister into money!

> Laban and Bethuel answered, "This is from the LORD; we can say
> nothing to you one way or the other." *Genesis 24:50*

But wasn't the father, Bethuel, dead? He had to be, since "the father could not be mentioned after the son."[22] Maybe *this* Bethuel was a younger brother, a *son* of Bethuel, named after his late father. Or maybe Laban was simply acting on his deceased father's behalf, hence the mention of his name here. If by chance Bethuel was alive, he was "completely overshadowed by an ambitious son and dominating wife."[23]

Whoever was speaking, their answer was swift: "The LORD has obviously brought you here, so what can we say?" (NLT). What they said was *yes*.

> "Here is Rebekah; take her and go, and let her become the wife of
> your master's son, as the LORD has directed." *Genesis 24:51*

Did Rebekah's heart leap at the news, envisioning foreign lands and a wealthy husband? Or did her spirits sink, thinking of leaving behind all she knew and loved? So far we've learned more about Laban than Rebekah as we've observed his questionable character at work and his eagerness to trade his sister for a profit: "Take her; she's yours."[24]

Abraham's servant bowed down to honor the Lord once more, then stood to dress the bride in riches.

> The servant brought out gold and silver jewelry and articles of
> clothing and gave them to Rebekah;... *Genesis 24:53*

Though her wardrobe was not described, we're told he brought "lovely clothing" (NLT) for Rebekah's journey. Slipping the fine threads over her head, did she think fondly of the man she would soon marry, or did his wealth alone woo her? Expensive jewelry and designer clothes have captured women's hearts for centuries. Because the Bible includes this scene, we can be sure it's significant, revealing something of Rebekah's character: money mattered.

And look who else benefited from this little trunk show.

> …he also gave costly gifts to her brother and to her mother.
> *Genesis 24:53*

"Costly gifts"? Details, please. Ah, but they're not to be had. We must be satisfied knowing they were "precious things" (NASB), "costly ornaments" (NRSV), "valuable presents" (NLT), and "expensive gifts" (NCV). But no trinkets for Dad: further proof Bethuel wasn't on hand.

After eating, drinking, and sleeping their fill, Abraham's men were eager to return home—none more so than his head servant.

> When they got up the next morning, he said, "Send me on my way
> to my master." *Genesis 24:54*

Considering Abraham's age, haste was prudent. Or perhaps the servant couldn't wait to see the look on Isaac's face when he met his charming bride.

> But her brother and her mother replied, "Let the girl remain with us
> ten days or so; then you may go." *Genesis 24:55*

What was that about? Were they hoping for more jewels, more costly gifts, more fancy clothes for Rebekah? Ten days of hospitality for such an entourage would be expensive. What did Laban and his mother hope to gain?

Time was what they were after. Time to honor the custom of the day, requiring the bride to tarry with her family a bit longer.[25] And time to make sure this praying servant qualified as an able escort, since leaving the protection of her family would involve considerable risk.[26]

When the servant begged them to reconsider, Laban and his mom made a surprising suggestion.

> They said, "Let's call the girl and ask her about it." *Genesis 24:57*

In an era when women were traded like livestock, it's remarkable they chose to "consult her wishes" (NASB) and "ask her what she thinks" (NLT). A further clue to Rebekah's personality. We already know she was beautiful, chaste, intelligent, energetic, charitable, and enthusiastic. Now we see she had a mind of her own, or her family wouldn't have sought her opinion.

> So they called Rebekah and asked her, "Will you go with this man?"
> *Genesis 24:58*

Her family gets points for asking a straightforward question—"Will you go?"—and leaving room for her to say, "Yes," "No," or "Later." They didn't mention their request for ten more days or the servant's plea for haste, nor did they try to persuade her one way or the other. Could be they knew how this strong-willed sister would respond.

> "I will go," she said. *Genesis 24:58*

Bold and decisive, that's our Rebekah.

She demonstrated in a single Hebrew word—*aylach,* meaning "I will go"—that she was "just like her future father-in-law, willing to take the journey on faith."[27] Abraham at least had his family with him when he packed up his tents and followed God. But Rebekah fearlessly left everything she knew to marry a man she'd never met, and embarked on "the only journey of her life."[28]

What a gutsy, get-things-done young woman, worthy of carrying on the covenant. In this generation, Rebekah stood out as "the mover and shaker, the risk-taker, the doer, the pioneer."[29] Our kind of girl.

Yet we also know women who move people who didn't ask to be moved and shake things better left untouched. Was Rebekah the sort who ignored others' feelings in her headlong approach to life? Another concern: Rebekah left her family with disturbing ease. Not a word of regret, not a teary farewell, not a moment's hesitation.

It seems inside our Mostly Good Girl lurked a Slightly Bad Girl eager to set her plans in motion.

> So they sent their sister Rebekah on her way, along with her nurse
> and Abraham's servant and his men. *Genesis 24:59*

With her family's blessing ringing in her ears, Rebekah prepared to leave with several maidservants and Deborah,[30] her "childhood nurse" (NLT), who accompanied her much like a lady's maid might in later centuries: as a trusted servant, a suitable chaperone, and an indication of Rebekah's social status.

So the servant took Rebekah and left. *Genesis 24:61*

Again we find no description of the long journey itself. The servant simply "departed" (NASB) and "went his way" (KJV), taking Isaac's future bride on a trek across deserts and mountains, valleys and plains.

You'll never guess who was on hand to greet them.

Well Groomed

Now Isaac had come from Beer Lahai Roi, for he was living in the Negev. *Genesis 24:62*

Sure, we remember the place where Hagar named her heavenly visitor El Roi—God Who Sees Me. A place where God also watched Isaac venture forth, a young man unaware of who was headed in his direction.

He went out to the field one evening to meditate… *Genesis 24:63*

What a contemplative fellow, walking in "the open country" (AMP) at dusk. Far above him the stars blinked into view as he offered his musings to God. In a single brush stroke, our narrator has painted the adult Isaac for us: a quiet, thoughtful, solitary man of faith.

Then something in the distance caught his eye. Cue the violins, please.

…and as he looked up… *Genesis 24:63*

The phrase "he lifted up his eyes" (KJV) appears some thirty times throughout the Bible, often at the introduction of a noteworthy event. This one certainly qualified.

…he saw camels approaching. *Genesis 24:63*

Donkeys were used for short jaunts; these camel-riding travelers had come a long distance. Isaac no doubt recognized his father's caravan. But who were all those women?

> Rebekah also looked up... *Genesis 24:64*

You *can* hear the violins, yes? The romance of this scene makes me sigh.

> ...and [she] saw Isaac. *Genesis 24:64*

When Isaac lifted his gaze, he saw camels. But when Rebekah raised her eyes, she saw Isaac. The difference between men and women in a nutshell.

> She got down from her camel. *Genesis 24:64*

Legend has it Rebekah "was so smitten and dazzled when she saw Isaac for the first time that she fell off!"[31] We know better: she wanted to manage the ungraceful act of dismounting before the man got any closer. Whether Rebekah "slipped quickly from the camel" (NRSV) or "jumped down" (NCV), our girl quit that beast in a hurry. Abigail did the same when she approached her future husband: "She quickly got off her donkey and bowed down before David with her face to the ground."[32] To show respect, the scholars say. To not let your fiancé see your awkward dismount, Lizzie says.

> [Rebekah] asked the servant, "Who is that man in the field coming to meet us?" *Genesis 24:65*

Always good to be certain, though she must have instinctively known.

> "He is my master," the servant answered. *Genesis 24:65*

His true master was Abraham, though any servant in the household would bow to Isaac as well. The servant might have said, but sagely did not, "He is soon to be *your* master." Rebekah got the message nonetheless.

> So she took her veil and covered herself. *Genesis 24:65*

Custom dictated a bride be modestly veiled in the presence of her bridegroom until the wedding,[33] though don't picture this as a lacy, peekaboo affair. Rather, this veil was a large wrapper "of ample dimensions, so that it might be thrown over the head at pleasure."[34]

Honey, after a five-hundred-mile camel ride, I'd throw a queen-size quilt over myself and hope the man stood upwind.

Then the servant told Isaac all he had done. *Genesis 24:66*

While the servant gave his report, Isaac must have stolen a few glances at the young woman by his side, admiring her lithe body and conjecturing what sort of face her veil might conceal. Or perhaps this meditative man thought not of the flesh but of the spirit and wondered how compatible they might be in that regard.

Whatever Isaac's thoughts, his actions revealed his eagerness to marry Rebekah.

Isaac brought her into the tent of his mother Sarah... *Genesis 24:67*

Since Sarah's death three years earlier, her tent had remained vacant, a shrine to the woman Abraham had loved and Isaac had cherished. Jewish midrash tells us the four sides of Sarah's tent were kept open so all might "see her hearth fire burning, its warmth welcoming travelers from every direction."[35] One traveler in particular was about to take residence and assume the role of mistress of the household.

...and he married Rebekah. So she became his wife... *Genesis 24:67*

No engraved invitations, no long line of groomsmen and bridesmaids, no expensive reception, just the "simple taking of a woman for a wife before all witnesses."[36]

Yes, Isaac married her. And, yes, he slept with her, making Rebekah his wife. But this added touch warms our hearts.

...and he loved her;... *Genesis 24:67*

Indeed, he "loved her very much" (NLT). What began as a lifelong commitment grew into love—a relationship model worthy of consideration. At age forty[37] Isaac offered Rebekah a love shaped by maturity. He was a man who'd experienced both great joy and deep sorrow, a man who'd observed the mutual respect of his parents, a man who knew the God of Abraham, a man who understood love's source: "We love because he first loved us."[38]

Did Rebekah return his affections? We're never told and so must judge the attitude of her heart by watching her behavior toward her husband as the years unfolded. She was savvy enough to please him so thoroughly that he never sought another wife. Nor did she thrust another woman into his arms. For that, Rebekah was wiser than Sarah or Rachel.

Here's some hint of Rebekah's feelings: she consoled her still-grieving husband and helped his wounded heart begin to heal.

> …and Isaac was comforted after his mother's death. *Genesis 24:67*

Those of us who have buried our mothers know this pain well. The sense of loss refuses to pass. Weeks, months, years go by, and still our eyes well when a vivid memory arises. Rebekah, for all her youth, had a strong maternal instinct and "crept into the vacant spot"[39] only a woman can fill.

Seeking Answers

As the years passed, a fresh ache—and a familiar one for this family—surfaced. Like her mother-in-law had once been, Rebekah was barren. "Almost twenty years later, Rebekah still had no children."[40]

Unlike Sarah, Rebekah didn't take matters into her own hands. Not yet. Instead, her husband turned to the only One who could remedy the situation.

> Isaac prayed to the LORD on behalf of his wife, because she was barren. *Genesis 25:21*

Abraham was a man of action, but his son Isaac was a man of prayer. And so he "pleaded" (NLT) and "entreated" (KJV) and "appealed to the LORD" (NEB), knowing the promise made to his father was meant for him as well. Isaac might have chosen another wife, but he chose instead to honor his commitment to Rebekah and trust God. He may have been a taciturn guy, but still waters ran deep with Isaac, "the only patriarch who was monogamous."[41]

Jewish tradition holds that Isaac took his wife to Moriah, the sacrificial mount his father once called "The LORD Will Provide,"[42] the spot where God promised to multiply Abraham's seed. There Isaac "pleaded the promise made in that very place."[43] Compared to all of Sarah's machinations with Hagar, prayer certainly seems the easier method. And far more effective.

> The LORD answered his prayer, and his wife Rebekah became
> pregnant. *Genesis 25:21*

Ta-da! God "yielded to his entreaty, and Rebecca conceived" (NEB), though the Hebrew literally says God " 'let himself be entreated,' not just because Isaac asked but because it was in his own will."[44] Adding "Lord willing" to our prayers can sound trite, but if we sincerely mean "Thy will be done," we may discover, as Isaac did, that our heart's desire and the Lord's are the same.

Since Rebekah was still of childbearing age, hers was not a miraculous conception like Sarah's, but it was thrilling nonetheless. Just to prove that "God often outdoes our prayers,"[45] Rebekah had *two* children in her womb.

> The babies jostled each other within her… *Genesis 25:22*

Ouch. My firstborn weighed eleven pounds, twelve and a half ounces at birth, so one jostling baby in my womb was quite enough. But Rebekah had *two* babies bouncing inside her. They "pressed hard" (NEB) and "struggled" (NASB) and "clashed."[46] Mothers of twins have assured me this description is accurate; they, too, felt as if their babies were "crushing each other."[47]

Naturally, Rebekah panicked. Unaware that she carried twins, she knew only that her pain was excruciating. God's chastisement of Eve comes to mind: "I will greatly multiply your grief and your suffering in pregnancy."[48] Even knowing that to be true, every pregnant woman with indigestion, swollen ankles, and a gymnast in her womb eventually moans "the primeval cry of 'Why?' "[49]

...and she said, "Why is this happening to me?" *Genesis 25:22*

The Hebrew literally reads, "Wherefore, then, am I?" perhaps meaning "she saw no future in her pregnancy."[50] No wonder she felt anxious: after twenty years of barrenness, Rebekah desperately wanted to see this pregnancy through. Did she fear her pain was a portent of doom? We can almost hear the whispers circling her tent: *Something is wrong. The child is cursed.*

Not only were the babies inside her struggling; Rebekah must have struggled as well, wondering why God's blessing had become a painful burden, why "God's frown had so suddenly replaced His smile."[51] Hadn't Isaac, the kindest and best of husbands, diligently prayed? And hadn't his entreaty been answered? Rebekah fretted aloud, "If it is so [that the Lord has heard our prayer], why am I like this?" (AMP).

Good question, sister—and one we've all asked the Lord at some point. We pray for the perfect job, then are dismayed when it's not everything we'd hoped for. We pray for the ideal mate, only to be taken aback the moment his less-than-ideal traits surface. We pray for God to bless us with children, then balk when motherhood isn't filled with endless Gerber Baby moments.

We understand why Rebekah wanted an explanation for her pain and applaud her courageous move.

So she went to inquire of the LORD. *Genesis 25:22*

Rebekah sought "guidance" (NEB) not from her husband or a midwife or another expectant mother. Not this intrepid soul. She wanted "an answer from the LORD" (NCV).

Where did Rebekah *go*? we wonder. Judging by the language used here, she went to "a special shrine,"[52] a place where one might expect to find God in a listening mood.

In Rebekah's case, he not only listened; he answered.

The LORD said to her... *Genesis 25:23*

Let's pause and revel in the moment. God spoke directly to a woman—one-on-one—about her pregnancy. Does the Lord care about our every need? Count on it. No need to begin our prayers, "I know this is silly, but…" Nothing is trivial to God.

…"Two nations are in your womb…" *Genesis 25:23*

And "rival nations" (NLT) at that. Most of us are content starting a family. Imagine starting a whole *nation*. Make that two.

"…and two peoples from within you will be separated;…"
Genesis 25:23

This didn't mean her babies would be torn asunder—only that they would be "incompatible."[53] Some consolation there, except we have no biblical record of a mother before Rebekah bearing twins. If she was the first, think how frightening a prospect that would have been! Who could survive such a thing?

While Rebekah tried to grasp the reality of two children in her womb, God kept on talking.

"…one people will be stronger than the other, and the older will
serve the younger." *Genesis 25:23*

The Lord neatly turned man's law on its head. In that time and culture, the older was always favored. Now, by "God's sovereign choice,"[54] the younger would be honored. Come to think of it, God also chose younger Isaac over older Ishmael and preferred young Abel's offering to that of his older brother, Cain.[55]

What was going on here?

The Almighty was "countering human presumption and arrogance"[56] by simply being God. Nearly three hundred times in Scripture he bears the name "Sovereign LORD." David exalted him, saying, "How great you are, O Sovereign LORD! There is no one like you, and there is no God but you, as we have heard with our own ears."[57] And seen with our own eyes. And read in the stories of Sarah and Hagar and Rebekah. And experienced in our own lives. The favor God bestowed on this unborn child—and on us as well— "came from the sheer grace of God himself."[58]

Rebekah, clutching her heaving abdomen in pain, returned home with more questions than answers. God had told her *what* but not *why* or *how* or *when.* Since she's the first woman in the biblical record to carry twins, such a birth may have been a strange and rare occurrence. Did she keep this foreknowledge of the twins to herself? Or was Isaac the first to know and her girlfriends soon after? The Bible is silent on the subject. But I suspect Rebekah held God's promises close to her heart, waiting for the day when her younger son would be the favored one.

> When the time came for her to give birth, there were twin boys in her womb. *Genesis 25:24*

No surprise to God. No surprise to Rebekah. Possibly a big surprise to Isaac. "Really? Two?"

> The first to come out was red, and his whole body was like a hairy garment; so they named him Esau. *Genesis 25:25*

Not just a little hair here and there. The boy was covered in so much red hair "one would think he was wearing a piece of clothing" (NLT), "like a hairy robe" (NCV). So they called him *Esau,* which means (you got it) "hairy."[59]

Forgive me as I burst into song: "I'm just wild about Hairy…"

> After this, his brother came out… *Genesis 25:26*

How effortless this sounds, as if Rebekah calmly watched while "his brother followed" (MSG) "immediately afterwards" (NEB). Oh sure. It's called *labor* for a reason.

> …with his hand grasping Esau's heel;… *Genesis 25:26*

The twins were born almost simultaneously, one hanging on to the other. *Ouch.*

> …so he was named Jacob. *Genesis 25:26*

Unlike his brother, Jacob was neither red nor hairy when he entered the world with "his fist clutched tight to Esau's heel" (MSG). Originally his name meant something like "God follows after,"[60] but the meaning soon shifted to suit his personality. Jacob became known as a supplanter, a schemer, a wrestler, a finagler, a "heel-grabber."[61]

Behold the twin sons of Rebekah: Hairy and Heel.

> Isaac was sixty years old when Rebekah gave birth to them.
> *Genesis 25:26*

Since she was young when they married, perhaps no more than fifteen years of age, we now have a thirty-five-year-old mother and a sixty-year-old father. (Think Catherine Zeta-Jones and Michael Douglas.) A common scenario throughout history yet one that foreshadows the troubles to come.

Playing Favorites

> The boys grew up… *Genesis 25:27*

No news to report here apparently. They simply grew up. And apart.

> …and Esau became a skillful hunter, a man of the open country…
> *Genesis 25:27*

We get the picture: Esau was "a man addicted to his sports,"[62] a rough-and-ready outdoorsman, and an aggressive hunter, "loving hardship and courting danger."[63] Ishmael Jr., if you will.

> …while Jacob was a quiet man, staying among the tents. *Genesis 25:27*

That would make him Isaac Jr.: "a mild man" (NKJV) rather than a wild man, "the kind of person who liked to stay at home" (NLT), who "settled down and became a shepherd" (CEV). The Hebrew text suggests qualities like being levelheaded, mature, and dependable—traits that made Jacob a "formidably cool opponent."[64]

Raising sons who were different from hair to heel wasn't an uncommon challenge. What wreaked havoc in this family of four was the divisive game of playing favorites.

Isaac, who had a taste for wild game, loved Esau... *Genesis 25:28*

Better put, "Isaac loved Esau because he hunted the wild animals that Isaac enjoyed eating" (NCV). It was the *food* Isaac adored and, secondarily, the son whose bow and arrow nabbed dinner.

...but... *Genesis 25:28*

No, that's not a typo, nor have I resorted to studying the Bible one word at a time (though if I thought you could stand it, sis, I'd go for it!). Whenever you see *but* in Scripture, it's significant; some vital comparison is about to be made. Even if there are positive statements on either side of the word, *but* alerts us to a problem.

This verse might have been written, "Isaac loved Esau, *and* Rebekah loved Jacob."

Unfortunately, it wasn't.

...but Rebekah loved Jacob. *Genesis 25:28*

It seemed she loved Jacob *instead of* loving Esau, meaning all her maternal affection ran in one direction. No denying it, "Jacob was his mother's favorite son" (CEV). Larger portions at meals. Fancier trim on his tunics. More eye contact, more physical contact. An ever-available lap when he was small, a listening ear as he grew older. Whenever you saw Jacob, he was wearing that T-shirt his mother ordered from the Smothers Brothers' Web site: "Mom Likes Me Best."

Rebekah doted on Jacob, fussed over Jacob, and protected Jacob—not unlike Sarah, who mothered Isaac with the ferocity of a lioness guarding her cub.

Sarah's ill will toward Ishmael, while unkind, was at least understandable.

But Rebekah withholding love from her own flesh and blood strikes us as unconscionable. As one scholar mused, "How can a mother who would do this be lifted up as a role model?"[65]

Say hello to our third Slightly Bad Girl.

Maybe Isaac made his preference known first since the oldest son "is the first sign of his father's strength."[66] Or Isaac may have seen in Esau "his alter ego—a wild, emancipated soul,"[67] thereby prompting Rebekah to take up for Jacob, defending and protecting her "gentle, industrious shepherd."[68]

But I think it more likely that Rebekah favored Jacob from the day God revealed his plan for her younger son. After all, "only one could be the hero of the story."[69]

While both boys were still in her womb, Rebekah had already made up her mind: whoever was born second would have her undivided attention. Surely that was what God meant for her to do...wasn't it? She would keep Jacob close to home, make him "her companion at chores,"[70] and teach him how to cook a lentil stew so fragrant his ravenous brother would sell his birthright for a bowlful.

Though she didn't make an appearance, Rebekah's influence was felt on the day "Esau came in from the open country, famished."[71] Common sense and spiritual discernment go out the window when a growling stomach takes over. Esau demanded food, and Jacob demanded payment. In short order Esau "swore an oath to him, selling his birthright to Jacob."[72]

The birthright was no small prize: it meant Jacob "succeeded to the father's official authority."[73] That was precisely what Rebekah wanted for her son: "the older will serve the younger,"[74] just as God had said.

No matter how sorry you feel for Esau later (and you will), remember that at this critical juncture Esau threw away his future with both hands. The Bible doesn't say, "Thus Jacob cheated his brother out of his birthright."[75] No, Jacob was merely the clever son of a clever mother, doing all she'd taught him to do. On that day he lived up to his name: Finagler. Schemer. Heel.

Imagine the fallout when Isaac heard the news! Did Rebekah secretly rejoice? Wink at Jacob over dinner? Disavow any knowledge of things when she lay next to Isaac that night? We can be sure of this: "family relationships crumbled because Rebekah made an idol out of Jacob."[76]

How many marriages can you name that have ended up like this one? The wife's strong nature slowly but surely usurps her husband's authority; the acquiescent husband surrenders without protest. Children, through no fault of their own, widen the gap between their parents, who begin showering affection on their offspring rather than on each other.

As to Rebekah, "whatever love she once bore her aged husband vanished when children came."[77] We never see the words "Rebekah loved Isaac" in Scripture, yet we find "Rebekah loved Jacob." And though there was a time Isaac "loved her," the day came when we can only be certain "Isaac loved Esau." Heartbreaking, isn't it? With a heavy sigh we must admit, "the sweetest love stories do not always last."[78]

Rebekah was no longer an innocent lass standing by the town well with a clay jar perched on her shoulder. In her place an older, more calculating Rebekah had emerged: a mother determined to see her favorite son inherit all God intended, no matter whose hearts she trampled in the process. Much as we wish it weren't so, "her love for Jacob made her hurt the other men in her life."[79]

Will our Slightly Bad Girl see the error of her ways? The truth awaits us in the next chapter of her colorful life.

What Lessons Can We Learn from Rebekah the Wife?

Strength can be a good thing.
Rebekah was "strong and masterful from the time she appears in the Scriptural narrative until she goes out."[80] Her strong body carried her up and down the steps of the well. Her strong courage gave her the fortitude to say, "I will go," and not look back. Her strong faith enabled her to trust the prayers of her husband to bless her womb. Strong-willed women can learn much from Rebekah—both what to do and what *not* to do. If we use our strength to barrel through life, ignoring the needs of others, that's not good. But if we use our strength for the benefit of those around us and for the glory of the Lord, that's goodness personified.

She is clothed with strength and dignity. *Proverbs 31:25*

It pays to take your questions to the top.

Faced with a challenge, we often turn to friends or books or experts for answers. Yet Rebekah went directly to the Lord with her question, certain he would respond. She didn't go to complain or ask for a refund; she just wanted to know "Why is this happening to me?" I've cried out those very words myself yet seldom waited for a heavenly response. "Why, God?" I groan. "Why me?" It's a cry of frustration, of anger, of weariness—not a genuine plea for answers. Rebekah, however, had a problem that needed solving and knew the Lord could and would explain what she needed to know. The angel of the Lord sought out Hagar, but brave Rebekah "went to inquire of the LORD" on her own (Genesis 25:22). That's an example worth following.

> Seek the LORD while he may be found; call on him while he is near.
> *Isaiah 55:6*

"What God has joined together, let man not separate."

A familiar verse, Matthew 19:6. One often included in marriage ceremonies. What to do with Jacob and Esau, then, who were "born to divide husband and wife"?[81] The fault rested not with the children but with their parents. When Bill and I married, he vowed, "The best thing I can do for our children is to love their mother," and he's proceeded to do exactly that. (I know, I know, I'm one blessed woman!) Sadly, with Isaac and Rebekah, each parent chose one son to love, separating the family in multiple ways—husband from wife, mother from child, father from child, brother from brother. For those of us who are wives and mothers, one of the greatest gifts we can give our children is loving, honoring, and respecting their father. And even more so, loving, honoring, and respecting their heavenly Father.

> Each one of you also must love his wife as he loves himself, and the
> wife must respect her husband. *Ephesians 5:33*

Inner beauty needs cultivating too.

When Isaac first met Rebekah, she was "a beautiful young girl with a gold nose ring and lots of chutzpah,"[82] chosen by Abraham's servant, not for her outward appearance, but for her character. As the years passed, Rebekah's strengths, allowed to grow unchecked, became her weaknesses. The same can happen to us. Having a mind of our own is good, but single-mindedly pursuing a goal to the detriment of our trust in God and our treatment of others is foolhardy. Being bold is useful, but running roughshod over others is cruel. "A strong-minded, decisive girl" can turn into an "autocratic matriarch"[83] before she realizes it. However attractive Rebekah might have been, her character took an ugly turn.

> Like a gold ring in a pig's snout is a beautiful woman who shows no discretion. *Proverbs 11:22*

Good Girl Thoughts Worth Considering

1. One scholar described Isaac as having "a sedate, contemplative, and yielding disposition," the sort of man who "followed, but did not lead."[84] What incidents in Isaac's early years might have shaped his laid-back personality? In what ways might go-go Rebekah have reminded him of his mother? What are the pluses of marrying someone who is your opposite? And what are the minuses?

2. The servant asked God for a specific sign—"If that happens, I will know she is the right one" (Genesis 24:14, ICB)—thinking a woman willing to go the extra mile would make a good wife for Isaac. Did asking for a sign mean the servant lacked faith, or was he simply seeking direction? What makes you say that?

3. Rebekah *did* go the extra mile (and a zillion extra steps!) to water the servant's ten camels. How would you explain her benevolent effort? Youthful enthusiasm? Heartfelt generosity? A prompting from the Lord? Or could her motivation have been less than altruistic? To impress the men? To earn a fistful of coins? To shame the other women who were watching? Think of a recent incident when you were exceedingly generous or hospitable. What

were your underlying motives? And other than a happy recipient, what was the outcome of your action?

4. Describe how you envision Rebekah's conversation, her facial expressions, and her body language when she hurried to tell her mother's household. Do you see any hint of the character flaws that surfaced later in her life? Compare your younger self to the woman you are today. How has your character changed for the better over the years? And in what ways have your flaws gained ground?

5. How might Rebekah have seen her relocation to a distant land as a calling from God? And why did she seem so ready to marry a stranger? Several members of Rebekah's household accompanied her. How might that make such a venture easier for you? Or would you rather take off solo? What would convince you that such a journey was God's idea and not yours?

6. Why do we have no recorded conversation between the betrothed parties on that enchanted evening when Isaac and Rebekah first gazed at each other across a crowded field of camels? However reticent his personality, Isaac wasted no time in marrying Rebekah. In what ways did he demonstrate his love for her from that day forward? And how did the Lord—not Isaac, not Rebekah—solve her problem with barrenness?

7. When pregnant Rebekah "went to inquire of the LORD," his promise was clear: "the older will serve the younger" (Genesis 25:22–23). Was that sufficient justification for Rebekah to love Jacob (and, it would seem, not love Esau)? Which aspects of Rebekah's personality do you recognize in Jacob? In Esau? If you have children, do you ever struggle with favoring one over the other(s)? What are some healthy ways to balance parental affection?

8. What's the most important lesson you learned from our visit with Rebekah, a young wife who said "I will" with gusto?

Using Her Wits

Man forgives woman anything
save the wit to outwit him.
MINNA ANTRIM

Rosalind Seaver grasped the letter with both hands, wishing it were the administrator's stiff neck so she might throttle the man. What did he *mean* only one child per household was eligible?

She scanned the contents again. Perhaps she'd misunderstood.

No, there it was, plainly stated: *The foundation's policy allows one student per family.* "No exceptions," she grumbled aloud, tossing the letter onto the cluttered desk in her husband's study. The foundation had approved their fourteen-year-old twins for an exclusive student-exchange program yet included only one acceptance form. Even Eric's overflowing bank account couldn't buy a second spot, and a summer in New Zealand was not something the boys could flip a coin over.

She dropped into Eric's leather desk chair with a noisy sigh, then reached for the phone, hitting the speed-dial button for her husband's private line at the office.

He answered on the first ring. "Eric Seaver."

"Darling, we have a problem." She didn't bother to ask if he was in a meeting. Nothing mattered more than her sons. "We've heard from the foundation."

"I assume they approved Ethan?"

Her jaw tightened. "*And* Jackson." Had that possibility never occurred to him? Rosalind heard him sorting through papers on his desk as if he were only half paying attention.

Finally he said, "No reason we can't send them both."

"I'll give you one." She read aloud the pertinent section of the letter, which fueled her anger further. "Now do you see the problem?"

"But Ethan has his heart set—"

"So does Jackson!" Tears stung her eyes. "This is not the time to play favorites, Eric."

"I know, dearest. I know."

Hearing the resignation in his voice, she pressed her point. "If only one of the twins can participate, shouldn't it be our straight-A student?"

"But New Zealand is a sportsman's paradise…"

"And our summer is their winter," she countered, though cold weather would hardly deter Ethan. Her gaze landed on the collection of framed photographs on her husband's desk: Ethan fly-fishing in Montana, Ethan lining up a shot with his new BowTech Commander, Ethan hiking Red Rock Canyon.

Not so much as a snapshot of Jackson in sight.

A cold fury settled in her heart. What sort of parent ignored one son and championed the other? Eric never missed one of Ethan's games, yet he skipped last week's academic award ceremony where Jackson received several honors. Was her husband blind? Could he not see the damage he inflicted, the pain etched on Jackson's face?

"Rosalind," he was saying, "I'll be home by four o'clock. Can we discuss this then?"

"We can." *And we will.* She stopped herself from hanging up without a proper good-bye. Eric was her husband, after all; she couldn't dismiss him.

But she could persuade him.

With a firm resolve, she reached for the acceptance form: a sea of words in small print and only a few lines to fill out. The student's name was required along with both parents' signatures.

Rosalind reached for a pen, then thought better of it. Forging Eric's signature was not only unwise; it was illegal. God was on her side in this; she didn't need to break the law.

Might she convince Ethan to forgo the trip? Offer him something in exchange? Such a trade-off had worked before when he wanted to wear his brother's Eagle Scout medal and settled for a Sacramento Kings jersey instead.

But what could she offer that would compare to this? For weeks Ethan had talked about nothing but tramping, caving, and kayaking. Yet Jackson intended to pursue a PhD in agricultural research. Surely he would benefit from exploring a country where sheep outnumbered people twenty to one.

Young as he was, Jackson had a sense of mission, a long-term view of things, and far more potential than his brother. Hadn't she sensed God's hand on him practically from birth? More to the point, she'd prayed daily since the boys turned in their applications. When she did, it was Jackson she envisioned walking down the Jetway, sending postcards from Auckland, and returning home with a suitcase full of priceless kiwi memories.

For that prayer to come true, she needed to act quickly. Once Ethan learned of his acceptance, he would claim the trip for himself, with his father's blessing.

Rosalind tucked the letter and form in her purse and pulled out her car keys as a foolproof plan took shape.

"Wow, Mom." Jackson leaned in the passenger-side window. "What smells so good?"

"Dinner." She gestured toward an aromatic package of her husband's favorite gourmet barbecued chicken, perched on the backseat. "Come, we're holding up the carpool line." She waved her fingers in the rearview mirror, catching the eye of the mother parked behind her, then touched the gas pedal and pointed the Porsche Cayenne Turbo toward home.

Jackson had inherited her russet hair, her pale, freckled skin...and her avid curiosity. He stared at the white bag with the chef's signature in a bold, red logo. "Since when did you start buying takeout chicken?"

"My, aren't we the private-school snob?" she chided him. "I thought I'd bring home a treat for your father. You must admit, Angelo's is hardly fast food."

He shoved his books off his lap and onto the floor. "Hope it still tastes decent by the time Dad gets home at…what, eight?"

"Oh, he'll arrive long before that. Your father has an eye-doctor appointment this afternoon. I'm expecting him about four o'clock for an early dinner."

"But Ethan will still be at archery practice."

"I know," she said with a sigh. "Your brother will have to make do with leftovers." She reached into her purse and withdrew the folded papers, then pressed them into Jackson's hands. "Good news from the foundation."

As he skimmed the letter, she watched his face mirror her own initial reactions: elation, then dismay.

"Mom, how's this going to work? We can't both go."

Rosalind eased to a stop at a traffic light, weighing her words. "Are you willing to give up your place?"

"No way!"

His vehement response told her all she needed to know. "Your father prefers to send Ethan."

"I'll just bet he does." Jackson slumped down in his seat, glowering.

Rosalind said nothing else, letting him stew.

By the time they pulled into the garage, Eric's silver Lexus was already parked there. Jackson carried his books under one arm, Eric's meal under the other, as they walked through the pristine mud room and into the house.

Rosalind slipped off her shoes and padded toward his study. "Eric?"

"In here."

She found him at his desk, shielding his eyes.

"They gave me those drops." Eric blinked, then turned off his desk lamp. "The ones that dilate your pupils. Apparently my eyes will stay like this for a few more hours. Can't read a thing."

"Really."

"Driving in the sun was brutal." He held up a disposable pair of sunglasses. "The latest in fashionable eyewear."

Rosalind took the cardboard shades and slipped them into her pocket. "We brought home a treat for you. Angelo's barbecued chicken."

He grinned like Ethan with a new quiver of arrows. "So that's what I smell."

"I'll have Jackson bring it to you in here." She turned to leave. "It's far too bright in the kitchen."

Rosalind found Jackson standing at the counter, practically drooling as he peered down into the Angelo's bag. "Is Dad hungry yet?" he asked.

"Listen," she said softly, "and do exactly what I tell you." She smoothed out the acceptance form on the granite countertop. "Print your name where it says 'student,' and add your signature at the bottom."

Jackson blanched. "Mom…"

She brandished a pen. "Do you want to go to New Zealand? Or shall we let your father send Ethan?"

"Okay, okay." Jackson did as she requested, then quickly shoved the paper in her direction. "How will you get Dad to sign it?"

"First you'll take him his dinner." She lifted out the chicken, careful not to spill the sauce, and began arranging it on an oversize dinner plate. "Then you'll ask him to sign this acceptance form for Ethan."

"*Ethan?* But he'll see my—"

"No, he won't." She handed him the plate of food and a setting of silverware. "Not for another hour or two."

"But what if—"

"Then I'll handle it, Jackson." She exhaled, impatient to have things over with. "Before you go in, let me sign my name."

She touched pen to paper and wrote her signature in a bold script. *Rosalind D. Seaver…*

Rebekah the Mother: Becky Goes Bad

Every book needs a groaner: *D. Seaver* should do it for this one!

Our Rebekah was older now and her hubby older still. We'll discover in a moment that her hearing was sharper than ever; the same cannot be said for her husband's eyesight.

> When Isaac was old and his eyes were so weak that he could no
> longer see... *Genesis 27:1*

The poor man was "almost blind" (NLT). Metaphorically, he'd lost his vision as well, no longer able to see the glaring truth before him: his son had sold his birthright for a bowl of stew and no longer deserved his father's favor. His father's love, absolutely; but not his father's spiritual inheritance.

> ...he called for Esau his older son and said to him, "My son."
> *Genesis 27:1*

Another word remained unspoken, yet we hear it in his voice: "My *favorite* son."

Esau proudly stepped forward.

> "Here I am," he answered. *Genesis 27:1*

As this volatile chapter unfolds, you'll notice each scene features just two actors at a time; "because of the deep rift in the family Esau never meets with Jacob or Rebekah."[1] The separation that began in Rebekah's body resulted in two brothers who could not bear the sight of each other and a mother estranged from her son and husband.

You may find your sympathies pulled in different directions and decide that all four characters had "both admirable and deplorable traits."[2] First, let's see what you think of the patriarch.

> Isaac said, "I am now an old man..." *Genesis 27:2*

Those familiar words would have caught Esau's ear since they served as a prologue for a "deathbed 'blessing.'"[3]

> "...and don't know the day of my death." *Genesis 27:2*

None of us does, of course. Isaac was merely saying, "I expect every day to be my last" (NLT). Hence, he wanted to take care of urgent matters using the legal terminology of ancient times. As it happened, Isaac lived many years beyond this day, but he wasn't taking any chances. A ceremonial meal befitted any solemn occasion, and Isaac knew what he was hungry for.

> "Now then, get your weapons—your quiver and bow—and
> go out to the open country to hunt some wild game for me."
> *Genesis 27:3*

Wild game might have included "venison" (KJV) or the meat of any number of beasts that roamed the land—ox, gazelle, roe deer, wild goat, ibex, or antelope[4]—the gamier, the better, from Isaac's perspective.

> "Prepare me the kind of tasty food I like and bring it to me to
> eat..." *Genesis 27:4*

Like his favorite son, Isaac was ruled by his appetite. We can almost hear the elderly man smacking his lips, as if catching a whiff of the "appetizing meat" (AMP), "savory and good" (NLT). Highly seasoned foods were preferred in the Near East, where aromatic herbs and spices like salt, onions, garlic, saffron, and mint were rubbed into the meats.[5]

Oh bother. Now I'm getting hungry. May it never be said of me, as it was of Isaac, "his palate...governed his heart."[6]

For Esau, providing the meal would come first. Then he'd receive his long-awaited dessert.

> "...so that I may give you my blessing before I die." *Genesis 27:4*

The blessing of one's father represented a verbal will, a spoken scepter, an invisible crown of words circling the son's brow. The ancients believed that a blessing held such power that "the words, once uttered, could neither be negated nor diverted from their course."[7] Potent. Mystical. And irrevocable.

Esau was not the only one who heard the word *blessing*.

Now Rebekah was listening as Isaac spoke to his son Esau.

Genesis 27:5

"Listening," eh? Had she simply "overheard the conversation" (NLT) while she worked at some task nearby? Or was she intentionally eavesdropping, waiting for the right moment to make her move? I vote for the second option, knowing Rebekah as we do: "She operates behind the scenes, but she controls the action."[8]

Control. That's Rebekah's most problematic issue.

And mine.

Like Rebekah, my control tendencies escalated when I became a mother. Our children *need* us to be in charge, don't they? Yes, in the early years. But it's a hard habit to break and often extends well beyond the nursery. Without meaning to, we start making decisions for our husbands. Our siblings. Our friends. Our peers at work.

Let's face it: anyone with a meeker personality is sure to be flattened by our steamroller approach. We make suggestions, then bristle when they're ignored. We do things for others, then get testy when our efforts aren't appreciated. We hand out to-do lists, then whine when we find them in the circular file. If people would simply follow our instructions—or, better yet, read our minds and respond accordingly—life would be so much easier.

Wait. *Our* lives would be easier.

Sigh.

Control issues plagued each of our Slightly Bad Girls—Rebekah most of all. A more assertive husband might have curbed her controlling nature, but she was married to a man who'd been "protected, pampered and pleased" by Sarah, leaving Rebekah little choice but to also mother Isaac.[9] Perhaps Rebekah lost respect for her husband and even "came to despise him."[10]

I pray that wasn't the case—that their relationship never sank so low—though this scene suggests all was not well between them. Once Esau left for the open country, Rebekah unveiled a plan that was "deep, dark, disconcerting."[11]

Do What I Tell You

> Rebekah said to her son Jacob, "Look, I overheard your father say to
> your brother Esau, 'Bring me some game and prepare me some tasty
> food to eat, so that I may give you my blessing in the presence of
> the LORD before I die.'" *Genesis 27:6–7*

She repeated Isaac's words almost verbatim, with one telling addition: "in
the presence of the LORD." Rebekah, perhaps more than her husband, understood the spiritual gravity of this act. One of her sons would receive not only
his father's blessing but also God's blessing as promised through Abraham.
Wasn't she—not Isaac—the one who'd heard God's prophetic words concerning her younger son? Then it was up to her to see God's will done.

Heaven knows the Lord couldn't manage without her help. Nor could
Jacob. (Nor Isaac, nor Esau, but they had to wait their turns.)

> "Now, my son, listen carefully and do what I tell you:…" *Genesis 27:8*

Make a note of that "do what I tell you" line; you'll hear it twice more
before the story is over. "Obey my voice," Rebekah insisted, "according to
that which I command thee" (KJV). "Command" was the word for it. Clearly,
"Rebekah dominated Jacob."[12] She also taught him everything she knew, as
evidenced in the trade-my-stew-for-your-birthright scene.

Both mother and son showed themselves to be quick, clever, and calculating, but she was the veteran. You'll notice Rebekah didn't say, "This is how
we're going to trick your father." She simply sent Jacob to get groceries.

> "Go out to the flock and bring me two choice young goats…"
> *Genesis 27:9*

Goat meat? Isaac wanted *game* meat. But Rebekah was no longer bent
on pleasing her husband, only on getting his goat.

> "…so I can prepare some tasty food for your father, just the way he
> likes it." *Genesis 27:9*

Women have been saying "The way to a man's heart is through his stomach" since 1853,[13] but the concept goes back at least to Rebekah, who contrived to butter up her husband with roasted goats, prepared "just the way your father likes them" (NCV). Hey, even the Bible commands, "If your enemy is hungry, give him food."[14]

> "Then take it to your father to eat, so that he may give you his
> blessing before he dies." *Genesis 27:10*

Again she echoed the words of her husband. That was his plan precisely, and hers as well. She wanted to make only one small change: the son.

If we dropped by Rebekah's kitchen at this crucial moment, we would find a woman convinced she was a Supremely Good Girl, "instrumental in carrying on the Divine purpose."[15] If we cried, "Becky, stop! You're about to deceive your husband," she would glare at us and claim, "On the contrary, I'm helping him do God's will."

Maybe Isaac wasn't the only sight-challenged person in that household. Self-righteous zeal blinded Rebekah into thinking "the end sanctifies the means."[16] How often have I done the same, exerting my will over a situation, convinced that as long as the outcome lined up with Scripture, the method didn't matter. Rebekah's motives were clear, but they weren't pure.

As for Jacob, he wasn't thinking about God's will *or* his mother's will. His concern was of a more practical nature.

> Jacob said to Rebekah his mother, "But my brother Esau is a hairy
> man, and I'm a man with smooth skin." *Genesis 27:11*

Some verses in the Bible stand on their own—powerful, meaningful, life changing. This is not one of them. Audiences chuckle when I read it aloud: "Behold, Esau my brother is a hairy man, and I am a smooth man" (KJV). Visually, it's a hoot.

Spiritually, it's a sham. Jacob had already figured out what his mother was tacitly asking him to do—impersonate Esau—yet he raised no objection to deceiving his father or stealing his brother's inheritance. No, Mr. Smooth worried only about breaking the eleventh commandment: "Thou shalt not get caught."[17]

> "What if my father touches me? I would appear to be tricking him…" *Genesis 27:12*

Forget appearances, son; you *would* be tricking him. You would in fact be "a deceiver" (KJV) and "a cheat and an imposter" (AMP). Unlike his mother, Jacob weighed the possible repercussions of this little masquerade. Single-minded Rebekah envisioned only the blessing to come, but Jacob considered the awful alternative.

> "…and would bring down a curse on myself rather than a blessing."
> *Genesis 27:12*

God had spoken to Jacob's grandfather about such things: "I will bless those who bless you, and whoever curses you I will curse."[18] We can imagine this family repeated that promise often—when they sat at home and when they walked along the road, when they went to bed and when they woke up.

If Jacob dishonored and deceived his father, wouldn't God curse him? Not on Rebekah's watch.

> His mother said to him, "My son, let the curse fall on me."
> *Genesis 27:13*

Let the *what?*

Rebekah, you weren't serious.

Oh, but she was. "If your father puts a curse on you, I will accept the blame" (NCV), she told Jacob. If necessary, "I'll take the curse on myself" (MSG). By agreeing to suffer any consequences, Rebekah "must have understood that if in the future she was despised for this act she would have to bear it."[19]

She was willing to be hated by her husband and cursed by God—all so her son might be blessed? Whatever are we to think of Rebekah? She seems as manipulative as "Off-with-his-head!" Herodias, as devious as "I'll-get-you-the-vineyard" Jezebel. Yet, unlike those Glad-to-Be-Bad women, Rebekah served the one true God, making her behavior here all the more inexcusable.

Rebekah's willingness to sacrifice herself for her son wasn't virtuous; it was blasphemous. God alone decides whom he will bless and whom he will curse. And only God's sacrifice is sufficient to cover our lies and deceptions. Not even a mother's love can match his definition of the word: "This is love: not that we loved God, but that he loved us and sent his Son as an atoning sacrifice for our sins."[20]

All our sins—even the most conniving, controlling ones—have been covered by the blood of the Lamb. And so we read on, whispering a prayer of gratitude, relieved that even flagrant sins like these are not beyond God's mercy.

> "Just do what I say; go and get them for me." *Genesis 27:13*

There's our second "do what I say" of the story. If nothing else, Rebekah's repetitive command that Jacob do her bidding assuaged her son's guilt. He could rightly protest, "It was Mom's idea." And if you've lost track after several pages, what she'd asked him to do was "Go out and get the goats" (NLT).

Cooking Up Trouble

> So he went and got them and brought them to his mother…
> *Genesis 27:14*

Jacob didn't need to go hunting in the distant forests like his brother since the family flocks grazed near the tents. His ability to select the choicest young goats reveals Jacob's adeptness as a herdsman—a skill that would be sorely tested in the years that followed.

However delicious Jacob's lentil stew recipe, Rebekah was wearing the chef's hat that day.

> …and she prepared some tasty food, just the way his father liked it.
> *Genesis 27:14*

Isaac could no longer see, but he could definitely smell this "delicious meat dish" (NLT) with its "delightful odor" (AMP). As the aroma wafted from the hearth in Rebekah's tent, Isaac must have pictured Esau poking at the roasting game with a stick.

Oops, wrong son.

> Then Rebekah took the best clothes of Esau her older son, which
> she had in the house, and put them on her younger son Jacob.
> *Genesis 27:15*

Since Esau was out hunting, he'd left at home his "goodly raiment" (KJV), something like a "festal robe,"[21] well suited for receiving the blessing.

The clothes fit Jacob. But there was still the problem of his smooth skin.

> She also covered his hands and the smooth part of his neck with the
> goatskins. *Genesis 27:16*

I've seen a few goats in my time, even petted one at a farm, and it did *not* feel human. But a particular breed called a camel-goat has hair that, if not humanlike, is less goatlike.[22] We're not told how Rebekah attached these animal skins to Jacob's hands and neck, though it matters little: Isaac couldn't see the stitches or strings that held the goatskins in place. If Jacob could befuddle the patriarch's other four senses, his dark deed was done.

> Then she handed to her son Jacob the tasty food and the bread she
> had made. *Genesis 27:17*

Jacob may have served as the delivery boy, but we're meant to attribute "this deliberately calculated initiative"[23] entirely to Rebekah, who "put herself in the place of God"[24] even as Jacob put himself in the place of Esau.

> He went to his father and said, "My father." *Genesis 27:18*

Can you believe Jacob spoke first? If I were wearing his sandals, I'd have entered in silence and started dishing out grub, only grunting when necessary. Surely his father recognized his younger son's voice.

> "Yes, my son," he answered. "Who is it?" *Genesis 27:18*

Isaac knew it was *a* son but nothing more. And so he asked, "Which one of my sons are you?" (CEV), "Esau or Jacob?" (NLT). The poor man really was blind. Maybe his hearing had started to diminish as well.

As we prepare to hear the seven lies of Jacob, we sense Rebekah listening intently, her dark eyes peering through the folds of the tent partition, her heart pounding as she mouthed a silent prayer for her favored son, convinced she was doing God's will.

> Jacob said to his father, "I am Esau your firstborn." *Genesis 27:19*

Lies One and Two. When he bargained with Esau for his birthright, at least Jacob was straightforward. Here he stole his brother's name and birth order in one breath.

> "I have done as you told me." *Genesis 27:19*

Nice try, but two more lies. Jacob wasn't the son to whom Isaac made his request. And while we're picking nits, he did what his *mother* told him, not his father: he didn't go hunting, nor did he cook the meat.

> "Please sit up and eat some of my game so that you may give me
> your blessing." *Genesis 27:19*

Take Five: Jacob hasn't got game; he's got goat!

Rather premature to mention the blessing, don't you agree? Rebekah, safely out of view, must have frowned at her son's impatience. Speaking of rushing things, her husband posed a pointed question.

> "How did you find it so quickly, my son?" *Genesis 27:20*

Isaac was nearly blind, but he wasn't stupid. Hunting wild game, then skinning the carcass, and hanging the meat to a high flavor—these things took longer than an afternoon. Jacob's face must have warmed as he searched for the right answer, then offered "the worst of his lies."[25]

> "The LORD your God gave me success," he replied. *Genesis 27:20*

Oh, that's rich. "Your God was kind to me" (CEV) and "cleared the way for me" (MSG). The nerve of that boy, dragging God into the middle of this mess. Still, our deceiver "spoke more truth than he realized:"[26] the Lord *did* clear the way for his blessing long before the child was even born.

Jacob also spoke the truth when he said "your God." Not "my God," not "our God," but "*your* God." It seemed Jacob did not fully share in the faith of his parents, at least not yet.

> Then Isaac said to Jacob, "Come near so I can touch you,
> my son, to know whether you really are my son Esau or not."
> *Genesis 27:21*

Jacob's one fear—"What if my father touches me?"—sprang to vivid life as Isaac waved him forward. "Come close and let me feel you" (NEB).

Hmmm. A sly visitor dressed in borrowed clothes bearing food for an unsuspecting invalid... You don't suppose this scene was the inspiration for "Little Red Riding Hood"? Okay, maybe not. Though we *do* have a wolf in goat's clothing.

Rebekah had to be holding her breath as Jacob drew closer to his father and let the patriarch touch him. "Hairy, like Esau," she might have whispered, hoping her husband would come to the same conclusion.

Our sympathy goes out to Isaac, whose advanced years worked against him, as did his trusting nature. "Isaac was so incapable of such duplicity himself, he did not really expect it of others."[27]

> "Are you really my son Esau?" he asked. *Genesis 27:24*

A last question from Isaac: "You're sure?" (MSG).

A last chance for Jacob to speak the truth. Instead, he told the seventh lie.

> "I am," he replied. *Genesis 27:24*

No, he was *not* Esau. He would never become Esau no matter how many times he claimed to be his brother.

After Jacob served his father meat and wine, Isaac tossed out an unexpected request.

"Come here, my son, and kiss me." *Genesis 27:26*

Jacob had held out his goatskin-covered hand for his father to touch, but a kiss required much closer contact. Our impostor had no choice but to comply with his father's request.

Betrayal and Blessing

So he went to him and kissed him. *Genesis 27:27*

Judas comes to mind. A kiss of betrayal. Greed at the heart of it, lies all around it. How could you, Jacob?

More to the point, how could you, Rebekah? You used your son to betray your husband. Only a wife would know how best to deceive the man who loved her, confusing his senses so thoroughly he made the wrong son his heir. Well, wrong from Isaac's point of view, quite right from Rebekah's.

When Isaac caught the smell of his clothes, he blessed him.
Genesis 27:27

Isaac "was finally convinced" (NLT), and the blessing unfurled, full of heaven's dew and earth's richness. What the Lord had once promised Rebekah, Isaac now revealed to Jacob.

"Be lord over your brothers, and may the sons of your mother bow down to you." *Genesis 27:29*

Esau would bow, all right, but only long enough to pick up his bow...

After Isaac finished blessing him and Jacob had scarcely left his father's presence, his brother Esau came in from hunting. *Genesis 27:30*

This verse reads like stage directions from a Broadway play, performed with impeccable timing. Jacob exited stage left even as Esau entered stage right, close on his brother's heels. No small irony there.

Neither Rebekah nor her ambassador appeared in the next exchange, but her scheming yielded its inevitable consequences. Though one man in her life was blessed, two other men would bear the fallout of her favoritism.

> "My father, sit up and eat some of my game, so that you may give
> me your blessing." *Genesis 27:31*

Word for word the very thing Jacob had said. Alas, "this was the ruin of Esau: he did not come in time."[28]

> His father Isaac asked him, "Who are you?" *Genesis 27:32*

We can hear the disbelief, the fear, the mounting terror in his voice. Isaac was "too grieved and shocked to say 'my son.' "[29] He only managed a single, awful question: "Who art thou?" (KJV).

When Esau responded, silence fell over his father's tent chamber as the truth sank in.

> Isaac trembled violently… *Genesis 27:33*

Mild-mannered Isaac "became greatly agitated" (NEB). He'd just been bested—not by Jacob, not by Rebekah, but by the Lord himself. Painful as it must have been for Isaac to accept, "he knew that God's will had been done."[30]

Isaac ground out the words.

> "I blessed him—and indeed he will be blessed!" *Genesis 27:33*

Esau knew what that meant: the deed was done. His father had conferred "an irrevocable blessing" (NLT) on his brother, a promise that could not "be taken back" (CEV). Fact is, Jacob was "blessed for good!" (MSG) since no ritual existed to undo a father's blessing.[31]

> When Esau heard his father's words, he burst out with a loud and
> bitter cry and said to his father, "Bless me—me too, my father!"
> *Genesis 27:34*

Those words tear at my heart. What child, feeling upstaged by a sibling, hasn't thrown his arms around his father's neck and sobbed, "Me, too, Daddy. Please?" Esau filled the air with "a great and exceeding bitter cry"

(KJV), like an animal caught in a hunter's trap, mortally wounded yet still alive to feel the pain.

Was Rebekah continuing to eavesdrop? Or had she abandoned her post to tend to Jacob's needs, stripping him of his goatskin gloves, hanging Esau's good clothes where she'd found them, the fabric warm and faintly smelling of Jacob? Did she give any thought to her other son? He must have known Jacob hadn't managed this heartless deception alone.

Though Esau had foolishly let his birthright slip through his fingers, the blessing had been wrenched from his grasp.

Isaac confessed as much.

> "Your brother came deceitfully and took your blessing." *Genesis 27:35*

Not "I was confused" or "I blew it"; Isaac insisted Jacob alone was at fault. Did Isaac suspect his wife's involvement in the affair? Perhaps not, for he never mentioned it. His first words were "Your brother," followed by descriptive phrases that painted a pitch-black picture: "Thy brother came with subtlety" (KJV), "with crafty cunning and treacherous deceit" (AMP), and "carried off your blessing."[32] If we wondered how Isaac felt about his younger son, those incriminating words say it all.

Isaac offered his grieving son a backhanded blessing, the very opposite of his brother's.

> "Your dwelling will be away from the earth's richness, away from the dew of heaven above." *Genesis 27:39*

As if living in an arid wilderness where nothing thrived wasn't misery enough, Esau would also be subject to his brother.

> "You will live by the sword and you will serve your brother."
> *Genesis 27:40*

Not hard to imagine how that went over. Was Esau angry with his father for being weak? Furious with his mother for her machinations? Distraught with God for turning his back on him? Maybe, though Scripture only records how he felt toward his brother.

Esau held a grudge against Jacob because of the blessing his father
had given him. *Genesis 27:41*

I dunno. "Grudge" seems pretty mild. "Seethed in anger" (MSG) sounds
closer to the mark. But "Esau hated Jacob" (NCV) "because he had stolen his
blessing" (NLT) sums it up best.

Without delay Esau began plotting revenge.

Run for Your Life

He said to himself, "The days of mourning for my father are near;
then I will kill my brother Jacob." *Genesis 27:41*

Esau was willing to bide his time, perhaps out of respect for the father
who'd favored him all his life. Or maybe Esau harbored an unspoken fear of
Jacob—not because his brother was stronger, but because Jacob was smarter
and had their mother's undivided loyalty. They made a formidable pair,
those two.

When Rebekah was told what her older son Esau had said...
Genesis 27:42

To her credit, she didn't eavesdrop that time; "someone got wind of what
Esau was planning" (NLT). Feckless Esau, broadcasting his intentions!

...she sent for her younger son Jacob and said to him, "Your
brother Esau is consoling himself with the thought of killing you."
Genesis 27:42

Not only consoling but "comforting himself" (NCV), all the while "plotting vengeance" (MSG). As always, Rebekah had a surefire solution.

"Now then, my son, do what I say:..." *Genesis 27:43*

Third time's the charm for that line. Of course, if Jacob hadn't done
what his mother said in the first place, he wouldn't be in such a fix.

Wouldn't you love to climb inside Rebekah's head? Wheels and gears must have spun in constant motion. Part of me admires her quick-witted style, always ready with plan B, C, or D. I love a woman who can think on her feet, adjust her plans on the fly, do whatever it takes to make things happen. Yet I cringe when I look at the emotional carnage around this queen of control—her distraught husband, her furious son. The woman "greatly underestimated the range of the mischief she had caused."[33]

Did she tend to their wounds later? We're not told in Scripture. At that moment Rebekah's only concern was saving Jacob's life.

"Flee at once to my brother Laban in Haran." *Genesis 27:43*

"Run for your life" (MSG) was more like it. Had brother and sister stayed in touch all those years? Or did Rebekah choose a blood relative because she knew Jacob would be safe within Laban's tents? Though the journey was long and grueling, she wanted Jacob well beyond the reach of his brother's bow. And his sword.

"Stay with him for a while until your brother's fury subsides."
Genesis 27:44

"Tarry with him a few days" (KJV), she suggested. Long enough for Esau to cool down.

"When your brother is no longer angry with you and forgets what you did to him..." *Genesis 27:45*

What *Jacob* did? Rebekah, wasn't the whole thing your idea? How blithely she shook any blame or guilt off her shoulders and onto Jacob's. She assumed Esau's anger would eventually subside and his memory of Jacob's treachery—and hers—would fade. But Rebekah "underestimated the memory of God."[34] Unlike Sarah and Rachel, Rebekah is not hailed in the New Testament as an example of wifely obedience or motherly devotion, nor does her name appear in the Hebrews 11 honor roll of faith.

Such is the danger of thinking only about *now,* one of Rebekah's weaknesses that hits uncomfortably close to home. I start fires without considering the ashes I'll have to sweep up later. I bandage problems without using a dab of antiseptic, only to watch infection set in. In our hurry to solve the crisis of the hour, we often fail to consider the long-range consequences of our short-term solutions.

It seems the only future that concerned Rebekah was Jacob's.

> "I'll send word for you to come back from there." *Genesis 27:45*

Rebekah couldn't bear to think of her son being gone for *good*. He just needed to make himself scarce for a season. She would send a servant to fetch him when the coast was clear. But if he stayed with her, death was certain.

> "Why should I lose both of you in one day?" *Genesis 27:45*

Her comment required a bit of research to sort out: "if Esau killed Jacob, a near kinsman would be obligated to kill Esau."[35] Such was the law of retribution: eye for eye, tooth for tooth, life for life.[36] Whatever her feelings for Esau, she couldn't bear to think of losing both her sons "on the same day" (NCV).

We also hear a desperate note in Rebekah's voice: "She knows now that her plan has achieved nothing."[37] Yes, Jacob had the blessing but for how long with a fire-breathing brother on his trail? Rebekah had to sacrifice Jacob's daily company and bid him farewell, not realizing she would never see her beloved son again.

Rebekah, true to form, thought only about the present dilemma. In order for Jacob to travel to Haran "openly and honorably"[38] and arrive in one piece, Rebekah had to enlist Isaac's help. How she did so was "a masterstroke,"[39] the finest example yet of her cunning mind at work.

She chose a subject they agreed on: their daughters-in-law, "a source of grief to Isaac and Rebekah."[40] Rebekah began the conversation with her husband—as I often do, sad to say—by breathing a sigh of complaint.

> Rebekah said to Isaac, "I'm disgusted with living because of these Hittite women." *Genesis 27:46*

Not just any Hittite women, but the two Esau had married: Judith and Basemath.[41] Esau had foolishly chosen wives who worshiped other gods, further spurning his birthright. Rebekah didn't hold back her opinion (but then, when did she ever?), whining to her husband, "Those Hittite wives of Esau are making my life miserable!" (CEV). Then she neatly segued into the subject of their *other* son's marriage plans.

> "If Jacob takes a wife from among the women of this land, from Hittite women like these, my life will not be worth living." *Genesis 27:46*

What a drama queen! And wait until you meet her niece Rachel.

I imagine young Rachel was exactly who Rebekah had in mind for her son, though she kept that juicy tidbit to herself a moment longer. First she had to convince Isaac that Jacob must not wed a local girl. Undoubtedly with the back of her hand pressed against her forehead, Rebekah wailed, "I'd rather die than see Jacob marry one of them" (NLT). We're reminded of when she was pregnant with the twins and groaned, "If this is the way it's going to be, why go on living?"[42]

Jacob's need of a bride was a cover-up; Rebekah just wanted her son on the road, pronto. But Isaac couldn't see through Rebekah's melodrama—or didn't want to—and so gave his wife what she wanted. Again.

> So Isaac called for Jacob and blessed him and commanded him: "Do not marry a Canaanite woman." *Genesis 28:1*

Since Abraham had said the same—no pagan bride—Isaac was following his father's example. In order to fulfill the covenant, a suitable wife was essential.

> "Go at once to Paddan Aram, to the house of your mother's father Bethuel." *Genesis 28:2*

"Leave at once" (MSG), he instructed Jacob, though he knew nothing of Esau's death threat. By sending Jacob north to Paddan Aram, Isaac thought Jacob would be hurrying *to* something, not running *away* from something.

"Take a wife for yourself there, from among the daughters of Laban, your mother's brother." *Genesis 28:2*

"Marry one of his daughters" (ICB), Isaac said, then offered his son a parting benediction. No final word from Rebekah is included in Scripture. Her son simply departed, leaving her "with a blind and broken husband whom she had betrayed."[43]

Even if Isaac never knew the truth, Rebekah did.

In Remembrance

Then Isaac sent Jacob on his way, and he went to Paddan Aram, to Laban son of Bethuel the Aramean, the brother of Rebekah, who was the mother of Jacob and Esau. *Genesis 28:5*

Oh, that's interesting: Rebekah was identified as "Jacob's and Esau's mother" (KJV) and *not* as Isaac's wife. Must be how God intended for her to be remembered: not as a good wife who comforted her husband when they married, but as a strong mother who was willing to sacrifice everything, including her marriage and her own happiness, for the son God chose to bless.

Her *why* was commendable but oh the *how*.

I've gone out on a limb, calling Rebekah a Slightly Bad Girl when some writers cast her with the full-tilt Bad Girls. Pummeled with words like "shrewd, unscrupulous,"[44] "folly and wickedness,"[45] Rebekah is written off as "a deceiving, lying woman,"[46] unaware of "how much God disapproved of her evil actions."[47]

Ugh. And to think we spent two whole chapters with such a person…

Yet other scholars sing her praises, viewing her as an Old Testament Good Girl who was "clever, active and energetic,"[48] "clear-sighted and courageous,"[49] "the active player in this family,"[50] and a woman "ahead of her time."[51]

Wow. Let's give her two more chapters and a few blue ribbons…

Or we could try a balanced view: Rebekah was all of the above, good and bad, just as we are. Though her story featured some shockingly bad behavior, it's worth noting what we *didn't* find. Rebekah's actions were not condemned in Genesis nor later in the New Testament. (Her son Esau—called "godless" in Hebrews 12:16—didn't fare as well.) Unlike Sarah, Rebekah sought the Lord's counsel about her pregnancy. And unlike Hagar, Rebekah didn't get into a catfight with another woman. Furthermore, Rebekah "begged for nothing for herself."[52] Only Jacob benefited from her actions.

At the end of the day, we're left marveling not at Rebekah but at God, who allowed our flawed heroine to stumble along this indirect course so "he might have the glory of bringing good out of evil."[53] Only a gracious God could use an imperfect woman to accomplish his perfect will. Only a loving God could embrace Isaac and Rebekah and claim them both as his chosen ones. As Job reminds us, "both deceived and deceiver are his."[54]

And what of our young deceiver, the son of Rebekah, sent off to Paddan Aram to seek a bride? Jacob found far more than he bargained for at journey's end. Make that *four* more than he bargained for…

What Lessons Can We Learn from Rebekah the Mother?

God is in control.

That's more than just the title of a Twila Paris song; that's a fact: God *is* in control. Yet those of us with controlling natures like to think we're helping God by nudging others along the path of righteousness. Or is that the path of *rightness*? As in "I'm right and you're not"? *Groan.* When I study Rebekah's life and realize she knew the Lord yet didn't fully trust him, I understand where my need for control gets me: nowhere fast. When we're running things, we often don't ask questions or admit mistakes, just as "Rebekah did not wait for God to show her the right way to go, nor did she walk in integrity."[55] But when we acknowledge God's sovereignty, when we realize he's in control of everything, we can r-e-l-a-x. What a concept!

> The LORD has established his throne in heaven, and his kingdom rules over all. *Psalm 103:19*

Strength can be a bad thing.

In the last chapter, we considered some of Rebekah's positive traits. Now we've watched her strengths turn into weaknesses. When the Word tells us, "Be strong in the Lord,"[56] the key phrase is *in the Lord*. Rebekah, however, relied on her own strength and her quick mind. Imagine if she'd instead stepped back and said, "I will wait for the LORD,"[57] then gave God the glory when he brought his will to pass, perhaps by changing Isaac's heart, so that the patriarch willingly bestowed his blessing on Jacob. Ah, but it takes a woman who is strong in the Lord to wait and to trust.

> This is what the Sovereign LORD, the Holy One of Israel, says: "In repentance and rest is your salvation, in quietness and trust is your strength, but you would have none of it." *Isaiah 30:15*

Lord, have mercy.

The Lord included troublesome stories like this one in his Word, not so we might criticize the actions of Rebekah and others, but so we might discover similar failings in our lives, confess the truth about them, and be set free. Lord, for all the times we've tried to garner blessings for our children rather than teaching them patience, have mercy on us. For all the moments we've been Slightly Bad Wives in order to seem like Really Good Moms, have mercy on us. For all the hours we've wasted plotting and planning when we could have been praying, have mercy on us. For the myriad ways we resemble our sister Rebekah, have mercy on us, O Lord!

> Remember, O LORD, your great mercy and love, for they are from of old. *Psalm 25:6*

Christ, have mercy.

The apostle Paul explained to the churches in Galatia that Abraham, Isaac, and Jacob weren't the only ones who'd received God's blessing: "those who have faith are blessed along with Abraham, the man of faith."[58] That would include believers in Abraham's day, believers in the first century, believers in the twenty-first century, and all the generations in between. Furthermore,

God's plan of mercy can be found in every book of the Bible—Genesis in particular—demonstrating how humankind's sin is covered by God's unfailing grace. The Law would have punished Rebekah for her treachery, yet God forgave her; the Law would have punished Jacob for his deceit, yet God blessed him. All through the ages, God's message has been the same: he offers mercy in abundance to those who believe.

> He redeemed us in order that the blessing given to Abraham might come to the Gentiles through Christ Jesus. *Galatians 3:14*

Good Girl Thoughts Worth Considering

1. Did your mother or father speak a blessing over you—offer a prayer on your behalf, serve a special meal, present you with a family heirloom—to launch you into the world? How might such an event impact a person's life? If you didn't receive a parental blessing, how could that be remedied—if not by your parents, then by someone you esteem? And if you are a parent, how could you bless your children now—whatever their ages—and what sort of response would you expect?

2. Rebekah was so in control she was out of control! What have you observed about people with control issues—their motives, their methods, and their results? In light of Rebekah's personality, how would you differentiate between these words: control and manipulation; confidence and arrogance; determination and obsession? What areas of your life might benefit from less control on your part and more control on the Holy Spirit's part?

3. Do you think Rebekah carefully conceived her deception of Isaac in advance or overheard her husband talking with Esau and made a sudden decision to intervene? From an ethical standpoint, does it matter whether Rebekah's approach was premeditated or spontaneous? Had Rebekah *not* taken matters into her own hands, what might have happened? If you've ever tried to help God, what was the result?

4. Why did Jacob not refuse to do Rebekah's bidding from the start? Based on what we've seen so far, describe the character of Jacob, both his strengths and his weaknesses. How would you parent Jacob if he were *your* son? Would you go to any lengths, as Rebekah did, to help him get the blessing promised by God? Or would you teach him the virtues of trusting the Lord?

5. I kept waiting for Isaac to realize he was conversing with Jacob rather than with Esau. You too? Other than attributing it to his failing eyesight, how would you explain Isaac's inability to discern—or accept—the truth? Was Isaac at all to blame for his misdirected blessing? If so, in what ways? Have you ever been deceived by someone you trusted? What did you think of that person—and of yourself—when the truth was revealed?

6. In the New Testament we read of Esau, "He could bring about no change of mind, though he sought the blessing with tears."[59] Did you feel sympathetic toward Esau in this scene, or did he deserve to lose his inheritance? After Jacob's departure, what might Rebekah's relationship with Esau have been like? If you've wronged a family member, even in a small way, how did you make amends?

7. Rebekah wanted Jacob to flee to Haran and manipulated Isaac into thinking it was his idea. Have you ever done such a thing on a smaller scale—perhaps helping a loved one embrace a decision you'd already made for him or her? Why did you think such machinations necessary at the time? How do you envision Rebekah's relationship with Isaac after Jacob left? Do you think Isaac knew about her involvement behind the scenes, or was her husband truly in the dark?

8. What's the most important lesson you learned from our second visit with Rebekah, a mother who cared only about the end, not the means?

The Night Has Eyes

Come, drink the mystic wine of Night,
Brimming with silence and the stars.
LOUIS UNTERMEYER

Laura Sullivan lay draped across her favorite overstuffed chair, paperback novel in hand, reveling in the moment. How many late nights had she spent at MSU, cramming for exams or cranking out term papers, longing for the day when she could goof off and not feel guilty?

She stretched her limbs, like a cat too long in one position, her arms reaching toward the open window beside her. A soft evening breeze lifted the brown wisps of hair framing her face as she drank in the smell of honeysuckle. Her first teaching position began in August, but, until then, summer and all its lazy delights awaited her.

What a relief to return home and find her bedroom unchanged. Some of her college friends had gone home to a different house, some to the shock of a different parent. Her own parents, Brian and Sue Sullivan, hadn't even traded in their cars. Naturally, her father had his own ideas about how Laura should spend the next few months. *Find a husband. Find a job. Find a husband with a job.* She agreed on that last one but intended to wait for Mr. Right, sticking by the motto that had served her well all through college: better no man than the wrong man.

For the moment she'd entrust her heart to the dashing hero safely captured between the covers of a novel. Her glasses forgotten on the dining room table downstairs, Laura held the book inches from her nose, until the slam of a car door snatched her back to the present.

Her sister's voice floated up through the open window: Chloe, home from her part-time job at Target. Laura heard another voice as well, vaguely familiar. A younger man. One of Chloe's friends from the University of Michigan, maybe. Or from work.

Curious, Laura leaned over the windowsill and peered into the fading twilight, wishing she had her glasses. Leafy maple trees, crowding the edge of the driveway, blocked her view. Whoever the guy was, Chloe apparently knew him well, because she was chiding him about something as they neared the house.

Laura started to call out a greeting, then hesitated. Her hair was a mess, her clothes were worse, and she hadn't bothered putting on makeup. Feeling foolish, she pulled back inside and listened more intently, picking out a few words here and there. A friend of her parents? Someone from church?

Then a name caught her ear. *Jeffrey.*

Suddenly his voice sounded very familiar indeed.

Laura scrunched down in the cushions of her chair. As if they could see her, as if it mattered. Jeffrey Garner was their former next-door neighbor— practically a member of their family growing up—and one of her high-school classmates. Laura hadn't seen him in four years, not since his family moved to Louisiana and he started at LSU. No doubt he'd just graduated and come back to Ann Arbor for a visit.

Jeffrey and Chloe were laughing about something. Laura knew she should either announce herself or move away from the window. Listening in on a conversation had to be a sin. Wasn't that in the Bible somewhere? "Don't eavesdrop on others"? Oh yeah, she was sure of it.

But Laura stayed put, propping her chin on the upholstered arm of her chair, feeling somewhat less culpable because she couldn't pick out every word. Their voices mingled with the evening birdsong: Chloe's, high and bright, one note short of irritating, and Jeffrey's, low and warm, one note short of dangerous.

Laura's feelings for him, long dormant, stirred to life. How many years had she carried a torch for Jeffrey Garner? Six? Seven? Back in high school he'd been crazy about Chloe, who was too young for him then and teased him unmercifully. Judging by what Laura could hear, nothing much had changed there.

Chloe, being Chloe, had never realized how much Laura cared for their neighbor, not because of his striking good looks, but because he was both intelligent and kind. Jeffrey also had seemed clueless about Laura's crush on him—a blessing if he was back in Ann Arbor to stay.

"Hey, Laura! You up there?"

Her mouth went dry. Had he seen her?

Laura eased her head over the windowsill. Maybe she looked more presentable from a distance. "Hey yourself, Jeffrey," she called down, trying to see him better, resisting the urge to squint. The details were blurry. Blond hair. Jeans. Taller than she remembered. "So, are you an official LSU grad now?"

"I am." She heard the smile in his voice. "And you?"

"MSU. Last week. No more trips to East Lansing." Laura paused, letting the truth of it sink in. She truly was home. "I'll be teaching this fall at Burns Park Elementary."

"You always did love kids." Still smiling. "Chloe and I are headed for pizza. Wanna come?"

"Um…" Laura looked down at her shorts stained with strawberry juice from lunch, then touched her frizzy, unwashed hair, and found her answer. "I'm kinda wiped out. You two go ahead. We'll get together another night, Jeffrey."

"Promise?" He sounded disappointed.

"Absolutely," Laura told him. And they *would* get together, she realized. Absolutely.

Chloe knocked on her bedroom door just before midnight. "You awake, sis?" she asked, then walked in without waiting for a response.

Laura looked up, still drying her hair. "So how's Jeffrey?" She kept her towel in motion—anything to prevent Chloe from seeing the truth in her eyes. Three hours of thinking about Jeffrey Garner had reduced Laura to a lovesick teenager all over again. How embarrassing. She was twenty-two, for heaven's sake.

"Jeffrey's fine." Chloe threw herself across Laura's bed, kicking off her shoes as she landed. "He's staying with the Wilsons down the street for now. Glad to be back in Michigan, he said. Plans on talking to Dad about a job."

Laura's hands stilled. "I didn't realize Jeffrey changed his major to accounting." If he joined their father's small firm, he really *would* be part of the family.

"Yup." Chloe pulled off her earrings and tossed them on the dresser. "I told him about the master's program at U-M. He could work for Dad this summer, then start back to school in the fall."

Laura hated what she was feeling: envious of Chloe's time with him; jealous of their easy friendship; miserable for not joining them, even if she had looked awful. "Sounds like you've mapped out Jeffrey's whole future," she said petulantly, then chastised herself for that too. *Grow up, Laura.*

"Well, I *think* he's still in love with me," Chloe said breezily. "And he *is* a fine-looking man." When Laura didn't respond, Chloe's eyes narrowed. "Admit it. You just don't want another U-M student hanging around."

Laura rolled her eyes. "Here we go." A sophomore at U-M, her sister took the rivalry between the two Michigan universities very seriously. Still, anything was better than talking about Jeffrey. "I'll remind you that MSU has more students, more buildings, and far more acreage than *your* school."

Chloe shot to her feet. "And U-M has more faculty members, more library books, and more...Starbucks!" She flounced out of the room, slamming the door in her wake.

Laura shook her head. *Drama queen.* For a twenty-year-old, Chloe seemed all of fourteen sometimes.

Circling the room to turn off the lights, Laura considered closing the window, then decided against it. The night air was perfect for sleeping: dry and mild with only a faint breeze. Kneeling by the low window in the darkened room, she couldn't resist leaning out far enough to catch another whiff of honeysuckle and to admire the sprinkling of stars against the black sky. *Well done, Lord.*

Footsteps, then a masculine voice. "Lovely night."

She nearly hit her head on the window sash. "Jeffrey?"

"Down here."

Even with her glasses, she couldn't see more than a shadowy form in the driveway. "What are you...um...doing?"

"Couldn't sleep. Too many late nights my senior year, you know?"

She smiled down at him. "Yes, I do."

"So I thought I'd go for a walk. Just to the park and back." He came a few steps closer. "I hate to ask twice in the same night, but..."

Laura was already half standing. "Two minutes."

She quickly exchanged her pajamas for jeans and a T-shirt, then slipped downstairs, her heart pounding. Now who was acting like a fourteen-year-old? Leaving the back door unlocked, she followed the brick walk around to the driveway, where Jeffrey stood waiting.

Taller, yes. Broader shouldered. And far more handsome.

"Hi," she said in a soft voice, tucking her hands in her jean pockets. "Shall we head for the park?"

He frowned, looking behind her. "Isn't your sister coming? I thought..."

Laura's heart sank. "No. I'm afraid you're stuck with me tonight..."

Leah the Unseen: Lady in Waiting

Were this whole chapter focused on that Blessed Boy of the Bible, Jacob, rather than our Slightly Bad Girl, Leah, we would linger on the road to Paddan Aram and marvel at all that happened there.

Instead, we'll study one life-changing experience on Jacob's journey, then press on to Uncle Laban's house, where his two daughters were blithely going about their business, unaware of the husband-to-be aimed in their direction.

Jacob left Beersheba and set out for Haran. *Genesis 28:10*

No mention of anyone traveling with him, and he'd not had much time to pack. Traveling north by northeast, Jacob headed toward the ancient city of Damascus and the Euphrates River beyond it, bound for the plain of Aram.

He stopped for the night because the sun had set. *Genesis 28:11*

How Jacob slept after all that family drama is a minor miracle, especially with a stone for a pillow. But he *did* nod off, soundly enough to fall into a deep sleep.

> He had a dream in which he saw a stairway resting on the earth,
> with its top reaching to heaven, and the angels of God were
> ascending and descending on it. *Genesis 28:12*

Very vivid, that dream. Captured on canvas by artists through the centuries.

Rather than a modern stairway or ladder, picture a stepped pyramid, like the ziggurat in old Ur. Far more important than the structure were the creatures "going up and going down on it" (MSG). A multitude of angels, all in motion: earth to heaven, heaven to earth.

And then, poised at the top, the One they served.

> There above it stood the LORD, and he said: "I am the LORD, the
> God of your father Abraham and the God of Isaac." *Genesis 28:13*

Like Saul on the road to Damascus, Jacob was a man living in denial, trying to outrun his sins. An encounter with the Lord was the *last* thing on his wish list. Yet here stood the God of his grandfather and the God of his father. *The* God.

Scripture doesn't tell us that Jacob was trembling violently, but *I* would have been, knowing my sins. Did I ever deceive my dad, as Jacob did? Oh my. As a teenager I lied dozens of times about where I'd gone, whom I'd been with, what we'd done. Jacob's sins were no worse than mine. Much as I dreaded facing my earthly father after a night of debauchery, I couldn't have imagined facing my heavenly Father.

When Jacob did so, something incredible happened: God did not admonish him, punish him, or banish him. *God blessed him.* And made no reference to the fiasco back home.

Only one word explains it: *grace.*

Saul wasn't punished or banished either; he, too, was blessed by God: "This man is my chosen instrument."[1] And on the day I finally faced God—as we all must—my sins were forgiven, my soul was washed clean, and I was sent forth, a woman reborn. In the apostle's own words, "Thanks be to God for his indescribable gift!"[2]

Jacob never forgot what happened that night and told his son Joseph many years later, "God Almighty appeared to me...and there he blessed me."[3] Once you've met the Lord, you simply can't keep the good news to yourself.

After vowing to give Jacob the land beneath his feet and countless descendants, the Lord made "the greatest promise God can make to anyone."[4]

> "I am with you and will watch over you wherever you go."
> *Genesis 28:15*

"I am with you." God spoke those same words to Isaac and to Joshua, to David and to Isaiah, to Jeremiah and to us, beloved: "Surely I am with you always, to the very end of the age."[5] God is *with* us. Not simply present by the power of the Holy Spirit, he is *with* us, he is *for* us, he is *on our side.* And "whom God loves he never leaves."[6] The Lord offers no sweeter encouragement to his followers than this: *you will never be alone.*

> When Jacob awoke from his sleep, he thought, "Surely the LORD is in this place, and I was not aware of it." *Genesis 28:16*

Hear the sense of wonder in his voice? Until now we've seen no evidence of godliness in Jacob. Quite the opposite. Rabbis of old believed Jacob was transformed because he'd "never before known the Holy Spirit, the Shekhinah,"[7] a Hebrew word expressing "the reverent nearness of God to his people."[8]

In response, Jacob turned his stone pillow into a pillar, anointed it with oil, and called the place Bethel, or "House of God."[9]

> Then Jacob made a vow, saying, "If God will be with me..."
> *Genesis 28:20*

Don't read this as a conditional statement with a big *if.* He already knew God was with him. "Jacob wasn't making a bargain with God; he was affirming his faith in God."[10] Like when we tell someone, "Well, if you say so…" What we really mean is *since,* not *if.*

Jacob wasn't worried about God being there for him, but he *was* Rebekah's son, and so he produced a short list of demands. Okay, requests.

> "…watch over me on this journey I am taking and…give me food
> to eat and clothes to wear so that I return safely to my father's
> house…" *Genesis 28:20–21*

Well, all righty then. Food, clothing, safe travel, shelter. Anything else, Jacob?

> "…then the LORD will be my God…" *Genesis 28:21*

My God. Not his grandfather's God, not his father's God. *My God.*

Consider this Jacob's confession of faith, as powerfully stated as anything in Scripture: "I will make the LORD my God" (NLT).

For those among us who grew up in homes where Christ was honored, the time comes when we must claim our parents' faith as our own and declare our "new-born spiritual liberty,"[11] just as Jacob did.

"My God." Jacob's relationship with him moved to a deeper, more personal level that night in the desert. Ours can, too, with those same heartfelt words: "the Lord will be my God."

Next Stop, Haran

Set free from the burden of his sin, Jacob "hurried on" (NLT), "briskly and cheerfully" (AMP).

No, really. That's what it says.

> Then Jacob continued on his journey… *Genesis 29:1*

"Continued" doesn't do the Hebrew justice, because the literal meaning is "Jacob lifted up his feet."[12] This is the only time you'll find that phrase in the Old Testament. The Lizzie Revised Version? Jacob had *happy feet*! He was almost dancing, his heart was so light. Good thing, with hundreds of miles to cover and no Fodor's travel guide to point out the best places to eat (by the fire) or sleep (on the ground).

After a long month, our road warrior arrived at his destination, "scorched by the sun, and footsore and weary,"[13] yet he *did* find his way there, as God had promised—fed, clothed, and watched over.

> There he saw a well in the field… *Genesis 29:2*

Not the same well where Rebekah hauled all that water years earlier. This well was some distance from town,[14] surrounded by flocks of sheep and covered by a stone.

> The stone over the mouth of the well was large. *Genesis 29:2*

Take note: it was a "huge" (MSG) rock.

Where there were sheep, there were shepherds watching over their flocks. A herdsman himself, Jacob chose his words of greeting carefully. Who knew what kind of reputation his Uncle Laban had?

> Jacob asked the shepherds, "My brothers, where are you from?"
> *Genesis 29:4*

My brothers. Mr. Smooth, back to his slick tricks, trying to win their trust. When they told him they were from Haran, Jacob inquired if they knew Laban.

> "Yes, we know him," they answered. *Genesis 29:5*

Oh, that was helpful. *How* did they know Laban? Was he friend, family…or foe? Jacob continued his game of twenty questions without offering his own identity. The man was nothing if not cagey.

> Then Jacob asked them, "Is he well?"
> "Yes, he is," they said… *Genesis 29:6*

The Hebrew is better translated "And they said, 'Well.'"[15] So their conversation would have sounded more like "Well?" "Well." Very amusing, since the men were standing near a *well*.

Everything hinged on the herdsmen's answer. If they'd replied, "Laban is dead," the story would have taken quite a different turn.

> …"and here comes his daughter Rachel with the sheep." *Genesis 29:6*

At the sight of his cousin, Jacob's heart must have leaped in his chest. Family at last! His exhausting journey was over. From a distance he could not discern the girl's beauty, but he knew her name. *Rachel.* Was she the woman he was meant to marry? If so, Jacob had much explaining to do, preferably without an audience, especially not a flock of curious shepherds.

> "Look," he said, "the sun is still high; it is not time for the flocks
> to be gathered. Water the sheep and take them back to pasture."
> *Genesis 29:7*

Kinda pushy for an out-of-towner. But Jacob was "primed for romance"[16] and determined to get rid of any onlookers.

The shepherds weren't having it.

> "We can't," they replied, "until all the flocks are gathered and the
> stone has been rolled away from the mouth of the well. Then we
> will water the sheep." *Genesis 29:8*

That was the custom in the Near East, meant to keep "any one herdsman from monopolizing the scarce water supply."[17] Plus, it took several men to move the rock.

At least that was how it usually worked.

> While he was still talking with them, Rachel came with her father's
> sheep, for she was a shepherdess. *Genesis 29:9*

The only shepherdess so named in the Bible, Rachel wasn't just strolling beside the flock: "she was the shepherd" (MSG). And the meaning of her name? Appropriately, "ewe."[18] (If your name is Rachel, I can hear you going, "Eeww!") Not to worry. A shepherd like Jacob loved sheep and would have considered *Rachel* a fine name.

> When Jacob saw Rachel daughter of Laban, his mother's brother,
> and Laban's sheep... *Genesis 29:10*

The family connections are critical, of course, but note that Jacob didn't see just her "comely face."[19] He also saw her uncle's fine sheep. The combination of lovely Miss Ewe and her lovely flock proved "irresistible to Jacob."[20] Not unlike when my grown son sees a long-legged brunette climb out of a low-slung sports car.

Once he got a good look at his cousin, Jacob was "dazzled."[21] As quick-thinking and shrewd as his mother, Jacob knew at once how to impress both his female cousin and her flock.

> ...he went over and rolled the stone away from the mouth of the
> well and watered his uncle's sheep. *Genesis 29:10*

That huge stone? Yup, he rolled it away "single-handedly."[22] Just as Rebekah had watered Abraham's camels, so Jacob watered Rachel's sheep, though she would never have asked him to do so since opening the well and helping yourself was "in defiance of local custom."[23] Not a very smart move for the new guy in town.

Honey, we've seen this movie: a beautiful young girl approaches a group of guys, and within minutes the males are falling all over themselves trying to outdo one another, trying to impress her. What better means than a "feat of great strength,"[24] especially if some measure of risk was involved—breaking the town's water laws, for example.

I'm still trying to figure out how Jacob moved that big stone. Had the arduous journey turned him into a buff outdoorsman? Did he whisper "God is with me" and summon an extra measure of strength? Might Jacob have had a little angelic assistance?

His adrenaline must have been flowing, because as soon as the rock was rolled and the sheep were watered, our Former Bad Boy claimed his prize.

> Then Jacob kissed Rachel... *Genesis 29:11*

No violins, please. No dozen roses. No chocolates. Sorry.

This was *not* love at first sight but a kiss of greeting, common between family members. Whatever social freedoms people enjoyed in that time and place, "men could not kiss women who were not their relatives."[25] Period, end of discussion. (And in case you were wondering, Jacob and Rachel did *not* inspire the phrase "kissing cousins." That Americanism is no older than our Civil War.)

I *do* think some deep-seated emotion prompted him to kiss Rachel, because of what came next.

> ...and [he] began to weep aloud. *Genesis 29:11*

As we say in the South, "Bless his heart." We've not seen Jacob's feelings on display before, yet here "he was moved to tears" (NEB), no doubt "because he was so happy" (CEV). He'd found his way to Haran, he'd found his relatives, and he'd found his beautiful bride standing beside a well just as his mother had once stood. (You *know* Rebekah told that story beside the family fire a hundred times.)

I also believe Jacob's newfound faith accounts for his expressiveness. The Lord had said, "I am with you," and he was. Jacob could already see the hand of God at work in his life.

> He had told Rachel that he was a relative of her father and a son of Rebekah. *Genesis 29:12*

To avoid any misunderstanding, Jacob had introduced himself to Rachel before he kissed her. And to say he was "a relative of her father" was an understatement: Jacob was "both Laban's nephew (through his mother Rebekah) and his second cousin (through his father)."[26] To date, their family tree resembled a bramble bush: low to the ground with rough, thorny branches thickly intertwined.

Meanwhile, Rachel's own keyed-up emotions sent her running home to Haran to tell her father, leaving her flock in Jacob's able hands.

> As soon as Laban heard the news about Jacob, his sister's
> son, he hurried to meet him. *Genesis 29:13*

Déjà vu all over again. Decades earlier when Laban went out to meet Abraham's servant, he'd ended up with one less sister and lots more silver. No wonder this time Laban "rushed out"[27] to meet Rebekah's son.

> He embraced him and kissed him and brought him to his
> home... *Genesis 29:13*

Again, these actions were true to social custom: the welcoming embrace, the family kiss, the offering of hospitality. Rabbinic tradition adds a tantalizing spin on this greeting, suggesting that when Laban threw his arms around his nephew, he hoped to find money and gems![28]

> ...and there Jacob told him all these things.
> *Genesis 29:13*

All *what* things? Did he mention his controlling mother, his angry brother, his stolen blessing, his ziggurat full of angels, his promises from God? "Everything that had happened,"[29] the scholars say. Not only a confession of his successes and failures but also an oral record of his family life, which established him as Laban's nephew. Important stuff if you plan to marry the man's daughter.

Unfortunately, Jacob had just met "his match in craftiness"[30]—an uncle whom rabbis of old paint "as a true rogue, none of his motives or actions having merit."[31]

Laban saw the joy on sweet Rachel's face, the promise in young Jacob's strength, and the vulnerability of an heir on the run, and his mental gears began to grind. A father of daughters had to choose sons-in-law wisely. If one of his daughters married his nephew Jacob, his land would remain in the family. Like it or not, "women simply served as blood links to pass property from male to male within the family line."[32]

A Tale of Two Daughters

After Jacob had stayed with him for a whole month... *Genesis 29:14*

A full month, measured new moon to new moon. Long enough for Jacob to settle into a daily routine and become well acquainted with Laban's household.

...Laban said to him, "Just because you are a relative of mine, should you work for me for nothing?" *Genesis 29:15*

Laban made his honored guest *work* for room and board? You bet. Jacob was kin, and everybody in the family worked. Some domestic servants, however, received a stipend; so did shepherds. Laban told him, "You are my relative, but it is not right for you to work for me without pay" (NCV). Even across a span of four thousand years, our taste buds sense Laban buttering up his nephew.

"Tell me what your wages should be." *Genesis 29:15*

A safe offer, even for a tightwad. No family member would ask for gold or silver. "What would you like me to pay you?" (NCV). After a month of living with his nephew, Laban must have known what sort of payment Jacob would request.

Now Laban had two daughters;... *Genesis 29:16*

As with all Scripture, the proximity of the words "wages" and "daughters" was no accident. And *two* of them? Why have we not heard of this second daughter before? Because in biblical narrative, characters are often not introduced until needed.

...the name of the older was Leah, and the name of the younger was Rachel. *Genesis 29:16*

Older and younger siblings. Sound familiar? One writer warns, "Our suspicions should be high."[33] I'm also thinking about their ages. How *much* older? How *much* younger? We're not told here, and nothing in the text gives us a hint. Esau and Jacob were older and younger by seconds, but it's hard to pinpoint the ages of the girls.

The older of the two sisters was Leah, whose name in Hebrew means (I hate this) "cow." But a related meaning in Akkadian, an ancient Semitic language, is "strong."[34] Better, yes? Plus, cows were a symbol of fertility.[35] I'd much rather see Leah as a strong, fertile woman than as a cow. Then again, her sister was a ewe.

What *was* this family thinking to name their daughters after livestock?! "Kindly meet my daughters, Baaa and Mooo."

Blink and you'll miss this: Leah is described in a single, two-word phrase.

Leah had weak eyes... *Genesis 29:17*

Mind if we spend a little time on this one? Because when you consider various translations, "weak" (RSV) and "dull-eyed" (NEB) don't give us the full story on Leah.

Since the Near Eastern standard of beauty favored lively, glowing eyes enhanced by cosmetics,[36] dull eyes were considered "a great blemish."[37] That might explain why modern writers have expanded this single word about her eyes, calling her "old squinty Leah,"[38] suggesting she was "rather plain"[39] and her whole being lacked "the luster of sexual appeal."[40]

Easy does it, sisters. Let's look more carefully at the Hebrew word describing Leah's eyes: *rakkoth.* The meaning is "tender, delicate, soft," like a slender twig.[41] Which explains why some of the newer translations tell us, "Leah had pretty eyes" (NLT) or "nice eyes" (MSG). The Talmud argues there could be "no physical blemish in the righteous Leah,"[42] and, furthermore, she's "not to be thought of as ugly in any way."[43]

Time for a new view of Leah.

"Older" doesn't mean ancient. And "tender-eyed" doesn't mean unattractive. Since God's Word declares, "The eye is the lamp of the body,"[44] perhaps

Rachel's orbs snapped and sparkled while Leah's eyes were dreamy and tender, hinting at the two women's dispositions.

Whatever their color or shape, Leah's eyes were apparently her only distinguishing feature. Her sister was another story.

> …but Rachel was lovely in form, and beautiful. *Genesis 29:17*

There it is again: "but." The little word that says so much.

In comparison to Leah, "graceful" (NEB) Rachel was "beautiful in every way, with a lovely face and shapely figure" (NLT).

We know the type.

In fact, we went to high school with Rachel (even if her name was Jennifer, Angie, or Michelle). You remember, "the pretty one, the one used to all the attention."[45] The girl we loved to hate even as we longed to be her twin.

No need to look up a dozen translations of *beautiful*; this is a word we understand. From culture to culture, epoch to epoch we might define it differently, but beauty itself is timeless. Wisely, Scripture doesn't include specifics like hair color, facial shape, or body type for Sarah, Rebekah, or Rachel. We can use our imaginations: *beautiful* says it all.

Physical description in Scripture often reveals character. Given what we've been told about Leah's eyes, we can surmise she was "sensitive and kind,"[46] "meek, submissive, and gentle."[47]

Some men are wise enough to find such qualities appealing.

The favored son of Rebekah was not one of them.

Truly, Madly, Deeply

> Jacob was in love with Rachel… *Genesis 29:18*

The Bible doesn't state Jacob loved Rachel because she was beautiful, but the juxtaposition of her appearance and his affection certainly points to it. So does family history. Jacob had grown up with a beautiful mother; no doubt his goal "was to find another woman exactly like her."[48]

Only a month had passed since they met at the well. Most parents today would flip out if their grown children found a partner for life so quickly. But Jacob and Rachel had a marriage made in heaven—in Yiddish, "a *beshert* relationship."[49] We've all known couples who became engaged after a handful of dates, married soon thereafter, and recently celebrated twenty years or more of wedded bliss.

Love happens.

In Jacob's case, he was a man on assignment from his father: "Take a wife...from among the daughters of Laban."[50] Regrettably, Isaac had neglected to provide a bride price for such a wife, leaving Jacob no recourse except to earn her hand in marriage.

> "I'll work for you seven years in return for your younger daughter
> Rachel." *Genesis 29:18*

Let there be no mistake. Jacob meant Laban's daughter Rachel, not "some other woman from the marketplace named Rachel."[51] Jacob also stated the duration of his labor in no uncertain terms: seven years. He must have been "madly and romantically in love with her"[52] to have made such an outrageous offer.

A shepherd earned ten shekels a year. The bride price—*mohar* in Hebrew—was thirty to forty shekels of silver.[53] So Jacob should have worked three and a half years for Rachel's hand in marriage. Instead, he promised to pay his future father-in-law double that amount in labor. (Maybe this is where we got the notion "I'm not losing a daughter; I'm gaining a son!")

Isaac was blinded by age, but Jacob was blinded by love. He was also taking no chances on a refusal. And how did his uncle respond?

> Laban said, "It's better that I give her to you than to some other
> man." *Genesis 29:19*

I don't hear a *yes* in that, do you? Verbal agreements were made by restating the terms. But Laban didn't repeat the offer—not the seven years, not Rachel's name. His cryptic answer no doubt hid his glee: seven years of unpaid labor at his nephew's expense!

At the time of betrothal, no one mentioned a dowry for Rachel. Did Jacob have some expectation? If so, it was not stated here, nor was anything offered by stingy Laban.

"Stay here with me." *Genesis 29:19*

Another odd statement and with no time frame. How long did he expect Jacob to stay in Haran? Far longer than Jacob ever intended, I can promise you that.

So Jacob served seven years to get Rachel... *Genesis 29:20*

Finally our hero did something honorable, even sacrificial, by working for his uncle as a lowly shepherd, "earning his livelihood in a way that was anything but 'romantic.'"[54] All the while Jacob and Rachel remained chaste—no easy feat, living among the same tents. My husband and I were engaged for all of four months before we married, and God wisely made sure we lived not only in different houses but also in different *towns* seventy miles apart!

Jacob kept busy tending sheep, counting each year as it passed.

...but they seemed like only a few days to him because of his love for her. *Genesis 29:20*

In all of romantic literature, you'll not find a more heartfelt declaration of "the purest love that can be."[55]

In Scripture the number seven represents completion; during that lengthy courtship, Jacob also finished his apprenticeship with the Lord. After seven years he was truly made new, conformed to God's image. "No man who loved that unselfishly could be an essentially self-centered person."[56]

Were this a movie, we would end here with Jacob and Rachel standing at the altar—bells ringing, birds singing, flowers blooming—as the couple leaned forward to exchange a tender kiss.

Oh, but this is the Bible, not Hollywood.

And, as everyone knows, "long engagements seldom turn out well."[57]

For seven long years Jacob worked and Rachel waited. What did Leah do all that time? She watched. Watched her cousin mature physically and spiritually. Watched her sister prepare to be his bride. Watched the moon wax and wane without anyone asking for her hand in marriage, and all the while she grew older.

Other than learning of her gentle eyes, we've heard nothing about Leah since Jacob's arrival. She stood in the wings, watching in silence until her time on stage drew near.

> Then Jacob said to Laban, "Give me my wife. My time is completed, and I want to lie with her." *Genesis 29:21*

My, what an eager fellow.

He spoke "so curtly, so roughly, disregarding common courtesy"[58] that it's clear Jacob's patience must have run out. Seven years was, after all, seven years.

"I'm ready to consummate my marriage" (MSG), he blurted out. Marriage was definitely on his mind, especially the wedding night. "Give me my wife so that we may sleep together" (NEB) is closer to the Hebrew wording, which is "clearly meant to express his—understandable—sexual impatience."[59]

But our impetuous bridegroom made a fatal mistake. He asked for his wife, but he did not ask for her by name. "Rachel" does not appear in the original Hebrew text.

With an uncle like Laban, Jacob should have been more cautious.

Nighttime Was the Right Time

> So Laban brought together all the people of the place and gave a feast. *Genesis 29:22*

That last feast we attended turned into a fracas, with Sarah casting Hagar and Ishmael into the wilderness. If you were hoping for a happier ending this time, dear sister, prepare to be disappointed.

"Everyone in the neighborhood" (NLT) came to Laban's shindig, where the groom was the man of the hour and, by tradition, the bride was not present.

No Rachel on hand? Already I'm uneasy.

Feasting also meant imbibing, since the Hebrew word for "feast" is derived from a root meaning "drink."[60] Noah and Lot could both attest to the dangers of drinking too much. As one writer sagely put it, "When wine flows in the Bible, a plot twist is almost inevitable."[61]

But when evening came... *Genesis 29:23*

"When it was dark" (NLT), the time came for the business at hand: the procession of the bride being escorted to the tent of her anxious groom. Not only was the night sky black, but by custom the lamps in his tent also remained unlit.

For the bride, darkness was compounded by a thick veil that thoroughly obscured her face and most of her figure.[62] The veil remained in place until after the marriage was consummated, "a very ancient custom, indicating modesty, and subjection to the husband."[63] Her voice, too, was hidden since the bride was to be presented in utter silence.[64]

Something happened on that dark evening. Traditions were inverted, thrown out of joint. Rather than being sacred, the tent became a place of secrets. Truth remained hidden beneath the covering of night as Uncle Laban did the unthinkable.

...he took his daughter Leah and gave her to Jacob... *Genesis 29:23*

No, poor Rachel was not lost in translation.

Laban "took" his firstborn daughter and "gave" her to a man who didn't love her, to a man who didn't want her, to a man "who had never shown her the least regard."[65] Her father gave Leah away as if she meant nothing to him.

I wept the first time I read this story, and I'm teary eyed again. How could Laban do such a thing—this "monstrous blow," this "shameless treachery"?[66] Had he planned the wedding-night deception all along? Or had he expected Leah to marry during those seven years but then at the last minute foisted her on the nearest bridegroom, not caring how many lives he ruined as long as she was duly wed?

Whatever his reasons—none of them valid—we can imagine Laban disguising Leah, just as Rebekah disguised Jacob, and shoving her younger sister's wedding clothes into her arms, demanding, "Do as I say." Did Leah have any choice in the matter? *Took* and *gave* make us doubtful. And where was Rachel? Bound and gagged in her father's tent?

This man so disgusts me that I refuse to examine Laban's motives or methods for at least another page and will trust the Lord to deal with him severely. "God of vengeance, shine forth!"[67]

But Leah, dear Leah... She's the one who tugs at my heart. Come the morning light, Rachel would still be loved, Laban would still be crafty, and Jacob would still be Isaac's heir. But Leah would surely be the most hated woman in Haran for stealing her sister's husband.

We know Jacob stole his brother's blessing willingly. Yes, Jacob was manipulated by his mother, but once she solved the problem of Mr. Hairy versus Mr. Smooth, he deceived his father with chilling efficiency.

Did Leah do the same? Did she slip on her sister's veil with calm hands, step into her gown with a light foot and a lighter conscience, and zip her lip as she headed for Jacob's tent, glad for a veil that hid the smile on her face? If so, she would qualify as a *Very* Bad Girl indeed.

Or did she fall at her father's feet and beg him to change his mind? Did she dress with trembling hands, wiping away tears of shame, then slowly walk to Jacob's tent on legs that barely held her upright? If so, we'd count her among the Sad Girls of the Bible, the many faceless victims whose stories haunt us long after they're read.

Nothing before or after verse 23 hints at how this tragic scene came down. All of Leah was concealed under that veil—her appearance, her emotions, her intentions, her desires, her hopes, her fears—leaving us with far more questions than answers.

Was she a "willing participant in this deception" or "merely an obedient daughter"?[68] Did Leah say to herself, "Better the wrong man than no man at all,"[69] or did her father make promises only Jacob could keep? Even at the last when she had Jacob to herself, could she not have warned him, re-fused his advances, called out to God, or fled from his tent under cover of night?

Because these are questions we cannot answer, Leah earns her place among the Slightly Bad Girls. *Something* untoward happened. Even if Laban was the one who *took* and *gave*, Leah was party to his deception.

After all, Jacob might have been in the dark. But Leah wasn't.

> …and Jacob lay with her. *Genesis 29:23*

Another translation puts it more bluntly: "they had sexual relations" (NCV). Got it. What it *doesn't* say is of far greater interest. Even the King James Version doesn't use the more common biblical phrase "he knew her." Because Jacob didn't know her at all!

Despite the heavy veil, Leah's unique mannerisms should have been rec-ognizable. How was it possible that Jacob mistook her for Rachel? Was he drunk with wine? Quite possibly. Was he drunk with lust? Almost certainly.

Simply put, Jacob expected Rachel. Who else dared come into his tent but his bride?

Leah dared.

Whether by choice or coercion, Leah risked everything that night. Could she have done so if she had no feelings for this man? I find it unlikely. And so this possibility must be considered: "Hidden deep in her heart a love grew for Jacob."[70]

> And Laban gave his servant girl Zilpah to his daughter as her
> maidservant. *Genesis 29:24*

Decades earlier, when Laban had shipped Rebekah off to Canaan, he'd sent along several maidservants. For Leah, he provided only one, yet another "sign of his greed."[71] This verse may be parenthetical in your Bible, like an afterthought, yet it foreshadows the role this maid would play in the follow-ing years. Laban intended her to be a nursemaid, but Leah later required much more of Zilpah.

Mercifully, we know nothing of Jacob and Leah's illicit coupling except that it occurred and that Jacob remained unaware of her identity. If indeed Leah cared for him, the last hours before dawn were the happiest of her life. And then they ended, as we shall soon see.

What Lessons Can We Learn from Leah the Unseen?

Here's looking at you, sis.
We all know a few Rachels—drop-dead gorgeous women who turn heads everywhere they go—yet "most of us are just plain Leahs,"[72] at least by the world's standards. When we glance at such women, they appear flawless. But when we gaze in our mirrors, flaws are all we see. Just as we need a new view of Leah, we need a fresh outlook on ourselves, one that's closer to how God sees us. You can be sure he finds you beautiful, dear sister, since you were created in his image and for his pleasure.[73] Make a list of all your positive attributes—physical, mental, emotional, relational, and spiritual—thanking the Lord for each one and asking him to bring out your true beauty, to his glory.

> "The LORD does not look at the things man looks at. Man looks at the outward appearance, but the LORD looks at the heart."
> *1 Samuel 16:7*

In God we trust. In Laban we don't.
The Lord agreed to provide everything Jacob needed: food, clothing, safe travel, shelter, and his guiding presence. But when Jacob arrived in Haran, he turned to his uncle for provision rather than to God. Jacob also trusted Laban to give him the wife he wanted instead of seeking the Lord's will for a bride. In the same way, rather than trusting her father, Leah should have trusted in the God of Abraham to find her a husband in an honorable way. When the Labans in our lives try to lead us astray, let's be wise to their dubious ways and put our faith in the One who deserves our trust.

> Trust in him at all times, O people; pour out your hearts to him, for God is our refuge. *Psalm 62:8*

Actions speak louder than words.

We didn't hear a single syllable from Leah in this chapter; her behavior alone told her tale as she crept "stealthily and silently towards a dark goal."[74] Had Leah refused to wear Rachel's bridal veil, she would have ended her father's nefarious plan before it began. Had Leah fled from Jacob's tent rather than climbed into his bed, she would have spared them both a lifetime of heartache. Even if we're caught in a situation where we cannot speak up, we can act in a manner worthy of our calling as women of God, knowing people see what we do far more clearly than they hear what we say.

> For it is God's will that by doing good you should silence the
> ignorant talk of foolish men. *1 Peter 2:15*

God's light penetrates the darkness.

Laban delivered Leah to Jacob's unlit tent under the cover of night, hiding her identity beneath a thick veil of fabric. Father and daughter both knew the truth...and so did God. Loving Jacob as he did, God might have revealed the subterfuge right then; instead God allowed the light of day to expose the truth. Even in permitting this disappointment, God still showed his love for Jacob, a man who needed to learn to put God's desires above his own. We'll soon see how God demonstrated his love to Leah, a woman meant to carry on his covenant no matter how miserly her father, no matter how misguided her own desires. Even in the dark, God's light shines.

> If I say, "Surely the darkness will hide me and the light become
> night around me," even the darkness will not be dark to you;
> the night will shine like the day, for darkness is as light to you.
> *Psalm 139:11–12*

Good Girl Thoughts Worth Considering

1. Of all God's promises to Jacob, this one inspires us most: "I am with you and will watch over you wherever you go" (Genesis 28:15). How can we know without a doubt that God will watch over us? What evidence do we

have of his presence? How can a perfect, holy God have fellowship with imperfect, unholy people? Does the fact that God forgave Jacob so freely make you mad or give you hope? Why is that?

2. At the well outside Haran, Jacob was outgoing and talkative with the shepherds, then impulsively moved the rock, kissed Rachel, and burst into tears. What reasons might you offer for his exuberant behavior? Do you keep your emotions under wraps, as quiet Leah seemed to, or are you the effusive type, like Rachel, who rushed home to Haran, bursting to share the news of her cousin's arrival? How can God use each personality style for his glory?

3. Esau and Jacob were defined by their labors: a long-range hunter, a close-to-home shepherd. Yet Leah and Rachel were defined by their appearance: one with gentle eyes, the other with beautiful everything. Are women today still defined by their looks? What makes you say that? In describing yourself, is your *first* thought what you do ("I'm a mother," "I'm a teacher") or how you look ("I'm blond," "I'm petite")? Why might that be the case?

4. At this point in the story, which sister garners your sympathy more, and why? One scholar noted, "Beneath the rivalry is the story of the struggle for self-esteem."[75] Is that how you see it? If you have a sister (or two), what are your differences and similarities? As you grew up, did people compare you to each other? In what ways did you compare yourself to your sister(s)? What is your relationship with your sister(s) like now?

5. Before you began this study, how did you picture Leah—her age, body type, features? What reasons would you suggest for Jacob favoring Rachel over Leah *other* than appearance? Why would he offer twice the usual bride price and then after seven years' labor carelessly not ask for Rachel by name? In what ways does love sometimes blind us?

6. Did Leah indeed show us her Slightly Bad Girl side on the wedding night? Or did Laban leave her no choice since fathers held sway over their

families in these ancient societies? What could Laban have told Leah to force her into Jacob's tent? In the New Testament we're told, "Anyone, then, who knows the good he ought to do and doesn't do it, sins."[76] How might that verse apply to Leah's situation that night? What would you have done in her sandals?

7. This deception scene hearkens back to the earlier tragedy in Isaac's tent. Compare the stories from Genesis 27:5–29 and Genesis 29:15–24, taking these into account: the scene of the crime; the players involved; the wardrobe changes; the food and drink served; the conferring of a blessing. What similarities in style do you see between the true deceivers in these stories: Rebekah and Laban?

8. What's the most important lesson you learned from our initial visit with Leah, an unseen sister veiled in darkness?

Morning Has Broken

Far off I hear the crowing of the cocks,
And through the opening door that time unlocks
Feel the fresh breathing of To-morrow creep.
HENRY WADSWORTH LONGFELLOW

L aura slowly opened her eyes, aware of a sour taste in her mouth and a dull
ache spreading between her temples. Darkness shrouded the cramped
room. Against her bare skin, the bedsheets felt scratchy, the mattress unfamiliar.

But she recognized the scent of the place. Her parents' motor home. And
she knew without looking who slept next to her. *Jeffrey.*

Shame washed over her like an icy shower. How had it come to this?

Laura remembered where it had begun, many hours earlier, at a neighborhood block party on a sultry August afternoon. The Pattons, three doors
down from her parents, had tapped a keg and fired up their mammoth grill,
broadcasting the tantalizing aroma of sizzling burgers and the irresistible beat
of dance music until the whole neighborhood found themselves at the Pattons' doorstep ready to party.

Laura's father, who seldom drank beer, downed one plastic cupful after
another in the oppressive heat. Sundown found him weaving from one clus-
ter of friends to the next while her embarrassed mother tiptoed home. Chloe
had to work, but Laura and Jeffrey were there, dancing barefoot in the grass,
gulping from the same cup. They were both of age, but she still felt vaguely
guilty.

Her father, however, was feeling very little. Standing before a group of
Burns Park newcomers, he lifted his beer in a toast to his older daughter and
his newest employee. "Wouldn't these two make a fine-looking couple?"

Jeffrey, a bit unsteady, threw his arm around Laura's shoulders and pulled her close. "I've been thinking the same thing."

"Me too," Laura whispered, seven years of longing welling up inside.

They slipped away, giggling like naughty children, and ended up in her parents' motor home that was parked behind the house. One friendly kiss led to another until they found themselves unbuttoning each other's clothes, throwing caution to the wind.

As she looked at him now, sprawled across the bed, tears pooled in her eyes. Did Jeffrey truly care for her, or were his heated words last night borne of passion and Miller Lite? *C'mon, Laura. You know how I feel about you.*

"No," she said softly, tracing the contours of his back with her gaze. "I don't."

Their relationship had grown through the summer with Jeffrey working for her father and living in their spare bedroom. Believing the Lord had brought him to her doorstep, Laura nevertheless kept her feelings for him under wraps whenever Chloe was around. Pride, mostly, and self-protection. Her sister had a cruel habit of exploiting her insecurities. But when Laura had Jeffrey to herself, she wore her heart on her sleeve, hoping he might claim it.

Instead, he'd taken something else. Something she could give only once, to one man. After waiting all through college, saving herself for some future, nameless husband, she'd not hesitated when he reached for her. Not for a moment. Not for Jeffrey. Not for the man God intended her to marry.

Now with dawn almost upon them, she was less certain of his commitment. When Jeffrey woke, would he gather her in his arms or turn away in disgust? Had their friendship evolved into love overnight, or had she ruined everything?

Dread filled her heart as Laura touched his bare shoulder. "Jeffrey?" He grunted but didn't move.

"Jeffrey, please. It's almost morning." The motor-home bedroom didn't have a clock, but its one narrow window grew lighter by the minute. Without the cover of darkness, they'd have a hard time slipping unseen into their respective rooms.

Fears held at bay through the wee hours of the night wrapped their tentacles around her heart. *Chloe.* If her sister found out, she would never forgive her, never stop chastising her. And what of her parents, who'd taught her to honor God? "How *could* you, Laura?" her mother would say. As to her father's reaction, Laura couldn't bear to think of it.

"Please..." With a rising sense of panic, she clasped Jeffrey's shoulder more firmly. "Please, we need to go."

"Huh?" He awoke with a start, then lifted his head from the crumpled sheets and slowly turned toward her.

Laura held her breath. *Don't say you're sorry. Please don't...*

A loud clatter from the next room startled them both. "Who's in there?" a tired voice called out.

Father.

She pressed her hand to her mouth, frantically looking at Jeffrey. He was frozen in place, eyes wide. If they didn't move, if they didn't breathe...

She heard her father banging around the tiny kitchen, searching for something. A cabinet door creaked open and closed. In the shadowy bedroom Laura held perfectly still, her face hot, her entire nervous system on alert. She longed to take Jeffrey's hand, needed his support. If her father came looking for them, if he opened the bedroom door...

"Look, kids. Just come out." He was standing on the other side of the folding door, not five feet away. "As long as you haven't done any damage, I won't tell your parents."

Kids. He thought they were a couple of youngsters from the neighborhood.

The folding vinyl door began to move. Desperate, Laura grabbed her cotton top and struggled to pull it over her head. *Please, please.* She couldn't be naked when her father found her, couldn't be so exposed.

But it was too late. By the time her head poked through the neckline, her father stood in the open doorway, a muffin tin in his hand, a look of disbelief on his haggard face. "Laura?"

Jeffrey cleared his throat. "Sir, we...I..."

Her father seemed not to hear him. "Your mother..." He held up the baking pan as if in a stupor. "She wanted to make muffins. For breakfast."

"Daddy…"

"I thought…" His features hardened as he turned toward Jeffrey. "I thought I could trust you, son. With my business. With my daughters."

Jeffrey abruptly sat up, covering himself with the sheet. "Mr. Sullivan—"

"Don't." Her father tossed the pan aside, and they both flinched. "Don't lie to me. Don't pretend to be sorry. You've been working for me all summer while behind my back—"

"No, Daddy." Laura held out a hand, determined to stop his tirade. "Jeffrey did nothing behind your back this summer. Neither did I. Last night just…happened. We were together. At the party… You remember? You called us a fine-looking couple…"

When her father looked at her, she saw the pain in his bloodshot eyes. "Then this is *my* fault, I suppose."

"No sir, it's mine." Jeffrey had managed to pull on his jeans and was twisting his T-shirt in a knot. "If there's anything I can do to…uh, to earn back your trust…"

"Yes, there is." Her father bent to retrieve the pan. "You can marry my daughter. In case you aren't aware of this, Laura is in love with you. Has been for a very long time."

Laura stared at the woven bedspread in shock. Had she been as obvious as that?

Her father didn't wait for Jeffrey to respond. "In my generation, if a man bedded a good woman, he did the honorable thing and made her his wife." He took a step back. "I'll tell her mother to start making plans."

With that, her father was gone, leaving them alone in the deafening silence. Jeffrey shook out his T-shirt as she pulled on her shorts with trembling hands. Morning light streamed into the room, making it impossible to hide anything, least of all her emotions.

Only when they were both dressed could she truly look at him. "Listen to me, Jeffrey. You don't have to do this. My father is—"

"Your father is right." His jaw was firm, yet tears glistened in his eyes. "I knew you loved me. Knew you would say yes."

She laid her hand on his forearm. "We're both to blame."

"No, Laura." Jeffrey shook his head as he shook free from her touch. "We're not…"

Leah the Unloved: Wake-Up Call

Some days it doesn't pay to get out of bed.

> When morning came, there was Leah! *Genesis 29:25*

Imagine the utter shock on Jacob's face, the sick feeling in his stomach, the anger that shot through his veins when "behold, it was Leah!" (NASB). No question, "Jacob woke up to his worst nightmare."[1]

Many grooms have awakened to a morning-after surprise. The expensive wedding gowns and filmy veils, the carefully applied makeup and fancy hair-dos—all have disappeared, leaving them with the women they truly married.

But Jacob didn't find a different-looking woman in his bed; he found a different woman entirely. If this happened today, the man would phone his attorney before breakfast and have the marriage annulled by noon. But in old Haran, a consummated marriage was a done deal.

Did Jacob blame Leah for deceiving him?

Ohhh, no. He knew exactly who was responsible.

> So Jacob said to Laban, "What is this you have done to me?"
> *Genesis 29:25*

Jacob not only "confronted Laban" (MSG), he "raged at Laban" (NLT), employing the very same words Pharaoh once used to charge Abram with trickery. "What have you done to me?" (NCV). Jacob's anger was justified. Hadn't Laban breached their agreement? No question "this was Laban's sin; he wronged both Jacob and Rachel."[2] As for Leah, her father's actions were "no small wrong to her too."[3]

With heated words, Jacob reminded his uncle of their terms.

"I served you for Rachel, didn't I?" *Genesis 29:25*

If only Jacob had spoken her name when he first asked for his wife! Too little, too late, like Esau arriving with a second platter of roasted meat. We can hear the desperation in Jacob's voice—"I worked hard for you so that I could marry Rachel!" (NCV)—but his words fell on deaf ears.

And what of the woman he'd slept with? What of Leah?

One glimpse of her at sunrise, and Jacob had bolted from their bed. Since we have no recorded exchange of words, it's possible Jacob left the tent before she awakened; "there was Leah" suggests she might still have been asleep. His bitter diatribe to Laban made it clear "there was no place for Leah in his heart."[4] If Leah had secretly hoped by complying with her father's demands that she could earn Jacob's affection, that he might awaken after their night of passion and say, "You'll do," she now understood the bitter truth: only Rachel would do.

Jacob, meanwhile, was still hammering away at Laban, giving him no time to respond between verbal blows.

"Why have you deceived me?" *Genesis 29:25*

We can hear him spitting out the words: "Why then have you deceived and cheated and thrown me down like this?" (AMP). Rather ironic, coming from Jacob the Deceiver. When we're wronged, we don't care *how* someone managed to trick us; we want to know *why* we've been "beguiled" (KJV).

What a wake-up call for Jacob! Once the deceiver was deceived, perhaps he understood how his father and brother once felt. "Until we ourselves are injured we do not see how mean and evil it is to injure someone else."[5] So wounded, Jacob might have realized how he'd wounded Isaac and Esau. A painful lesson indeed, watched over by a loving God.

Laban, however, was thinking not of Jacob's best interests but of his own. And so he offered a lame excuse for switching Leah for Rachel.

> Laban replied, "It is not our custom here to give the younger
> daughter in marriage before the older one." *Genesis 29:26*

Pulled that one out of a hat, didn't he? *If* it had been the custom, surely Jacob would have known that after seven years of attending local weddings. And *if* it had been the custom, Laban should have said from the outset, "We don't do it that way in our country" (MSG). True, in modern India it's considered "disgraceful in the extreme—a crime—for a father to permit a younger daughter to get married before the elder."[6] But not in Laban's time and place. His "excuse was frivolous."[7]

Just as Jacob didn't pause during his accusations, so Laban kept talking as he spun out a solution.

> "Finish this daughter's bridal week;…" *Genesis 29:27*

"Finish the week." Doesn't *that* sound romantic?

Not unlike a honeymoon, the bridal week allowed a newlywed couple to enjoy a respite from their daily duties—and enjoy each other, increasing the chances of a pregnancy early in the marriage.[8] Laban expected Jacob and his daughters to produce grandsons without delay.

Yes, both daughters.

> "…then we will give you the younger one also…" *Genesis 29:27*

Shame on you, Laban. He didn't even use their names—just "this daughter" and "the younger one"—as if they truly were livestock being traded at market. "First take Mooo, then take Baaa." Centuries ago John Calvin groused, "If Laban had ten more daughters, he would have been prepared to treat them all this way!"[9]

This proposal was even crueler to Leah than the wedding-night scheme. Laban could have found another suitor for Rachel, rather than force her to share Jacob with her sister, and given Leah a chance to turn Jacob's heart toward hers. But Laban didn't care about his daughters or about Jacob; Laban cared only about Laban.

And what Laban wanted was more free labor.

> "…in return for another seven years of work." *Genesis 29:27*

If the next verse read, "And Jacob threw himself in front of an ill-tempered camel," we would all understand. Seven more years? Look at your calendar and think about working seven full years—364 weeks in a row—for a man who'd deceived you and destroyed any hope of wedded bliss. Doubtless Jacob had planned to marry Rachel and take her home to Canaan. Now if he wanted Rachel, he had to remain in his uncle's tents, shepherd his uncle's flocks, and sleep with both his uncle's daughters.

Did Jacob protest this abominable plan? He did not.

> And Jacob did so. *Genesis 29:28*

That's right: "Jacob agreed" (MSG) just as his grandfather Abram once had. (Think Hagar.) Perhaps because he believed he was getting what he deserved for having deceived his father, Jacob was drawn "into the sin, and snare, and disquiet, of multiplying wives."[10]

Honeymoon from Hades

> He finished the week with Leah… *Genesis 29:28*

Jacob "complied and fulfilled" (AMP) his obligation to Leah. How dreadful even to contemplate what such a week might have been like with "a bitter bridegroom, an unhappy bride, and a grieving sister"[11] waiting her turn in the next tent.

The week must have flown for Leah, striving to earn her husband's affection. And the days must have crawled for Jacob, longing to be with the woman he loved. Was Jacob angry with Leah? Or, knowing Laban orchestrated the deception, did Jacob feel sorry for her? Tempers cool with time, but "pity in a marriage relationship can be deadly."[12] We don't know what that week held for these two ill-matched partners, but we can be certain sorrow and shame played a large part.

The last day finally came.

...and then Laban gave him his daughter Rachel to be his wife.
Genesis 29:28

Not seven years later, but seven *days* later Rachel became Jacob's secondary wife. No wedding feast, no procession, no bridal week. Jacob was hers but not exclusively: Leah held preeminence as his first wife.

Now we feel sorry for Rachel. None of this was her idea, for in no way did she benefit. Only Laban gained from this sordid marriage triangle. Since her father had the right to choose her future husband, Rachel had to submit to his wishes.

As to a wedding gift, he was hardly creative.

> Laban gave his servant girl Bilhah to his daughter Rachel as her
> maidservant. *Genesis 29:29*

A second marriage meant a second wedding night.

> Jacob lay with Rachel also... *Genesis 29:30*

Please, no details. It's already more than we can bear.

Though the patriarchs practiced polygamy, God never ordained it. On the contrary, when he first instituted marriage in the Garden of Eden, it looked like this: "a man will leave his father and mother and be united to his wife, and they will become one flesh."[13] Two become one, not two become *three*. Polygamy was a purely human, purely selfish convention, "and the desire for sons was the most prominent factor."[14]

Later, Mosaic Law included a prohibition against a Leah-Jacob-Rachel situation: "Do not take your wife's sister as a rival wife and have sexual relations with her while your wife is living."[15] After the sixth century BC, "marriage to two sisters was strictly forbidden."[16] But those laws came too late for Leah.

On the eighth night of her marriage, Leah slept alone, listening to the sound of lovemaking in a nearby tent, steeling herself for the look of triumph she would see on her sister's face come morning.

...and he loved Rachel more than Leah. *Genesis 29:30*

Much as it grieves me, "he loved her rather than Leah" (NEB) is closer to the mark. Jacob had loved Rachel to distraction for seven years; he wasn't about to stop now. As to his loving Leah, we have no record of him even noticing her until the night she slipped into his bed. Come to think of it, he didn't notice Leah then either.

Once again the sisters competed with each other—not about looks, but about love—and Rachel emerged the victor. From Jacob's viewpoint, "one wife can't do anything wrong, and one wife can't do anything right."[17]

Remember how quickly those first seven years flew by for Jacob? Funny how time can grind to a halt.

And he worked for Laban another seven years. *Genesis 29:30*

No mention of "they seemed like only a few days." Not this time. Toiling for a crooked boss like Laban had to be a pain, Rachel surely required every spare minute he could muster, and Leah as his first wife deserved some of his time and attention, if not his affection. His wives with their maidservants would have lived in separate tents; well trampled was the path between them.

The first seven years Jacob had worked to earn Rachel's hand in marriage. Now that he'd been paid in full, as it were, only hard labor remained. If you've ever received payment for something *before* you did the work, you know how enthusiasm can fade without that carrot dangling at the end.

Surprisingly, the main character of this story has been absent from the early verses of Genesis 29. We've missed his presence, his wisdom, his guiding hand, and we have longed for his intervention when things got ugly.

Lord, please don't wait a moment longer. We haven't heard Jacob cry out to you even once since he arrived in Haran. Did Rachel turn to you for comfort? Leah concerns us most of all. Couldn't you do something for her?

Yes, he could. And he did.

Beloved, just because the Lord is silent doesn't mean he's distant. God misses nothing. "His eyes are on the ways of men; he sees their every step."[18]

At that juncture in history, his gaze fell on a quiet, unassuming woman who needed what only he could provide.

Seen by God

When the LORD saw that Leah was not loved… *Genesis 29:31*

It's painful enough to be "unloved" (NLT), but the truth is "Leah was hated" (RSV) and "despised" (AMP) compared to Jacob's feelings for Rachel. Those words cut like a newly sharpened knife, sliding between our ribs to pierce our hearts. Poor Leah! Our only consolation is knowing this phrase "doesn't imply active abuse."[19] Not physical abuse, perhaps, but emotional neglect creates just as much wreckage.

Of those who knew Leah, it's hard to say who hated her most. Jacob loathed her for appearing to have been "a willing tool in his deception."[20] Rachel reviled Leah for stealing her bridal week, her husband, and her happiness. Laban probably detested his daughter for being so pliable; manipulative types have little respect for those they can control. And if Leah was "no better than an adulteress,"[21] the people of Haran abhorred her as well.

Think how many times Leah must have mentally revisited the hours before her wedding night. *If only I'd refused. If only I'd revealed myself to Jacob. If only I'd run away rather than walking into that tent. If only… If only…* We all live with regrets, made even worse if we're still mired in the consequences of our disastrous choices. What a comfort to know God is *with us* in the midst of our mess. Any hate aimed in Leah's direction didn't come from the Lord.

And there's more than meets the eye here. "Hated" was also a "technical, legal term for the unfavored co-wife."[22] As the rejected spouse, Leah was due special compensation. In Deuteronomy we're told, "If a man has two wives, and he loves one but not the other…he must acknowledge the son of his unloved wife as the firstborn by giving him a double share of all he has."[23] Apparently God had little patience with men who favored one wife over another.

And when we read, "Under three things the earth trembles, under four it cannot bear up,"[24] Leah comes to mind, since one of those unbearable situations is "an unloved woman who is married."[25]

Unloved by Jacob perhaps, but dearly loved by God.

It's the first part of this verse that matters most: "When the LORD saw…"[26] Nothing escapes his gaze, especially not people who are maligned unjustly; yet "the hardest thing to believe when you are suffering rejection is that anyone is noticing you at all."[27]

We see you, Leah. We don't know all that happened behind the scenes, but we can clearly see the end result: a husband who doesn't love you. Some of your sisters understand all too well what it feels like to live with a man who leaves the house early and comes home late, who never makes eye contact when he is home, who only makes physical contact when necessary—a cold and perfunctory act without passion. It's a sort of walking death. Feeling invisible, overlooked, discounted, ignored.

Know this, Leah: "the eyes of the LORD range throughout the earth to strengthen those whose hearts are fully committed to him."[28] God looked at you because you belonged to him.

Jacob loved Rachel, yes. Yet God loved Leah.

And here's how he proved it.

…he opened her womb… *Genesis 29:31*

We didn't realize Leah's womb was closed, but *she* knew. Out of compassion, God "made it possible for Leah to have children" (NCV). In a word, he blessed her. Not because her husband prayed on her behalf, but simply because God loved her and knew that childbearing was "the only way for a woman to achieve status in her own family and community."[29]

Hard to say how long Leah and Jacob had been married at that point. A few months, perhaps even a few years. We can imagine Leah keeping close track of her menstrual cycle, hoping Jacob would visit her tent on the opportune night and despairing when another month passed by without a pregnancy.

Then God intervened for Leah's sake, and "the LORD let her have a child" (NLT).

> …but Rachel was barren. *Genesis 29:31*

Another well placed "but." One sister was fertile; the other was not. "He gave children to Leah, but not to Rachel" (CEV).

Was the Lord playing favorites? Not at all. Rachel would have her turn eventually and produce a remarkable son. God was merely exercising his divine will: "I will have mercy on whom I will have mercy, and I will have compassion on whom I will have compassion."[30] He chose to have mercy on Leah. He had, in fact, chosen her from the beginning just as he had ear-marked Jacob.

By leaving Rachel's womb empty for a season, the Lord declared his love for Leah, even as he rebuked Jacob "for making so great a difference between" his wives.[31]

> Leah became pregnant… *Genesis 29:32*

One morning the truth must have dawned on Leah sure as the sunrise warming her tent. How else to account for the nausea in her stomach and the tenderness in her breasts? *Pregnant!* It was too good to be true. Yet it *was* true. She had all the assurance she needed growing inside her.

Whom do you suppose she told first—Jacob or Rachel? Not her smug father, who would have taken credit for it somehow. Was her maid, Zilpah, a trustworthy confidante, or did even she spurn her mistress?

Until her expanding waistline required an explanation, Leah may have kept the news to herself, relishing the truth like a private stash of chocolate, each bite sweet and satisfying. *Eight months to go. Seven months to go.*

What did others think of Leah's gift from God? The Bible remains silent on the subject yet blessedly lets us experience things from Leah's perspective. She who'd stood quietly in the wings moved to center stage at last.

> …and gave birth to a son. *Genesis 29:32*

Thanks be to God! A healthy heir for Jacob. And some long-awaited respect for Leah.

> She named him Reuben... *Genesis 29:32*

The fact that Leah, rather than his father, picked the name gives no cause for alarm; the mother often did the naming.[32] Her choice was Reuben, which does *not* mean a grilled sandwich with corned beef, swiss cheese, sauerkraut, and Russian dressing on rye. *Reuben* means "Look-It's-a-Boy" (MSG) or "Look, a son!"[33]

Leah knew why she'd been given such a gift.

> ...for she said, "It is because the LORD has seen my misery."
> *Genesis 29:32*

A biblical character's first recorded words are meant to reveal his or her true nature. What did Leah say first? "The LORD." Not "help me," not "poor me," not "give me." She honored God and his blessing on her life from her *first words.* Whatever happened on her wedding night, however Slightly Bad she might have been, Leah knew the Lord, loved the Lord, and blessed the Lord who'd sought her out in the wilderness of her marriage.

El Roi saw Leah just as he'd seen Hagar. He saw not only her gentle countenance but her tender heart as well. In Leah's words, the Lord "looked upon my affliction" (RSV), "my troubles" (ICB), "my humiliation" (NEB), "my distress,"[34] then banished that sorrow with the birth of her first son, Reuben.

The credit and the glory went solely to the child's heavenly Father.

But Leah still longed to win the heart of his earthly father.

> "Surely my husband will love me now." *Genesis 29:32*

Like a whispered prayer, those words. *Surely now...* Whether or not she cared for Jacob on the night she stole into his darkened tent, "the emotionally neglected Leah"[35] certainly loved him now.

Since sons were "arrows in the hands of a warrior,"[36] Jacob should have been elated at Reuben's birth and should have honored the child's mother with a greater show of affection. But that's not what happened. He dutifully slept with her, but he did not love her.

Unrequited love stories in movies or novels tug at our heartstrings. But in real life one-sided relationships tie our hearts in knots, producing a pain almost beyond bearing. If you've been there, you can sympathize with Leah's plight. Longing for the one thing we cannot have. Asking more of someone than he can possibly give. Making ourselves—and everyone around us— miserable. The solution? Seeking God for the affirmation we need.

However slowly, Leah learned that difficult but valuable lesson.

Heard by God

She conceived again, and when she gave birth to a son she said, "Because the LORD heard that I am not loved, he gave me this one too." *Genesis 29:33*

Another pregnancy, another son. A handful of words in Scripture, yet a long year or more of this woman's life in which she was still "hated" (RSV), still "unloved" (NKJV).

Yet look how Leah blessed the Lord, giving him all the glory (and not even mentioning Jacob). With her first son, "the LORD saw"; with this son, "the LORD heard." God was not only watching; he was listening.

So she named him Simeon. *Genesis 29:33*

Once again Leah did the naming. *Sim* means "one who hears."[37] How carefully she chose her sons' names, each one reflecting her growing awareness of "God's close presence."[38] Now she had a child tucked in the crook of each arm: two robust sons, two gifts from the Lord. Still no response from Jacob other than the occasional appearance in her bed. "She felt erased and silenced when she so dearly needed him to recognize her, to hear her."[39]

Again she conceived... *Genesis 29:34*

Wow. When God opens a womb, order a boatload of Pampers. It appears Leah's pregnancies came in rapid succession. Almost, but not quite, miraculously. Though we know Jacob was involved in the process, the Bible doesn't include his words or actions in these passages. Instead, God's eyes and ears were trained on Leah.

> …and when she gave birth to a son she said, "Now at last my
> husband will become attached to me, because I have borne him
> three sons." *Genesis 29:34*

A final, desperate appeal from our Slightly Bad Girl, who must have felt she was doing penance for her sin as she produced son after son for a thankless husband. Though her children were a blessing, not a curse and certainly not a punishment, Jacob's indifference caused grief beyond bearing. Yet Leah did not ask God to change the man; she believed with all her heart that her labors alone would earn Jacob's affection. "At last," Leah said. "This time" (KJV). "Surely now" (NLT).

Leah wanted what every wife wants: "a very closely knit relationship, one in which the two mates are joined together so that they feel, think, and act as a unit."[40] Two become one: God's plan from the beginning. And so Leah confidently assured herself that Jacob would "be a companion to me" (AMP), "connect with me" (MSG), and "hold me close" (CEV). The name she chose for her son captured the desire of her heart.

> So he was named Levi. *Genesis 29:34*

The Hebrew word *lavah* means "cleave";[41] hence the name Levi for the son she prayed would draw her husband closer.

Still no response from Jacob.

Am I the only one who wants to throttle this guy? Tie his legs in a knot? Bend his arm behind his back until he cries, "Uncle Laban!"? The woman gave him *three sons,* yet he remained silent.

"Our hearts go out to Leah—locked into a loveless relationship, with no end to the bitterness, rejection, and hostility heaped upon her."[42] All true, and yet we've also watched Leah's unflagging faith mature through her ordeal.

Leah knew she was not alone, knew her life was not without purpose. "Leah's inward beauty grew under pressure."[43] Her God was with her. Her sons were with her. And before another season passed, her womb was full again.

Loved by God

> She conceived again, and when she gave birth to a son she said…
> *Genesis 29:35*

Yeah, yeah, we've seen those words before. Three times before.

Yet something remarkable happened during those nine months. Leah looked at the children around her feet, gazed up at the heavens above, and realized how very much she was loved, how clearly blessed she was among women.

With a heart full of joy, Leah lifted her voice to the One who mattered most.

> …"This time I will praise the LORD." *Genesis 29:35*

What a woman! Instead of blaming God for what she didn't have, she began praising God for what she *did* have. "Now will I praise the Lord!" (AMP). Only the Lord, not Jacob. Only praise, not sorrow. Our emancipated Leah sang out, "This time let me praise Yahweh."[44]

Listen, if I gave a man four sons and he didn't give me the time of day, I'd be shouting, "This time I want him dead…"

Ah, but "this time" made all the difference for Leah. No more turning to Jacob, longing for him to respond. *This* time she turned to God, realizing "she could not change Jacob, but she could change herself."[45] Sister, you *know* that's right.

It's the first time in the NIV translation we find "praise the LORD," and it's spoken by a woman who could have complained to the Lord, pleaded with the Lord, railed at the Lord, yet she did none of those things. Instead, Leah, "the so-called unloved one," chose to "experience herself as the beloved of God."[46]

So she was. And so are you, dear one.

Each of us must come to that Leah place—a place where God is enough, where his grace is enough, where his love truly is enough.

I finally reached that place five years after I met the Lord and mere days after I met my wonderful Bill. Our first date was joy unspeakable. *He's the one!* my heart kept whispering. Yet when Bill left my house that evening, I called my best friend and said, "I just found the man of my prayers. And if he never calls me again, I'll be okay."

That was a *huge* step for a woman like me, who'd spent a lost decade looking for love and settling for sex. To find a terrific guy and yet be willing to let him go, knowing I was fully loved by God—that for me was the Leah place. (For the record, when Bill *did* call me again, I took that as a sure sign our courtship had the Lord's stamp of approval!)

Leah was abundantly loved, and her four sons and her changed heart were living proof.

So she named him Judah. *Genesis 29:35*

The very sound of his name was like the Hebrew word for "praise."[47] So fitting since God had given Leah "a garment of praise instead of a spirit of despair."[48] Her fourth son's name was lilting, like music: "This time I sing praise to the Lord."[49] Note, she praised God first and *then* named her son. The woman finally had her priorities straight.

Of course, the romantic in me wants Leah's story to have a traditional happy ending. Boy meets girl, boy marries girl, and after much travail boy loves girl. Sadly, those words aren't found in Scripture. But I find some satisfaction in this: of Jacob's wives, only Leah was laid to rest in the cave with Abraham and Sarah, Isaac and Rebekah. "And there I buried Leah," Jacob said just before he joined her in death.[50] Not a declaration of love but at least an indication of respect. As one commentator put it, "Ultimately Jacob seems to have had more lasting appreciation for Leah."[51]

If it's a happy ending you're looking for, Leah's finale was triumphant. The arrival of that fourth son of hers—that "praise the LORD" son—marked the start of something big. "For it is clear that our Lord descended from

Judah."[52] No wonder Judah's name sounded so familiar, eh? Jesus came "from him whose name was praise, for he is our praise."[53] Much as we admire godly Joseph, Rebekah's son, it was kingly Judah, Leah's son, whom God chose to bear the royal seed.

When we turn to the first chapter of the New Testament, the opening words tell the tale: "A record of the genealogy of Jesus Christ the son of David, the son of Abraham: Abraham was the father of Isaac, Isaac the father of Jacob, Jacob the father of Judah…"[54] If we listed the mothers rather than the fathers, it would be Sarah, Rebekah, Leah: two acknowledged beauties loved by their husbands and one older, tender-eyed woman loved by God.

Then she stopped having children. *Genesis 29:35*

Once again the word *barren* is not used of Leah. She simply "ceased bearing" (RSV). One commentator offered two possible explanations: "Leah had become infertile, or Jacob no longer slept with her."[55] Could be, though nothing in the previous scenes points to that. Leah was abundantly fertile and would be so again, and Jacob seemed very intent on performing his husbandly duties.

Here's a third possibility: perhaps Leah was content in her relationship with God and with her sons for this season of her life and no longer expected, nor demanded, Jacob's love and attention since the Lord met all her needs. As the psalmist wrote, "He gives children to the woman who has none. He makes her a happy mother."[56] And on the practical side of things, by nightfall a woman with four active boys would be too exhausted to do anything but sleep!

For whatever reason, her womb fell silent, though not soon enough to suit her barren sister, Rachel, as we'll soon see.

When we first met Leah, the woman was so featureless she almost disappeared. After her Slightly Bad Girl wedding night, we weren't sure we wanted to look any closer. Finally we've seen Leah as God saw her: a daughter who needed mercy, a wife who needed love, and a mother who needed a reason to sing again.

What Lessons Can We Learn from Leah the Unloved?

She resisted the urge to whine.

Though it's risky to teach from silence—from what's *not* in the Bible rather than what *is* there—it's worth noting all the things Leah didn't do. She didn't complain, she wasn't irritable or demanding, and she didn't become "an embittered woman, taking out her resentment and frustrations on others."[57] She may have pleaded, but she didn't whine. Nor did she speak ill of her sister or her father. In Leah we see Paul's words lived out: "Be joyful in hope, patient in affliction, faithful in prayer."[58] Though a modern Leah might seek escape from such an oppressive situation, biblical Leah deserves our respect for enduring with hope and faith, showing us how a godly woman can offer up praises rather than protests.

> She opens her mouth in wisdom, and the teaching of kindness is on her tongue. *Proverbs 31:26,* NASB

What's in a name? Lots.

For Leah, naming was "a rigorous spiritual discipline."[59] Each name was selected with care: Reuben, Simeon, Levi, and Judah. All four of Leah's meaning-filled names still appear among the list of the one thousand most popular baby names, Levi being far and away the favorite of the four.[60] Truly, "the names Leah gave her children testified to the miraculous faith God had planted in her heart"[61] and reflected her growing relationship with him. We can do the same for our children by choosing names that glorify the Lord. And we can worship God using the many names he bears in Scripture: Anointed One, Bridegroom, Counselor, Deliverer, and Everlasting Father, just to mention a few.

> A good name is more desirable than great riches. *Proverbs 22:1*

Beauty is in the heart of the beholder.

The longer we look at Leah, the more attractive she becomes, as the picture God's Word paints of her changes from a sketchy, colorless abstract to a handsome oil portrait done in warm, vibrant hues. Jacob judged the sisters' outward beauty and favored Rachel over her sister. But in the dark of night, he still went to Leah's bed. Marital duty? Perhaps. Yet Leah's enduring love for him, her patience with him, her tender eyes, and her fertile body all must have had their appeal. Things are no different today: we're still judged by our appearance. Yet the people we most admire, most want to be like, most enjoy being with, are often those the world calls plain…and God calls pleasing. Some sages have said, "Leah grew more beautiful as the years went by. Her hair turned white like the clouds but her face took on a wondrous look of strength…and her eyes became clear."[62] True or not, we know God found Leah beautiful.

> Your beauty…should be that of your inner self, the unfading beauty
> of a gentle and quiet spirit, which is of great worth in God's sight.
> *1 Peter 3:3–4*

Our sin cannot stop God's grace from flowing.
Laban may have shoved Leah into Jacob's tent against her will, showing himself to be one of the Baddest Boys in the Book. Or she may have tiptoed in gladly, more than earning her Slightly Bad Girl title. In either case, "the God of Jacob brought good out of evil, and caused His grace to abound over all the sin and folly."[63] However bad Leah's behavior might have been, God forgave her completely and graced her womb with four sons in a row. Again and again she honored the Lord, boasting not of her goodness but of his mercy. We find in Leah a role model for every woman who feels less than beautiful, less than loved, less than wanted. Suppose we give *her* a name: Chosen by God.

> He chose the lowly things of this world and the despised things—
> and the things that are not—to nullify the things that are, so that
> no one may boast before him. *1 Corinthians 1:28–29*

Good Girl Thoughts Worth Considering

1. Who had the ruder awakening: Jacob, discovering he'd married the wrong woman, or Leah, realizing her husband hated, despised, and rejected

her? If they spoke at all that first morning, what do you imagine the newly-wed couple said to each other? When Jacob cried to Laban, "I served you for Rachel, didn't I?" (Genesis 29:25), did he seem more upset about being deceived or about having Leah for a wife? Think of a time when you were betrayed or deceived in some way. Was it the motive or the method or the outcome that bothered you most? Why?

2. One commentator wrote of Leah, "She never seems more than tolerated, continuing to be Leah the unloved through the passing years."[64] Having read thus far in Scripture, is that how you see things? Based on your own experience or observation, describe what happens over time in a one-sided relationship. Do you agree Leah "couldn't squeeze more love out of Jacob than he could give,"[65] or should Jacob have tried harder to love both wives? What advice might a modern marital therapist give this unloved wife?

3. Matthew Henry noted, "Jacob was paid in his own coin."[66] Do you agree, or did all three suffer equally? Make a case for Jacob bearing the greatest burden, trying to please two women. And one for Rachel, sharing the husband she thought would be hers alone. Then one for Leah, married to a man who did not love her. When we're in a difficult situation, it's easy to see how we've been wronged. Choose a challenging relationship in your own life and consider what the other person has endured.

4. The pivotal verse in our story is this one: "When the LORD saw that Leah was not loved..." (Genesis 29:31). Does the realization that God sees inside your heart and knows the intimate details of your life encourage you or make you uncomfortable? Why might that be so? Leah is never called barren, yet God did open, or bless, her womb, altering her status from unloved to beloved. How could God best express love to you? What changes do you long for in your life that only God could orchestrate?

5. Even loved by God as she was, Leah longed for Jacob's love too. Was that a realistic expectation on her part or simply an indication of spiritual or

emotional immaturity? We have no record of Leah taunting Rachel during her pregnancies, as Hagar did Sarai, nor flaunting her newborn children in front of her barren sister. What does that tell us about Leah? If you were the older, unloved sister with a beautiful, much-loved sibling, how would you resist the urge to show off God's abundant blessings?

6. Leah's emergence from the shadows of her Slightly Bad Girl maidenhood to her Mostly Good Girl motherhood is encouraging to watch. What distinction do you find between "the LORD saw" and "the LORD heard"? Why do you suppose Leah looked to Jacob after Levi's birth rather than to the Lord? What do you most long for in a relationship with a man? If you've been disappointed, as Leah was, how might you come to a place of peace?

7. What a triumphant note Leah sang out at Judah's birth: "This time I will praise the LORD" (Genesis 29:35). How was this birth different for Leah? One commentator wrote, "Leah personified for every woman the crucial need to live primarily for God and His glory."[67] Why might doing so make a difference in our lives? Practically speaking, how can you put God first as Leah finally did?

8. What's the most important lesson you learned from our second visit with Leah, an unloved wife who was very much loved by God?

When All Is Said and Done

The jealous bring down the curse they fear
upon their own heads.
DOROTHY DIX

C hloe Sullivan stared at the baby announcement, swallowing hard. *Another son.*

She'd already heard the news, of course. Her sister had given birth to her fourth child nearly a month ago. Now here was further proof of Laura's fertility: a snapshot of her growing family in matching polo shirts and matching smiles. Chloe tossed the photo card in the wastebasket, then felt guilty two seconds later. She rescued the card, slapped it on her refrigerator, and planted a large magnet on Laura's face.

There.

Her sense of satisfaction lasted until she pulled on her running shoes and trotted out the front door of her condo. The sight of her neighbor Billie Hay pushing her twin stroller engulfed Chloe in another wave of envy. Did *everyone* have babies except her?

"Come see." Billie waved her closer, then bent over the stroller to fold down their pink and blue blankets. "Olivia lost the little rash on her face, and Patrick's finally starting to grow hair."

Chloe dutifully knelt by the stroller to get a better look. "They are indeed perfect," she agreed. And they were. Olivia, with her thick swirl of red hair, blinked at her like a baby doll with round eyes that opened and closed. And Patrick, with very little hair despite his mother's claim, had a handsome nose worthy of a child twice his age.

She stood, still gazing down at them. One of each in the same birth. Some women didn't know how blessed they were. "Gotta run," she said at last, glancing up at the sky. The forecast called for rain, and she'd promised to stop by Laura's house with a bucket of fried chicken for the boys.

Chloe took off at a sprint, pushing herself hard, her feet pounding against the concrete as she headed for the park. Mentally, she was running as well, going through the exercise that helped her deal with life as it really was. She was single, childless, thirty, and not getting any younger. But she was also a graduate of the University of Michigan School of Art & Design, a wildly successful interior designer, and the proud owner of a stylish new condo. Those were worthy accomplishments, weren't they?

Then why didn't her sister envy *her*? Because Laura Garner lived in a rambling old house on a shady Ann Arbor street with her hunky husband, Jeffrey, and their four adorable sons.

Jeffrey didn't pique her jealousy; Laura was welcome to him. Of course, Jeffrey *could* have been hers when he first came home from LSU. The man had mooned over Chloe all summer long. But she didn't love Jeffrey then, and she didn't want him now. Children? Those, she definitely *did* want.

Chloe balanced the bucket of chicken on her hip as she knocked, then pushed open the Garners' back door, knowing they expected her. "Dinner!" she sang out, walking through the dimly lit laundry room cluttered with basket upon basket of dirty clothes. From their family photo she recognized the bright blue polo shirts poking through one side of a torn plastic hamper. Doing laundry wasn't a priority at the moment, she imagined. Not with a new baby in the house.

"In here," Laura called from the family room, sounding exhausted.

When Chloe found her, she tried not to look shocked. Laura's face was ashen, and her hair needed washing. Seated in the old, overstuffed chair from her bedroom back home—her mothering chair, she called it—Laura was still wearing maternity clothes.

Nursing her new son, Judd, Laura waved her free hand toward the front room. "Can you gather up the boys and feed them in the kitchen?"

Chloe nodded, still trying to process what she was seeing. Not the neat and tidy family on the photo card, that was certain. She found Laura's three boys—all under age six—huddled on the couch in the living room, watching the approaching storm through the tall Victorian windows that faced the street.

Rufus, the oldest, greeted her with saucer-eyed enthusiasm. "Aunt Chloe, look!" He pointed to the dark line of clouds gathering above them. Simon and Lee hid their faces in their knees, folded against their chests. After venturing a brave peek, they ducked their heads as if any minute the storm might unleash its fury in their living room.

By the look of things, Chloe feared it might. "Let's go eat while the chicken's still hot."

The older boys made a dash for the kitchen, waving at their mother in passing, while Lee toddled behind as fast as his stout legs would carry him. Laura murmured her thanks to Chloe, preoccupied with her current task. "Save a piece for me in the fridge, okay?"

The old kitchen, larger than most, had room enough for a long oak dining table. And a playpen. And a high chair. And a booster seat. Chloe got the boys settled around the table, taking note of the dishes piled in the sink and on the counter.

While the boys finished their chicken, Chloe made up her mind—about several things. When Laura joined them in the kitchen, Chloe volunteered to bathe the boys.

"Jeffrey can do that when he gets home," Laura told her, the baby nestled in the hollow of her breasts, fast asleep.

Chloe glanced at the kitchen clock. *6:30.* "How much longer will he be?"

Laura's shrug told her what she needed to know. Jeffrey had his own accounting office now: longer hours, shorter nights.

"Then I'm doing baths now," Chloe said firmly, "or you'll have chicken grease from one end of the house to the other." When Laura didn't protest, Chloe rounded up the boys and made a game of it. "I need three able sailors to storm the high seas," she told them, then proceeded to have even more fun than they did, playing a lady pirate. She soaked the entire bathroom in the process, but at least her mariners emerged clean.

Bedtime went more smoothly than expected. Chloe read to them, prayed with them, and brushed kisses on their foreheads, then blinked away tears as she stood in the doorway before turning out the light. She was good with kids, wasn't she? Then why hadn't God brought her children of her own? Did he not hear her prayers?

She tiptoed down the stairs, listening to the rain beating on the tin roof above her. Laura sat at the kitchen table, nibbling on her cold chicken, with Judd tucked in a rocking baby carrier at her feet. She smiled, but the dark circles under her eyes clearly showed her exhaustion.

"Laura…" Chloe sat down next to her, determined to see to the boys' care however she could. "I think you need someone to help you. Shall I look into it? Or would you prefer Mother—"

"No," she said quickly. "Not Mom."

Chloe studied her for a moment. "What aren't you telling me?"

Laura averted her gaze. "Nothing, really. She's never… I mean, since the wedding…well, before that…"

"Before the wedding?" Chloe leaned toward her. "You've lost me, Laura. Did Mother not want you to marry Jeffrey?"

"Oh, she wanted me to marry him." Laura nodded absently. "So did Daddy. Right away."

"Really?" Vague memories of plans made in haste and an early autumn wedding began to surface. "Why the rush?"

After a long silence, Laura slowly raised her head. "Because Jeffrey and I slept together one night. When Daddy found us, he insisted…he told Jeffrey…"

"Wait." Chloe slumped forward, stunned. "He *made* Jeffrey marry you?"

"He couldn't force him to, of course. But Jeffrey worked for him…"

Chloe shook her head as if to dislodge the whole ugly scenario. "And Mother? I suppose she's been punishing you ever since."

Laura's chin began to tremble. "More or less."

Chloe stared at her sister, dumbfounded. For ten years she'd envisioned a happy marriage, a perfect family, an easy life for Laura. "I'm sorry, Laura. I…didn't know."

The back door banged open and closed. Jeffrey, finally home at nearly nine o'clock.

"I'd better get moving." Chloe stood to collect her things, grateful for an excuse to go. "On the way out I'll talk to Jeffrey about having a housekeeper come over for a couple of hours each day. That okay with you?"

Laura nodded, then bent to pick up Judd. "Tell him I've gone to bed."

Chloe hurried toward the back door to intercept him, each step strengthening her resolve. Jeffrey was still in the laundry room when she got there, drying his wet hair with a wrinkled towel.

His expression brightened when he saw her. "Of all the days to forget an umbrella."

"Jeffrey, we need to talk." She kept her voice low, listening for Laura's footsteps on the stairs. "I think it's time Laura had help with the house. Or with the kids. My sister—"

"I know." Jeffrey's smile faded. "It's a mess around here. She can't seem to keep up."

"Are you kidding? She's doing the job of three people. And one of those people should be you."

Now he was scowling. "Since when do you care what I do? Or don't do?"

"Since I found out ten minutes ago that you married my sister for all the wrong reasons."

He exhaled as if she'd knocked the wind out of him. "I married her because your father gave me no choice. And because I'd be close to you even if you married someone else."

"Jeffrey…" She didn't hide her shock; she couldn't. "Laura was the one who loved you."

"And I was the one who loved you. Or didn't I make that clear enough?" He moved closer before she could dodge him and took her by the shoulders. "I wanted you to be my wife, Chloe. I wanted you to have my sons."

She wriggled free of his grasp. "Don't say such a thing!"

"Why not if it's the truth?"

"Because it's cruel. And because…" She didn't dare say the rest—that she wished his sons *were* hers. *God, forgive me…*

Rachel: The Girl Turns Green

Reuben. Simeon. Levi. Judah. The names of Leah's sons "were like so many arrows shot into Rachel's tender flesh."[1] We sense them penetrating her heart and so share her sorrow.

A single woman who longs to wed, even as she watches friend after friend marry, or a married woman who longs for children, even as she attends everyone else's baby showers—such among us may identify with Rachel's plight: "her barrenness tormented her."[2] Whenever we compare our life to another woman's, we're bound to see something we want but can't have.

What Rachel wanted was a child. Oh baby, did she ever.

> When Rachel saw that she was not bearing Jacob any children…
> *Genesis 30:1*

A dozen years or more have passed since Jacob first laid eyes—and a cousinly kiss—on Rachel. She'd waited seven long years to marry Jacob, only to end up sharing him with Leah. Her sister gave birth as regularly as the ewes lambed every spring, yet Rachel couldn't conceive. Much as we've come to respect unloved Leah, our sympathy is also drawn toward infertile Rachel.

When her deepening pain caused her to respond in the most human of ways, Rachel donned her Slightly Bad Girl crown.

> …she became jealous of her sister. *Genesis 30:1*

Is it so bad, really, to be jealous?

In a word, yes. Jealousy eats away at us, robbing our joy and souring our spirits. And if we give vent to our feelings, the Bible reminds us, "Jealousy is cruel as the grave."[3] Because Rachel "envied her sister Leah" (NCV), commentators describe Rachel as "insecure, jealous,"[4] "peevish, and self-willed,"[5] "bitter, envious, quarrelsome and petulant."[6]

Right, right. We know what that looks like. On a bad day I've been all those things and more.

You'd think our next scene would show Rachel ranting at Leah, which she did soon enough. But first her husband bore the brunt of Rachel's frustration. (My hubby would murmur, "Now there's a surprise…")

So she said to Jacob, "Give me children…" *Genesis 30:1*

How like Jacob she sounds: "Give me my wife."[7] Or like hungry Esau: "Give me some of that red stew."[8] Rachel's words were every bit as impulsive, every bit as impatient: "Give me children." And not just *one* child, not when Leah had four. Rachel expected an equal or greater blessing—a common mode of thinking among Slightly Bad Girls.

Our drama queen wasn't quite finished emoting.

"…or I'll die!" *Genesis 30:1*

Strong words, those.

Since a woman without children was "accounted as dead"[9] in her culture, Rachel was not only jealous but desperate: "Give me sons, for if you don't I'm a dead woman!"[10] More evidence of her Slightly Bad Girl nature (and mine): tossing out dire ultimatums. "Give me what I want…or else!" We haven't worked out what "else" might be, but we're determined to go there if we have to.

And what was hubby's reaction?

Jacob became angry with her… *Genesis 30:2*

No kidding. We can feel the heat coming off the page. "Jacob's anger was kindled against Rachel" (KJV), and he "flew into a rage" (NLT). Bet this wasn't the first time they'd had such a conversation. After four, five, six years of marriage without a child in her womb, any little spark probably set Rachel ablaze: hearing Reuben call for his mother; watching Simeon take his first steps; catching wind of the rumors whispered about her; seeing her husband make tracks for Leah's tent.

Enflamed, Rachel lashed out at Jacob as if he were to blame for her barrenness. Instead of dousing her anger with a pitcher of cold water, Jacob added gasoline.

…and said, "Am I in the place of God, who has kept you from having children?" *Genesis 30:2*

"Am I God?" (NLT) he retorted. "Can I do what only God can do?" (NCV). Jacob knew his virility was not enough: God alone could open Rachel's womb and, to date, had not done so. The patriarch reminded his wife—and none too kindly—"He is the one who has kept you from having children" (NCV).

Perhaps from Jacob's viewpoint, Rachel had done something wrong to merit God's censure. Their childlessness was "her fault, not his."[11] Barren wives were expected to humbly seek out "a divine messenger or a man of God"[12] to plead their case. But we have no record of Rachel seeking God's counsel as her Aunt Rebekah once did.

What about Jacob? Did he pray on his wife's behalf as Isaac had? Hard to say, though certainly Jacob had to be as disappointed as Rachel was, if not more. Behind his unkind words we hear a bruised ego. His beloved wife had cried out "Give me children," not "Give me Jacob." That *had* to hurt. No husband wants to be treated like a sperm bank.

Not Again

When he fumed, "Am I the one who refused you babies?" (MSG), Rachel must have felt rejected by God just as Leah felt rejected by Jacob. To fear she was "not good enough for God, or not fit to be trusted with children"[13] surely grieved Rachel to the point of desperation. How else to explain her outrageous solution?

> Then she said, "Here is Bilhah, my maidservant. Sleep with her so that she can bear children for me…" *Genesis 30:3*

"Nooo!" we shout, waving our arms to get her attention. "Don't go there!" Rachel didn't see insolent Hagar, didn't hear mocking Ishmael, but we did. We know how this sleep-with-my-servant business can end up. Besides, Rachel's intentions weren't as honorable as her great-aunt's: Sarai wanted an heir for Abram; Rachel wanted children for Rachel, period. "Have intercourse with her" (AMP), she told Jacob. "Let her substitute for me" (MSG).

Groan.

"…through her I too can build a family." *Genesis 30:3*

That little word "too" is a giveaway: Rachel refused to be bested by Leah. Like a greedy child on Christmas morning counting the stash beneath the tree to make sure her sibling didn't receive more presents than she did, Rachel was determined to get her fair share. If another woman had to be sacrificed to her cause, so be it.

Bilhah "shall deliver it upon my knees" (AMP), Rachel declared, the customary gesture when claiming a surrogate child in her day.[14] Except the newborn was usually placed on the *father's* knees, signifying his acceptance of the child.[15] Rachel not only wanted Bilhah to substitute for her; Rachel wanted to substitute for Jacob.

The take-charge mother in me winces. How many times I have written an e-mail to friends, singing the praises of *my* son or *my* daughter and nearly hit Send before spotting my blooper. Make that *our* son and *our* daughter…

Rachel had made her decision, and Bilhah, like Hagar, had no choice in the matter.

So she gave him her servant Bilhah as a wife. *Genesis 30:4*

One commentator wrote of this scene, "Rachel resorted to plan B."[16] She sure did: B for Bilhah. And, yes, Bilhah became Jacob's wife; all the translations say so. In a later verse she's downgraded to a "concubine,"[17] but here Bilhah was very much a married woman.

Jacob slept with her… *Genesis 30:4*

Whether "to console his beloved Rachel"[18] or to put an end to her whining, Jacob did his duty by Bilhah. She did her part too.

…and she became pregnant and bore him a son. *Genesis 30:5*

What Leah thought of all this, we're not told. Nor do we ever hear from Bilhah, the birth mother. Rachel's response to this birth was triumphant, a confession "so mixed with ambition that it had little sincerity in it."[19] Bilhah may have given birth, but the boy belonged to her mistress, who claimed both the child and her right to name him.

> Then Rachel said, "God has vindicated me; he has listened to my
> plea and given me a son." Because of this she named him Dan.
> *Genesis 30:6*

Like her older sister, Rachel acknowledged God, but somehow her words don't communicate gratitude or humility. Instead they sound boastful: "God took my side" (MSG), and "God has judged me innocent" (NCV). *Innocent of what?* we wonder. Of the wedding-night wife swap perhaps? Rachel was decidedly guilty of envying her sister and also guilty of forcing her husband to take a third wife to bed. Truth is, Rachel "did not celebrate God's goodness but congratulated herself."[20]

Add another tarnished star to her Slightly Bad Girl crown.

I, for one, need a lifetime supply of such stars in my desk drawer for all the times I've taken credit when I should have honored the Lord. Even if I say, "Thanks be to God," in my heart I'm thinking, *Surely my hard work had something to do with it...*

No, Liz. All God, all the time.

In the same way, God blessed Bilhah's womb because it pleased him to do so, not because of anything Rachel did.

You'd think Rachel would have reclaimed her husband once she had a son. But since Leah had four lads, Rachel wanted at least two: an heir and a spare.

> Rachel's servant Bilhah conceived again and bore Jacob a second
> son. *Genesis 30:7*

Sigh. Are we there yet?

Even with six sons in Jacob's growing family, "hearts were still out of tune and unhappy."[21]

Then Rachel said, "I have had a great struggle with my sister, and I have won." So she named him Naphtali. *Genesis 30:8*

"Great struggle with my sister" makes it sound like Rachel and Leah were both waging war, yet through all four of her sons' births, Leah never once referred to her younger sister. I see this as a one-sided skirmish filled with "wrestlings" (AMP) and "grapplings"[22] and "an all-out fight" (MSG)—but only on Rachel's side of the battlefield. Don't be fooled. These aren't "the wrestlings of prayer";[23] God isn't even mentioned here. Perhaps this translation best captures Rachel's bitter spirit of competition: "I have played a fine trick on my sister, and it has succeeded" (NEB). Her father, aunt, and husband were all tricksters; Rachel learned from the best.

Though Rachel claimed she had won, "she must have known that she had not."[24] Surely she realized "in the eyes of the world, in the eyes of the Lord, in Jacob's eyes," she was a barren woman whose womb remained "closed, locked, empty."[25]

Et Tu, Leah?

Sadly, Rachel's jealousy may have stirred up similar feelings in her quiet sister, who did not speak but regrettably did act.

When Leah saw that she had stopped having children, she took her maidservant Zilpah and gave her to Jacob as a wife. *Genesis 30:9*

Remember the ancient law: after two years without a child, a dutiful wife gave her husband a servant to bear his offspring. Two years must have passed while Bilhah was busy having babies—and Leah was not. So perhaps she gave him Zilpah not to spite her sister but to honor the law and "give Jacob more joy"[26] by providing him still more sons.

Since no justification and no explanations are given in Scripture, I'm hesitant to give Leah another black mark on the Slightly Bad Girl roster for handing over Zilpah, though she does seem to behave as if she'd "never taken part in God's favor."[27] Following her sister's poor example, Leah "summoned her handmaid to the battle for her husband's affection."[28]

And like his grandfather Abraham before him, Jacob, the henpecked husband, did as he was told.

> Leah's servant Zilpah bore Jacob a son. *Genesis 30:10*

At least Sarah's servant, Hagar, spoke and was spoken to. These silent handmaidens, Bilhah and Zilpah, are treated like childbearing chattel. Even the meanings of their names remain uncertain: perhaps "simplicity" or "unconcern" for Bilhah[29] and "short-nosed" for Zilpah.[30] (Is it my imagination, or did these ancient folk have a *thing* about women's noses?)

Whatever the shape of Zilpah's features, she put a smile on her mistress's face.

> Then Leah said, "What good fortune!" So she named him Gad.
> *Genesis 30:11*

The bad news? No reference to God. The good news? No victory dance aimed at incensing Rachel. Just a positive statement, "I am lucky" (NCV), and a name for her son that meant "fortune" (AMP). Though Leah didn't "resort to complaining or deceitful actions,"[31] she, too, wasn't satisfied with just one surrogate son.

Here we go again.

> Leah's servant Zilpah bore Jacob a second son. *Genesis 30:12*

I know, I know, this is about as interesting as the begats of the Bible. Another birth, another son. *Yawn.* Leah, however, was delighted—as we would be if a new child were welcomed into our families under any circumstances.

> Then Leah said, "How happy I am! The women will call me
> happy." So she named him Asher. *Genesis 30:13*

Even if Jacob and Rachel withheld their approval and affection, Leah had earned the respect of the women of their region. She named her son

Asher, or "happy," convinced the women of Haran would call her "blessed" (AMP), in particular the young women of childbearing age who would "more greatly esteem her"[32] now that she had six sons on her scorecard.

While we're keeping score, Rachel was running a distant second in the baby parade—a situation she was determined to remedy. Of all her Slightly Bad Girl shenanigans, the next one takes the cake. And the mandrake.

Rooted in Misery

> During wheat harvest, Reuben went out into the fields and found some mandrake plants, which he brought to his mother Leah.
> *Genesis 30:14*

It was late spring, when wheat was harvested and mandrakes grew ripe in the fields. The tuberous plant would be hard to miss with its "large leaves, violet flowers, and yellow fruit."[33] Oh, and its fetid smell.

The ancients believed that if a woman gazed upon a mandrake root, she'd become fertile,[34] perhaps because the root was large and often forked, resembling the lower half of a person's body. The mandrake was thought to "cure fevers, heal wounds, and open the wombs of barren women."[35] Did Reuben—"about six years old"[36] at this point—bring the plants to his mother because she asked for them, hoping to start bearing children again? Or did he drag home a fistful of the funny-smelling plants as curious children are wont to do?

However the mandrakes ended up in Leah's hands, Rachel wanted them.

> Rachel said to Leah, "Please give me some of your son's mandrakes."
> *Genesis 30:14*

Heads up: this is the first time in the biblical account that Rachel and Leah actually engage in dialogue. Rachel certainly sounds polite: "Give me, I pray thee" (KJV) beats Esau's "let me have some of that red stew!"[37] She wasn't conceding defeat, just showing her sister the customary respect owed a primary wife. Leah now enjoyed "a position of power, perhaps as never before in her relationship with Rachel."[38]

That could be why Leah didn't hesitate to speak her mind. Finally.

> But she said to her, "Wasn't it enough that you took away my husband?" *Genesis 30:15*

Well now. I taste some pepper in those words. And pain too.

Leah once took away Rachel's husband. Then for a long time the women shared Jacob. Now it seemed he no longer visited Leah's tent, and Rachel had the man all to herself.

No wonder Leah was hurt; no wonder her tone was bitter. "Wasn't it enough that you got my husband away from me?" (MSG). Adding insult to injury, her sister wanted more.

> "Will you take my son's mandrakes too?" *Genesis 30:15*

Leah's words have that last-straw sound, revealing "the depth of her anger and exasperation."[39] She wasn't only unhappy with Rachel; Leah was also unhappy with herself. Drawn into her sister's baby battle, Leah had willingly given up her marriage bed to Zilpah, sending an unintentional signal to Jacob that he no longer mattered to her as he once had.

Men seldom overlook that kind of rejection.

Rachel took advantage of her sister's misery and offered her a shocking solution.

> "Very well," Rachel said, "he can sleep with you tonight in return for your son's mandrakes." *Genesis 30:15*

The woman traded a night with her husband for a *plant*?!

That's it. I'm rewriting *Really Bad Girls of the Bible* with Rachel as the lead chapter. Girlfriend, does this not beat all? Let's hope Reuben had already handed his mom the mandrakes and run off to play. I'd hate to think of little ones overhearing this unseemly discussion.

One writer suggested, "We have to admire Leah and Rachel for their forthrightness."[40] No we don't. There's nothing admirable about selling a husband's sexual services. Unbeknownst to him, Jacob was "bartered like a ram between two ewes."[41]

Leah didn't respond verbally, though she must have agreed to her sister's terms and handed over the mandrakes. No loss for Leah; their potency was rooted in superstition, not science. As time will soon prove, "Leah did not need the mandrakes, and they did Rachel no good."[42]

They also cost Rachel nothing but a night with her husband, which she apparently held in little esteem. Jacob was the one who had to fulfill her side of the bargain.

> So when Jacob came in from the fields that evening, Leah went
> out to meet him. *Genesis 30:16*

Was it sheer pent-up desire that sent Leah hurrying out to intercept him? Or did she prefer to tell Jacob privately, without an audience? Considering how many people had a claim on the man—including three other wives and eight sons—Jacob might have lingered in the fields that evening to savor a few moments alone.

Solitude was not on Leah's agenda for the night.

> "You must sleep with me," she said. *Genesis 30:16*

Oy! So much for "quiescent, vulnerable and self-deprecating Leah."[43] Her language couldn't have been more straightforward: "You will have sexual relations with me" (NCV). This particular idiom was usually reserved for first-time bedroom encounters, "a strong indication that Jacob has been sexually boycotting Leah."[44] No wonder she accused Rachel of taking away her husband and felt compelled to shamelessly buy him back.

Notice she said nothing about begetting children or building her family this time. I don't think Leah wanted another son; I think she wanted Jacob. Her heart was at peace with God, and mothering filled her life to the brim. But Jacob was still her husband, and she was still his wife. If only for one night, Leah intended to remind him of that.

"I have hired you with my son's mandrakes." *Genesis 30:16*

Whatever did he think, hearing such a thing? Yet when Jacob looked in Leah's tender eyes, "he saw in them a determination he had not expected. She would not easily be denied."[45]

So he slept with her that night. *Genesis 30:16*

You'll find few men in Scripture more obedient than Jacob. He'd grown up doing a woman's bidding—"Now then, my son, do what I say."[46] Then learned to do his uncle's bidding—"And Jacob did so."[47] Finally he did the bidding of his many wives.

Though two of them controlled Jacob's sexual activity that night, God alone controlled the outcome.

Blessings from Heaven

God listened to Leah… *Genesis 30:17*

We're relieved to know Leah was still seeking God's will, as evidenced here: "God answered Leah's prayer" (NCV). *What did she pray for?* we wonder. Some sign of Jacob's regard for her, perhaps? What she didn't do was plead for another arrow to add to her quiver solely to strike out at her sister. Nonetheless, a fine addition arrived.

…and she became pregnant and bore Jacob a fifth son.
Genesis 30:17

Once again God opened Leah's womb rather than Rachel's, "refusing to be manipulated."[48] Despite her Slightly Bad Girl moments, Leah continued to enjoy God's favor. And continued to give him glory.

Then Leah said, "God has rewarded me for giving my maidservant to my husband." *Genesis 30:18*

The Hebrew wording indicates that, although the ancient law called her to do so, "it was a difficult decision for Leah to share Jacob with yet another woman"[49] and that she'd been "struggling with her own conscience"[50] rather than struggling with her sister. From Leah's perspective, God rewarded her obedience by blessing her womb on a night of bartered lovemaking.

> So she named him Issachar. *Genesis 30:18*

She called her son "Bartered" (MSG), and so he was. Even without another mandrake exchange, Jacob returned to Leah's bed. How could he refuse, when her womb was so fertile and their sons so healthy?

> Leah conceived again and bore Jacob a sixth son. *Genesis 30:19*

I realize this is Rachel's chapter, but indulge me a moment longer to finish Leah's side of the story with the birth of Zebulun, meaning "Honor" (MSG) or "dwelling" (AMP) or "bridegroom's gift"[51]—all of which make sense, considering her response.

> Then Leah said, "God has presented me with a precious gift. This time my husband will treat me with honor, because I have borne him six sons." So she named him Zebulun. *Genesis 30:20*

She wanted Jacob to dwell with her, be protective of her, and honor her "like a princess."[52] Shades of Sarah there. But Sarah was beautiful and Sarah was loved, and our Leah was neither in Jacob's eyes, even though she'd borne him more sons than his other three wives put together.

Once again Leah had every human reason in the world to be bitter, jealous, and vindictive. Instead she prayed, trusted, and praised God. He rewarded Leah once more with a long-awaited addition to the family: a baby girl.

> Some time later she gave birth to a daughter and named her Dinah. *Genesis 30:21*

Fittingly, Dinah's name means "justice."[53] Though Jacob never treated Leah fairly, God certainly did.

As for Rachel, the mandrakes not only didn't work, they backfired: two more sons for Leah and a daughter as well. Would Rachel never have her heart's desire?

Finally, Finally

Then God remembered Rachel;… *Genesis 30:22*

Understand, God never forgot Rachel, not for a moment. He simply waited while she tried every scheme, every superstition, and every emotional trick in her well-thumbed book. Finally Rachel must have admitted to herself and to God that he alone could unlock her womb, and "she went and prayed on her own behalf."[54]

And so God remembered Rachel. "That remembering is the heart of the gospel. It will not be explained. It can only be affirmed, celebrated, and relied upon."[55] Joseph, Samson, Nehemiah, Hannah, Job, and Jeremiah all pleaded with God to remember them, as did David: "according to your love remember me, for you are good, O LORD."[56] When the criminal on the cross cried out, "Jesus, remember me when you come into your kingdom,"[57] he was asking for forgiveness; he was asking for salvation.

God did more than remember Rachel.

He forgave her. He saved her.

…he listened to her and opened her womb. *Genesis 30:22*

Rachel finally trusted in God rather than in human endeavors, and he "answered her prayer" (NCV) and "unclosed her womb,"[58] rendering her "a woman among other women, a creator of life."[59] Did she pray specifically for a boy? Count on it. Well and good for her sister to bear a daughter, but after so many years, Rachel longed for a man-child to place on Jacob's knees.

At long last it was Rachel's turn in the nursery.

She became pregnant and gave birth to a son… *Genesis 30:23*

Oh boy…and what a boy! When a barren woman is introduced in the Bible, "it is reasonable to anticipate the birth of a great hero."[60] This son would one day serve as prime minister of Egypt under Pharaoh and save his people when famine struck the land.

> ...and [she] said, "God has taken away my disgrace." *Genesis 30:23*

This time Rachel didn't take the Lord's name in vain when she confessed, "God has removed my shame" (NLT). Her need for forgiveness was clear, and her gratitude was genuine. "God has taken away my reproach, disgrace, and humiliation" (AMP). What a work God did in this woman's life! No more drama queen demanding, "Give me children, or I'll die!" No more bitter rival declaring, "I have had a great struggle with my sister, and I have won." No more desperate housewife deciding, "Very well, he can sleep with you tonight in return for your son's mandrakes."

When God remembered Rachel, "all the sorrows and disappointments of her life were forgotten."[61]

> She named him Joseph, and said, "May the LORD add to me
> another son." *Genesis 30:24*

A clever choice, since *Joseph* comes either from *asap,* meaning "take away," or from *yosep,* meaning "add."[62] After seven years of waiting to marry Jacob and seven years of longing to give birth, Rachel finally had her shame taken away, then admitted, "I wish the LORD would give me another son" (NCV).

I don't see this as a continuation of the Great Baby Battle. That struggle was over. From the moment God opened her womb, Rachel knew she was remembered, accepted, and blessed. Who wouldn't want another such blessing?

Moments after I gave birth to our first child and nestled him in the crook of my arm, I looked up at my husband through bleary eyes and said, "Let's have another one." Bill insists it was the anesthesia talking, but I know better: overjoyed by the miracle of birth, I couldn't wait to experience it again.

Jacob, on the other hand, was itching for a road trip.

> After Rachel gave birth to Joseph, Jacob said to Laban, "Send me on
> my way so I can go back to my own homeland." *Genesis 30:25*

Jacob had finished his second term of labor and so reminded his father-in-law, "You know how much work I've done for you."[63] Laban had to think fast if he wanted to keep his large, extended family—and his best shepherd—from disappearing into the sunset. He told Jacob, "Name your wages, and I will pay them."[64]

Uh-oh. "Wages"? We've heard that before.

Jacob the Deceiver was ready this time. He suggested a sly plan involving goats (again) and sheep, hoping to fleece Laban out of his livestock.

> "Let me go through all your flocks today and remove from them every speckled or spotted sheep, every dark-colored lamb and every spotted or speckled goat. They will be my wages." *Genesis 30:32*

Of course Laban promptly violated their bargain. He beat Jacob to the punch and spirited away said sheep and goats, then "put a three-day journey between himself and Jacob, while Jacob continued to tend the rest of Laban's flocks."[65] Naturally, Jacob anticipated his uncle's trickery and so resorted to "prenatal influence and selective breeding"[66] until he "grew exceedingly prosperous and came to own large flocks, and maidservants and menservants, and camels and donkeys."[67] Go, Jacob. Though we really should say, "Go, God." Only the Lord's blessing made such wealth possible, and Jacob knew that well.

Scripture doesn't tell us how Leah and Rachel (and Bilhah and Zilpah) occupied their time during those six productive years, but with eleven sons to raise, mothering duties must have claimed most of their waking hours. The only unhappy camper in the bunch was Laban. When "Jacob noticed that Laban's attitude toward him was not what it had been,"[68] he must have realized it was time to get outta Dodge—well, Haran—"before trouble broke out."[69]

Home to Canaan

As promised, God remained with Jacob all those years, prospering him and guiding him, even as he prepared to bring Jacob's time in Paddan Aram to an end.

> Then the LORD said to Jacob, "Go back to the land of your fathers
> and to your relatives, and I will be with you." *Genesis 31:3*

"I will be with you." Again that faithful vow bolstering Jacob's courage. He intended to take his family with him—all of his family—and so bravely put his plan in motion.

> So Jacob sent word to Rachel and Leah to come out to the fields
> where his flocks were. *Genesis 31:4*

What have we here? A scene with all three key players present. However sharply pointed this love triangle once was, time had softened the edges. Jacob needed a safe place out of Laban's earshot to confer with his wives to see if Rachel and Leah were willing to leave their father's house. Not only would such a move violate local custom, but the sisters had never lived anywhere but Paddan Aram.

When Sarai followed Abram, leaving her homeland behind, she didn't have children to consider. Moving a household in any epoch is difficult enough; relocating children makes things that much harder. New schools, new pediatricians, new play groups. Rachel and Leah had those concerns covered—homeschooling, herbal medicine, and enough sons to start a football team—but Jacob was still asking a great deal of his wives. Without God's clear directive he might never have departed Haran, but with it, Jacob was determined to go.

His speech to them sounded formal, almost rehearsed, as he described the situation: Laban's coldness, God's faithfulness, and his own hard labors. "Your father has cheated me by changing my wages ten times."[70] After recounting how God had prospered him despite their father's wiles, Jacob shared the words spoken to him by an angel of the Lord in a dream: "Go back to your native land."[71] He ended his speech with an unspoken question: *Are you coming with me?*

Jacob couldn't stay, yet he couldn't leave without them. How the sisters responded would "either confirm or deny God's plans for Jacob; their decision [was] binding."[72]

Then Rachel and Leah replied... *Genesis 31:14*

Are you seeing what I'm seeing? "Rachel and Leah answered" (AMP). True, Rachel was given pride of place over her older sister, but they spoke as one. My, how things have changed.

...“Do we still have any share in the inheritance of our father's estate?” *Genesis 31:14*

Not a question, really; Rachel and Leah knew the score: “Our father has nothing to give us when he dies” (NCV). The two sisters who'd once competed for Jacob's love were now “united in their hatred of their father,”[73] who'd squandered their inheritance.

“Does he not regard us as foreigners?” *Genesis 31:15*

Oh, that *was* bad. Daughters were not meant to be treated like “strangers” (AMP) or “outsiders,”[74] fed and housed but in no other way provided for.

“Not only has he sold us, but he has used up what was paid for us.” *Genesis 31:15*

Had Laban been a proper father, he would have returned a good portion of the bride price—Jacob's unpaid wages all those years—to each bride.[75] Instead, Laban “devoured” (AMP) their money, implying “ruthlessness of action.”[76] Not only had the man broken the family laws of their country;[77] he'd betrayed them as a father.

“Surely all the wealth that God took away from our father belongs to us and our children.” *Genesis 31:16*

Throughout Jacob's speckled-and-spotted lambs-and-goats project, God had neatly shepherded Laban's bounty over to Jacob's side of the pasture. Rachel and Leah wanted to be sure their wealth wouldn't be left behind. “Treated as partners, they emerge as partners.”[78] Thrilling to behold, isn't it? After so much domestic strife, the sisters were in accord.

Their loyalty to each other—and to Jacob—was clear. "If he was considering leaving without them, he could forget it."[79]

"So do whatever God has told you." *Genesis 31:16*

Rachel and Leah couldn't have stated their approval more strongly: "do it" (AMP).

Jacob "waited until Laban had gone away for a sheepshearing festival,"[80] then loaded the camels with his wives and children, packed up all the goods he'd accumulated in Paddan Aram, and drove his livestock ahead of him, bound for Canaan. Kinda sneaky on Jacob's part: "an act of fear and unbelief, not an act of faith."[81]

I'm sure Jacob justified his actions—to himself if not to others. "It's only fair I should have these things after all I've done." Or "My family wanted me to do this." Or "I had a clear word from God." I've said all those things to soothe my guilty conscience about iffy behavior. But when we choose our timing to avoid getting caught, something isn't quite…um, kosher.

And look at this: another trickster in the family took advantage of the situation. While Laban was gone, "Rachel stole her father's household gods."[82] Our Slightly Bad Girl returned for an encore. Even if Laban deserved to suffer, stealing from her father put Rachel on the Most Wanted list for breaking four of the Top Ten:
- "You shall have no other gods before me."[83]
- "You shall not make for yourself an idol."[84]
- "Honor your father."[85]
- "You shall not steal."[86]

Uh-oh. Even though the Ten Commandments wouldn't be written in stone until several centuries later, right and wrong are timeless, and what Rachel did was Bad-Girl wrong. Those wooden or metal *teraphim,* translated from Hebrew as "vile things,"[87] were abominations from God's perspective.

Ick, Rachel. Why run off with those?

Since no motive is given in Scripture, scholars have had a field day trying to pin down a definitive reason for Rachel's nabbing her father's statues. Did she have "a lingering attachment to these objects of her family's superstitious reverence"?[88] Or had she "not learned to trust in Jehovah to provide for her needs"?[89] Were they meant to provide "good fortune and fertility as well as protection during a journey"?[90] Or was it her "obstinate love of idolatry"?[91]

Maybe Rachel took them for less selfish reasons. Since "possession of the *teraphim* marked a man as the chief heir,"[92] she might've had Jacob in mind when she stole them, guaranteeing him Laban's lands and goods. The rabbis of old also believed Rachel's theft had a noble purpose: so she could steer "misguided Laban away from idolatry."[93] I'll buy the first option, but the second one doesn't sound like the feisty Rachel we know. I think she impulsively stuffed those Aramean idols in her goatskin purse to spite her father, then headed southwest with Jacob and company.

As for Laban, he had "no idea what was going on—he was totally in the dark."[94] Some justice there, I'd say. Three days later, when Laban got the news, "he pursued Jacob for seven days and caught up with him in the hill country of Gilead."[95] Naturally, he gave Jacob an earful, blaming the man for carrying off his daughters "like captives in war"[96] even though Rachel and Leah had gone willingly with their husband.

The longer Laban spoke, the more outlandish his words became.

> "Why did you run off secretly and deceive me? Why didn't you tell me, so I could send you away with joy and singing to the music of tambourines and harps?" *Genesis 31:27*

Oh please.

Laban called Jacob a fool, "a harsh indictment in that culture,"[97] then reminded him, "I have the power to harm you."[98] Not physical harm; Jacob no doubt had the advantage there. But Laban could legally punish Jacob for "contemptuous disregard of family customs."[99] How it must have irked Laban to confess with his next breath that he couldn't do a thing, because God had told him in a dream, "Be careful not to say anything to Jacob, either good or bad."[100]

When God promised Jacob he had his back, he wasn't kidding.

Relieved to know their husband was spared from imminent harm,

Rachel and Leah may have exchanged tentative smiles, thinking the worst was over.

Ah, but this is the Bible, remember?

All at once Laban demanded to know, "Why did you steal my gods?"[101] Yikes. Did Rachel's heart skip a beat? Did her hands grow cold? Did her gaze land on the bundle of idols barely hidden from view?

Caught off guard, Jacob promised, "If you find anyone who has your gods, he shall not live."[102] Not good, not good. "Jacob unwittingly pronounced the death penalty on Rachel,"[103] a foreshadowing of what was to come. Convinced no one in his party would have dared to steal the man's cherished idols, Jacob invited Laban to search their tents.

Idol Chatter

> Now Jacob did not know that Rachel had stolen the gods.
> *Genesis 31:32*

Now.

Our story has taken an unexpected—and uneasy—turn. Rachel must have been beside herself wondering how to hide the bulky statues. Did Leah know about her crime? Or did Rachel's maidservant, Bilhah? If so, the women remained tight-lipped while "Jacob's blissful ignorance" made things "unbearably tense."[104] Laban searched Jacob's tent, then the tent Bilhah and Zilpah shared, "but he found nothing. After he came out of Leah's tent, he entered Rachel's tent."[105]

Help.

> Now Rachel had taken the household gods and put them inside her camel's saddle and was sitting on them. *Genesis 31:34*

Rachel, Rachel. *Sitting* on your father's idols! Hearing this story, the ancients would have immediately understood what was implied by Rachel's "irreverent posture toward them"[106] and agreed "Laban's gods were judged with him."[107] Take that, teraphim.

Perhaps Laban studied his seated daughter and narrowed his eyes, for she felt compelled to explain herself.

> Rachel said to her father, "Don't be angry, my lord, that I
> cannot stand up in your presence; I'm having my period."
> *Genesis 31:35*

"The common lot of woman is upon me" (NEB), she told Laban. Readers of old surely laughed up their tunic sleeves at Rachel's audacious fib. Though it might have been the truth, Rachel wouldn't have hesitated to employ such a lie to suit her purposes. Guaranteed, her father didn't come near her. Even before Levitical laws were laid down, social rules set clear limits about such things.

Her husband, meanwhile, had had enough.

> Jacob was angry and took Laban to task. *Genesis 31:36*

Yes, indeed, he "contended with Laban" (NASB), he "lit into Laban" (MSG), he even "chode with Laban" (KJV), and am I ever sorry I missed *that.* Jacob was the man for the job, though Rachel had already put Laban in his place with her creative hide-the-idol scheme.

Our indignant shepherd was soon on a proverbial roll.

> "What is my crime?" he asked Laban. "What sin have I committed
> that you hunt me down?" *Genesis 31:36*

Jacob's poetic speech unfolded "solemnly and in exalted style."[108] Were Leah and Rachel both on hand? Surely they longed to see their father get his much-deserved comeuppance. Not a very charitable thought, I know. I'd hate to think of someone I'd sinned against giving me what-for with a tentful of people watching.

Uncle and nephew wrestled each other to the ground with words, finally resolving to make a covenant between them: "The LORD watch between me and thee, when we are absent one from another."[109] Pious sounding, though in a nutshell it meant they didn't trust each other.

With the night's drama behind them, Laban and Jacob parted company pleasantly enough the next morning. Before he left, "Laban kissed his grand-children and his daughters and blessed them."[110] Well, well. That's the first time we've seen Laban bestow a blessing on *anyone,* let alone his daughters.

We find very little of Laban in Leah's character yet quite a bit in Rachel's: the deception, the secrets, the whining, the stubbornness, the withheld affection, the possessiveness, the sharp tongue. Rachel, for all her beauty and charm, had more Slightly Bad Girl attributes than the four women we met before her (combined, some might argue).

Yet we can't overlook the good stuff: Rachel's strength and courage, her cleverness and determination, and her humble gratitude toward God for blessing her womb. If you have a daughter Rachel, you did not name her amiss. She was, after all, the mother of Joseph, "a man whose virtues and whose mind shine out over the last chapters of Genesis."[111] And she was the mother of Benjamin, which brings her chapter to a bittersweet close.

A Time to Be Born and...

Years passed. Jacob and his nomadic family found themselves traveling between Bethel and Bethlehem, or Ephrath. Rachel, at last pregnant with her second child, was nearing her time of confinement.

> While they were still some distance from Ephrath, Rachel began
> to give birth and had great difficulty. *Genesis 35:16*

Our hands press against our hearts. *We know, Rachel. We're sorry.* She suffered through "hard, hard labor" (MSG), a pain like no other. With Bethlehem beyond reach, Rachel "fell in travail by the way."[112] We hear remarkable stories of women giving birth in taxicabs and on front lawns and in grocery stores, stories with happy endings and amusing photos of passersby pressed into service, proudly displaying newborns for the camera.

Rachel's hard labor by the roadside was neither sublime nor ridiculous, but serious business. It was nothing less than a woman fighting for life—her son's, if not her own. She would see him born. She *would.*

And as she was having great difficulty in childbirth, the midwife said to her, "Don't be afraid, for you have another son."
Genesis 35:17

At the very moment "when her labor was at its hardest,"[113] the midwife
offered her a word of comfort, remembering Rachel's request for a second
son: "you shall have this son also" (AMP).

Finally he came forth, the child who cost Rachel everything.

As she breathed her last—for she was dying—she named her son
Ben-Oni. *Genesis 35:18*

With her dying breath, "as her soul was departing" (AMP), Rachel chose
a name that would have forever shrouded her child in grief: "Son-of-My-
Pain" (MSG), "Son of My Suffering" (NCV), "son of my trouble."[114]

Jacob could not bear to remember Rachel's sorrow every time he spoke the
boy's name, so he called his twelfth son—the only son whom Jacob named—
Benjamin: "Son-of-Good-Fortune" (MSG) or "son of the right hand."[115] The
hand a father extended in greeting, the hand a father rested on his staff, and
the hand a father used to bless his sons.

Rachel, the first woman in Scripture to die in childbirth, was buried by
the road—not inside the cave in the field of Machpelah with Abraham and
Sarah and Isaac and Rebekah, but en route to Bethlehem, where another Son
would someday come forth from his mother's womb.

Stricken with grief, Jacob set up a pillar over her grave, though we know
"Rachel's real tomb was in Jacob's heart."[116] Imperfect as she was—as we all
are—her husband "could not help loving her."[117] From the moment they
met by the well, Jacob never forgot his beloved Rachel.

Neither have all the generations that followed her.

When Boaz prepared to marry Ruth, the town elders blessed his marriage
with these words: "May the LORD make the woman who is coming into your
home like Rachel and Leah, who together built up the house of Israel."[118]
Together. We find it easy to applaud Leah, who said, "This time I will praise

the LORD." But we must also honor Rachel, however flawed her motives and actions, knowing God remembered her. And loved her. And blessed her—not because of any Good Girl deeds, but because of his great mercy.

A memorial to Rachel's tomb still stands on the road to Bethlehem in "a small room with a domed roof,"[119] guarded by soldiers. Women come there to pray for loved ones, to weep for lost ones, to seek the Lord. And "surely God is present there if only in the prayers of praise and of entreaty that rise above the soldiers' heads."[120]

Yes, God remembered Rachel. And so, beloved, should we.

What Lessons Can We Learn from Rachel?

We can grow old gracefully.

Comparing Rebekah and Rachel, related by blood as aunt and niece, it's easy to spot the family resemblance. Both were beautiful, intelligent, and desirable. As married women, they each suffered from barrenness: twenty years for Rebekah, fourteen for Rachel. Their personalities were also surprisingly alike: lively, expressive, temperamental…and devious. One writer noted, "They both form a charming picture in youth that changes in later life, as the less admirable qualities in their natures come to the front."[121] As we consider the similarities among women in our own families, it's worth noting what happens to us all as we mature. We either grow sweeter or turn more sour, become more generous or tighten our purses, draw closer to God or lose spiritual ground. Let's pray the Lord will make us more like him and less like our natural selves.

> Do not conform any longer to the pattern of this world, but be transformed by the renewing of your mind. *Romans 12:2*

Jealousy has two sides.

Rachel's jealous attitude toward Leah caused a painful rift between the two sisters, yet beneath it lurked a deeper problem: Rachel idolized, even worshiped motherhood, caring more about becoming a mother than loving her sister, respecting her husband, or honoring God. The Lord is also called jealous, and for good reason: he commands his followers to put away false idols and to worship him above everyone and everything else. Yet Rachel not only idolized her dreams of motherhood but also took her father's household gods with her, rather than destroying them, which raises doubts about her convictions. God doesn't mince words on this subject: we are not to be jealous of one another nor give the Lord cause to burn with jealousy toward us.

> Do not worship any other god, for the LORD, whose name is
> Jealous, is a jealous God. *Exodus 34:14*

Human love is never enough.

Leah and Rachel were both slow learners in this regard. Leah thought if Jacob truly loved her, he would stay in her tent 24/7 and her joy would be complete. Rachel thought if Jacob truly loved her, he would give her sons and *her* joy would be complete. Leah, at least, acknowledged God's presence in her life and praised him for seeing her, hearing her, blessing her. Rachel, however, sought out Jacob to demand that he fill her womb, when what needed filling was her heart. Jacob gave Rachel "all the love he could, but at the end of the day, as good as it was, he couldn't supply it all. He could not supply what was missing in Rachel's life, but God could."[122] Family and friends contribute greatly to our earthly joy, but it's unfair to expect them to meet all our physical, emotional, and spiritual needs. Only God has the resources of the world at his fingertips, and only God knows what we truly need.

> And my God will meet all your needs according to his glorious
> riches in Christ Jesus. *Philippians 4:19*

How good and pleasant it is when sisters live together in unity.

Rachel and Leah came a long way, from not sharing any dialogue, to having an honest, albeit painful, conversation about their husband, to standing together in the fields and speaking to Jacob in a unified voice. Though Germaine Greer once quipped, "The sight of women talking together has always made men uneasy,"[123] in this case Jacob's huge sigh of relief must have been heard across the plain of Aram. It's difficult to live with people who aren't communicating, aren't working toward the same end, aren't trying to get along. When Rachel held Joseph in the crook of her arm, she could finally stretch out her free hand to Leah, knowing God saw, heard, and remembered them both. Heated words and cold shoulders gave way to warm hands, clasped together as the two sisters stood side by side at last. What a fine way to remember these sisters, and what a worthy example of how we, too, can reach out to estranged family members or friends and rebuild those bonds in the name of Christ.

> How wonderful, how beautiful, when brothers and sisters get along!
> *Psalm 133:1, MSG*

Good Girl Thoughts Worth Considering

1. It's not enough to consider Rachel's jealous nature; we must also examine our own. What specific situations push your buttons, and why? We noticed that Rachel's envy sprang from the root of idolatry. What might lie beneath your envy? Are you ready to ask God to pull out that root—far more stubborn than a mandrake—and plant contentment in your life? How might you prepare the soil of your heart?

2. When Jacob asked his whiny wife, "Am I in the place of God?" (Genesis 30:2), he spoke in anger, but he also spoke the truth. He could not do what God could do; he could not take God's place. If you've ever put all your trust in someone, expecting that person, in essence, to be God for you, how did he or she respond? And what did you learn from the experience?

3. In the mandrake scene, were you rooting for Leah (pun intended), glad she'd finally spoken her mind, or dismayed to see the lengths to which these women went for children? In our day we may not amass offspring to impress our neighbors, but most of us surely collect something. What's your keeping-up-with-the-Joneses temptation? To what lengths have you gone to

add another one of those gotta-have-it items to your life? What might God be calling you to change about your behavior?

4. The Bible tells us, "God remembered Rachel." What does that mean to you, to be remembered by God? For Rachel, the Lord took away the societal disgrace of barrenness. The prophet Isaiah wrote, "The Sovereign LORD will wipe away the tears from all faces; he will remove the disgrace of his people from all the earth."[124] What tears, what sorrows, what shame in your life are you praying that God will take away today?

5. When Rachel and Leah joined Jacob in the fields, they finally revealed how they felt about their father. What did they object to most, and why? Were the sisters being greedy or demanding what was rightfully theirs? If you've been through any inheritance situations in your family, what did you learn about your parents? Your siblings? Yourself?

6. Why do you think Rachel stole her father's household gods? Was it a premeditated act, or did she grab them on impulse? If you've ever taken something from another person as an act of spite or revenge, what did you learn about yourself—and human nature—in the process? Jacob pledged to put to death anyone who had Laban's gods. Do you believe Jacob would have killed Rachel rather than break a solemn vow?

7. Rachel is one of the more memorable characters in the Bible, with *character* being the operative word. If you had the power to undo something Rachel did or to change something about her nature, what would that be, and why? Now look at your own life through a friend's eyes and answer the same questions. Which of your actions would you undo, and why? And what character trait will you step back and let God refashion for your benefit?

8. What's the most important lesson you learned from Rachel, the memorable mother of Joseph and Benjamin?

Endless Life

O, if we could tear aside the veil,
and see but for one hour what it signifies to be
a soul in the power of an endless life,
what a revelation would it be!
HORACE BUSHNELL

A revelation—that's what I pray our time together has been. Unveiling the truth about these ancient sisters and revealing our own Slightly Bad Girl moves in the process.

I shudder to confess how much of Lizzie I hear in Sarah's dismissive laugh, taste in Rebekah's mealtime deceptions, and see in Rachel's self-centered demands. Had I been Hagar, I would have perished in the desert just to spite my mistress and put an end to my master's hopes for a son. Had I been Leah, I would have strutted past Rachel's tent with a Baby on Board sign around my neck and a smirk on my face.

In other words, I'm worse than Slightly Bad: I'm wretched. Paul used that word to describe his flawed nature,[1] and we confess our wretchedness every time we sing the opening lines of "Amazing Grace." David said, "I am a worm and not a man";[2] Jacob told the Lord, "I am unworthy of all the kindness and faithfulness you have shown your servant";[3] and Job admitted, "I despise myself."[4]

Even those godly guys weren't utterly good. They recognized the immense gap between their sinful selves and a righteous God—a gap none of us can hope to bridge on our own.

No matter how beautiful the faces and figures (and noses) of Sarah, Rebekah, and Rachel, their actions were often ugly. No matter how fertile the wombs of Hagar and Leah, their lives sometimes yielded bitter fruit. And no matter how many church services we attend, how many dollars we contribute to God's kingdom, or how many good deeds we do in his name, we can never make up for the sins we commit on an hourly basis.

Is there any hope for Slightly Bad Girls like us?

Dear one, there is hope everlasting! "Against all hope, Abraham in hope believed."[5] Our spiritual barrenness prepares the way for God's blessing of grace to flow through our lives. "Therefore, the promise comes by faith, so that it may be by grace and may be guaranteed to all Abraham's offspring."[6] That includes us, sis. However bad we were, however bad we are, however bad we will be tomorrow, we belong to God. He isn't stuck with us; *he chose us.*

That was certainly the case for our five matriarchs. Chosen to bear the seed of Abraham despite their failings. Chosen to carry God's promise through three generations and beyond. "On the one hand the issue is one of *seed* or posterity, while on the other hand the Lord's sovereign will was operative."[7]

Count on it, beloved. Every time we say the Lord's Prayer, we affirm, "Thy will be done." Nothing that happened in Ur, Haran, Egypt, or Canaan surprised, bewildered, or in any way hindered God. The phrase "God's will" doesn't mean "what God hopes" or "what God prefers"; it means "what God has already ordained." And that's exactly what will come to pass.

The apostle Paul also used Rebekah's story to describe the sovereignty of God to a first-century Roman audience. "Rebekah's children had one and the same father, our father Isaac. Yet, before the twins were born or had done anything good or bad…," Paul explained, "she was told, 'The older will serve the younger.'"[8]

Rebekah was undoubtedly confused by God's promise at first, as some of us were. Yet God "made it perfectly plain that his purpose is not a hit-or-miss thing dependent on what we do or don't do, but a sure thing determined by his decision, flowing steadily from his initiative."[9] Paul went on to quote the prophet Malachi: "Just as it is written: 'Jacob I loved, but Esau I hated.'"[10]

Hated? Such a harsh word, also translated "rejected" (NLT) and "held in relative disregard" (AMP). Eugene Peterson calls it "a stark epigram" (MSG).

Before his Roman listeners protested, Paul continued, "What then shall we say? Is God unjust?"[11] I gotta be honest. At first glance the Lord's rejection of Esau felt unfair to me. Arbitrary. Like pulling petals off a daisy: "I love him, I love him not."

"Not at all!" Paul said.[12] He again turned to the Scriptures of old to explain why: "God told Moses, 'I'm in charge of mercy. I'm in charge of compassion.'"[13] Once more, this vital truth: God's in charge and we're not. Our attempts to earn his grace are a waste of time. It's not up to us; it's up to him. "It does not, therefore, depend on man's desire or effort, but on God's mercy."[14]

You mean we can't do *anything* good on our own?

Sorry, but we really can't. "Apart from me you can do nothing."[15]

Then are we stuck being Slightly Bad Girls forever? Trying to be good, yet failing? Messing up, then feeling guilty?

Not for a moment, my friend, let alone for eternity. Not if you have the same faith Sarah, Hagar, Rebekah, Leah, and Rachel had. The kind of faith that's "a pure gift,"[16] not something we stir up in ourselves.

God revealed himself to these women in unique ways, on special occasions, in particular places, and through specific acts. But he reveals himself to us even more abundantly through the gift of his Son and through his timeless Word. We can read for ourselves—absolutely and positively—that we are part of God's family because it pleased him to include us.

Whenever we struggle with those Slightly Bad Girl issues—trusting God completely, accepting his plan for our lives, resting in his sovereignty—here's one place we can turn for assurance: "God's gift has restored our relationship with him and given us back our lives."[17] Not your old Bad Girl life; your Forever Good Girl life, with a flawless God at the helm.

"And there's more life to come—an eternity of life!"[18] Abundant life. Endless life.

Your life, dear sister.

Study Guide

The questions at the end of each chapter are designed for both personal reflection and small-group use and are meant to stimulate our imaginations and spark lively discussions. Please don't make yourself crazy trying to come up with the "right" answer! What matters most is that you examine the biblical stories with care and apply what you've learned to your own life situations, seeking the Lord's leading.

The verses below will help keep your focus on God's Word as you consider your answers to each question. Opinions vary, but "the words of the LORD are flawless, like silver refined in a furnace of clay, purified seven times" (Psalm 12:6). May he richly bless the extra time you spend in his Word!

Sarai

1. Proverbs 31:11–12; Colossians 3:18–19; 1 Timothy 3:1–9
2. Luke 1:36–37; Isaiah 54:4–5; Matthew 10:29–31
3. Deuteronomy 13:4; Isaiah 58:11; Psalm 16:8
4. Psalm 91:9–10; Proverbs 31:30; Ecclesiastes 3:11
5. Ecclesiastes 7:8; Hebrews 6:12–15; Romans 12:12
6. Isaiah 47:10–11; Proverbs 14:1; Psalm 27:14
7. 1 Samuel 24:12; Lamentations 3:59; Proverbs 20:22

Hagar

1. Proverbs 3:34; Proverbs 11:2; Isaiah 5:15–16
2. Galatians 1:10; Matthew 10:22; Psalm 118:6
3. Leviticus 25:18; Psalm 119:60; Proverbs 17:28
4. Psalm 113:2–3; Psalm 33:13–15; 1 John 5:14
5. Proverbs 13:1; Proverbs 22:10; Proverbs 29:17

6. Psalm 63:1; Isaiah 41:17–18; John 4:13–14
7. Isaiah 45:5–6; Psalm 145:17; Isaiah 55:8–9

Sarah

1. Deuteronomy 30:19–20; Colossians 3:23–24; Romans 13:10
2. Hebrews 11:6; Psalm 78:38; 2 Corinthians 4:16
3. 2 Thessalonians 1:3–5; James 1:2–4; Ephesians 4:14–15
4. Psalm 29:4; Deuteronomy 5:24–25; Mark 4:22–23
5. Joshua 23:14; Acts 2:39; 2 Corinthians 1:20
6. Hebrews 11:17–19; James 2:21–23; Ephesians 5:1–2
7. Proverbs 5:18; Proverbs 31:23; Ephesians 5:33

Rebekah the Wife

1. Psalm 119:148; Ecclesiastes 9:17; Genesis 24:67
2. Judges 6:17; Psalm 86:17; John 2:11
3. Psalm 112:5; 1 Peter 4:9; Proverbs 16:2
4. 1 Corinthians 15:33; Ruth 3:11; Job 12:12
5. Isaiah 6:8; Isaiah 30:21; Isaiah 41:4
6. Proverbs 20:6; Proverbs 21:21; Psalm 85:10
7. Proverbs 31:28–29; Ephesians 6:4; 1 Corinthians 12:25–26

Rebekah the Mother

1. Genesis 49:28; Ephesians 1:3; 1 Chronicles 4:10
2. Proverbs 25:28; Psalm 19:12–14; 2 Peter 1:5–8
3. Proverbs 10:19; Proverbs 20:9; Acts 17:24–25
4. Psalm 34:13–14; Isaiah 3:12; Psalm 62:10
5. Leviticus 19:14; Proverbs 17:20; Micah 7:5–7
6. Deuteronomy 7:6–9; Proverbs 14:9; Psalm 38:18
7. Proverbs 21:8; 1 Corinthians 3:18–20; 2 Corinthians 4:2

Leah the Unseen

1. Isaiah 41:8–10; Titus 3:4–7; 2 Corinthians 5:21
2. Romans 12:6–8; Romans 11:29; 1 Corinthians 12:4–6
3. Ecclesiastes 2:22–23; 2 Corinthians 10:12; 10:18; Galatians 2:6
4. Galatians 5:26; 1 Peter 4:8; Matthew 18:15
5. 1 Corinthians 7:32–35; 1 Kings 11:4; Proverbs 29:20
6. Colossians 3:21; James 4:7; 1 Peter 5:8–10
7. Proverbs 14:8; John 3:19; Ephesians 5:17

Leah the Unloved

1. Psalm 69:19–20; Psalm 73:14; Psalm 88:13
2. Psalm 119:141; Proverbs 3:3–4; 1 Peter 3:1–2
3. Psalm 119:50; Romans 5:3–4; Ephesians 4:32
4. Hebrews 4:12; Jeremiah 17:10; Psalm 109:26–27
5. Matthew 11:29; Philippians 2:3; Ephesians 4:2
6. Psalm 34:15; Deuteronomy 26:7; Romans 15:13
7. Isaiah 37:16; Psalm 96:4; Revelation 15:4

Rachel

1. Proverbs 14:30; James 3:16; 1 Corinthians 13:4
2. Psalm 146:3; Psalm 20:7; Isaiah 26:4
3. Luke 12:15; Matthew 6:19–21; 1 John 3:17
4. Joel 2:12–13; Isaiah 50:7; Revelation 21:4
5. Proverbs 13:22; Proverbs 28:25; 1 Peter 3:9
6. Deuteronomy 29:17–18; Leviticus 19:18; Numbers 30:2
7. Ephesians 4:22–24; 1 John 3:2; 2 Corinthians 3:18

Notes

Introduction: Controlling Interest

1. Joseph Jacobs, ed., "Hercules and the Waggoner," Aesopica: Aesop's Fables in English, Latin and Greek, www.mythfolklore.net/aesopica/jacobs/61.htm.
2. Zephaniah 3:2
3. Romans 7:18
4. Romans 8:32
5. Naomi H. Rosenblatt and Joshua Horwitz, *Wrestling with Angels: What Genesis Teaches Us About Our Spiritual Identity, Sexuality, and Personal Relationships* (New York: Delta/Dell, 1995), 115.
6. 1 Peter 3:5–6
7. Janice Nunnally-Cox, *Foremothers: Women of the Bible* (New York: Seabury, 1981), 20.

Chapter One: Sarai

1. Julie-Allyson Ieron, *Names of Women of the Bible* (Chicago: Moody, 1998), 68.
2. Sherrilyn Kenyon, *The Writer's Digest Character Naming Sourcebook* (Cincinnati: Writer's Digest, 1994), 155.
3. Rose Sallberg Kam, *Their Stories, Our Stories: Women of the Bible* (New York: Continuum, 1995), 31.
4. Sue Richards and Larry Richards, *Every Woman in the Bible* (Nashville: Thomas Nelson, 1999), 31.
5. Harold John Ockenga, *Women Who Made Bible History: Messages and Character Sketches Dealing with Familiar Bible Women* (Grand Rapids: Zondervan, 1962), 21.
6. Tad Szulc, "Abraham: Journey of Faith," *National Geographic,* December 2001, 106.
7. Richards and Richards, *Every Woman in the Bible,* 31.
8. "The Royal Game of Ur: Historical Background," The Oriental University of the University of Chicago, https://oi.uchicago.edu/order/suq/products/urgamerules.html.
9. Ralph H. Elliott, *The Message of Genesis* (St. Louis, MO: Abbot Books, 1962), 102.
10. Sharon Pace Jeansonne, *The Women of Genesis: From Sarah to Potiphar's Wife* (Minneapolis: Fortress Press, 1990), 15.
11. Phyllis A. Bird, *Missing Persons and Mistaken Identities: Women and Gender in Ancient Israel* (Minneapolis: Fortress Press, 1997), 58.

12. Bird, *Missing Persons and Mistaken Identities,* 58.

13. Walter Brueggemann, *Genesis: A Bible Commentary for Teaching and Preaching* (Atlanta: John Knox, 1982), 116.

14. Szulc, "Abraham: Journey of Faith," 96.

15. George Matheson, *The Representative Women of the Bible* (London: Hodder and Stoughton, 1908), 61.

16. John H. Walton, Victor H. Matthews, and Mark W. Chavalas, *The IVP Bible Background Commentary: Old Testament* (Downers Grove, IL: InterVarsity, 2000), 43.

17. Brueggemann, *Genesis,* 118.

18. Georg Fohrer, *History of Israelite Religion,* trans. David E. Green (Nashville: Abingdon, 1972), 77–78.

19. John 12:26

20. Galatians 3:8

21. Galatians 3:8, MSG

22. Beth Moore, *The Patriarchs: Encountering the God of Abraham, Isaac, and Jacob* (Nashville: LifeWay, 2005), 15.

23. Derek Kidner, *Genesis: An Introduction and Commentary* (Downers Grove, IL: Tyndale, 1967), 117.

24. Kam, *Their Stories, Our Stories,* 34.

25. Genesis 19:26

26. LaJoyce Martin, *Mother Eve's Garden Club: No Halos Required* (Sisters, OR: Multnomah, 1993), 143.

27. Otto Kaiser, *Introduction to the Old Testament* (Minneapolis: Augsburg, 1977), 17.

28. Genesis 12:6

29. Gerhard von Rad, *Genesis: A Commentary* (Philadelphia: Westminster Press, 1972), 162.

30. Genesis 12:8

31. Walton, Matthews, Chavalas, *The IVP Bible Background Commentary: Old Testament,* 44.

32. Elliott, *The Message of Genesis,* 101.

33. Walton, Matthews, Chavalas, *The IVP Bible Background Commentary: Old Testament,* 44.

34. Carol Meyers, gen. ed., *Women in Scripture: A Dictionary of Named and Unnamed Women in the Hebrew Bible, the Apocryphal/Deuterocanonical Books and the New Testament* (New York: Houghton Mifflin, 2000), 34.

35. Naomi H. Rosenblatt and Joshua Horwitz, *Wrestling with Angels: What Genesis Teaches Us About Our Spiritual Identity, Sexuality, and Personal Relationships* (New York: Delta/Dell, 1995), 111.

36. Genesis 20:12
37. Claus Westermann, *Genesis 12–36: A Continental Commentary,* trans. John J. Scullion (Minneapolis: Fortress Press, 1995), 164.
38. Matthew Henry, *Matthew Henry's Commentary on the Whole Bible,* vol. 1, *Genesis to Deuteronomy* (1706; repr., Peabody, MA: Hendrickson, 1991), 71.
39. Brueggemann, *Genesis,* 126.
40. James G. Murphy, *Barnes' Notes: Genesis* (1873; repr., Grand Rapids: Baker, 1998), 270.
41. Margaret E. Sangster, *The Women of the Bible: A Portrait Gallery* (New York: Christian Herald, 1911), 41.
42. Meyers, *Women in Scripture,* 151.
43. Dave McAleer, comp., *The All Music Book of Hit Singles: Top Twenty Charts from 1954 to the Present Day* (San Francisco: Miller Freeman, 1994), 93.
44. Meyers, *Women in Scripture,* 150.
45. Jeansonne, *The Women of Genesis,* 17.
46. Matheson, *The Representative Women of the Bible,* 67.
47. Clyde Francisco, "Genesis," in *The Broadman Bible Commentary,* rev., gen. ed. Clifton J. Allen (Nashville: Broadman, 1969), 1:157.
48. Henry, *Matthew Henry's Commentary,* 71.
49. Henry, *Matthew Henry's Commentary,* 71.
50. Proverbs 31:30
51. John E. Hartley, *New International Biblical Commentary: Genesis* (Peabody, MA: Hendrickson, 2000), 139.
52. Hartley, *New International Biblical Commentary: Genesis,* 139.
53. Walton, Matthews, Chavalas, *The IVP Bible Background Commentary: Old Testament,* 44.
54. Hartley, *New International Biblical Commentary: Genesis,* 139.
55. Meyers, *Women in Scripture,* 143.
56. Kam, *Their Stories, Our Stories,* 34.
57. Anne Roiphe, *Water from the Well: Sarah, Rebekah, Rachel, and Leah* (New York: William Morrow, 2006), 45.
58. Von Rad, *Genesis: A Commentary,* 168.
59. Genesis 13:3
60. Genesis 13:3, NLT
61. Robert Alter, *Genesis: Translation and Commentary* (New York: W. W. Norton, 1996), 63.
62. Westermann, *Genesis 12–36: A Continental Commentary,* 219.
63. Murphy, *Barnes' Notes: Genesis,* 297.
64. Isaiah 64:6
65. Isaiah 64:8

66. Hebrews 11:1

67. John D. Currid, *Genesis* (Darlington, England: Evangelical Press, 2003), 1:301.

68. Westermann, *Genesis 12–36: A Continental Commentary,* 239.

69. Carolyn Custis James, *Lost Women of the Bible: Finding Strength and Significance Through Their Stories* (Grand Rapids: Zondervan, 2005), 87.

70. Hartley, *New International Biblical Commentary: Genesis,* 164.

71. Charles Henry Mackintosh, *Genesis to Deuteronomy: Notes on the Pentateuch* (1880; repr., Neptune, NJ: Loizeaux Brothers, 1972), 77.

72. Mackintosh, *Genesis to Deuteronomy,* 78.

73. Herbert Lockyer, *All the Women of the Bible* (Grand Rapids: Zondervan, 1967), 158.

74. Meyers, *Women in Scripture,* 86.

75. Matthew 22:21

76. Proverbs 16:3

77. Henry, *Matthew Henry's Commentary,* 85.

78. Westermann, *Genesis 12–36: A Continental Commentary,* 238–39.

79. Miki Raver, *Listen to Her Voice: Women of the Hebrew Bible* (San Francisco: Chronicle Books, 1998), 38.

80. John Calvin, *Genesis,* in *The Crossway Classic Commentaries* (1554; repr., Wheaton, IL: Crossway, 2001), 151.

81. Lockyer, *All the Women of the Bible,* 62.

82. Virginia Stem Owens, *Daughters of Eve: Women of the Bible Speak to Women of Today* (Colorado Springs: NavPress, 1995), 21.

83. Alter, *Genesis: Translation and Commentary,* 67.

84. Kidner, *Genesis: An Introduction and Commentary,* 126.

85. Kidner, *Genesis: An Introduction and Commentary,* 126.

86. Genesis 3:6

87. Barbara L. Thaw Ronson, *The Women of the Torah: Commentaries from the Talmud, Midrash, and Kabbalah* (Jerusalem: Jason Aronson, 1999), 23.

88. Katharine Doob Sakenfeld, *Just Wives? Stories of Power and Survival in the Old Testament and Today* (Louisville, KY: Westminster John Knox, 2003), 12.

89. Henry, *Matthew Henry's Commentary,* 86.

90. Alice Ogden Bellis, *Helpmates, Harlots, and Heroes: Women's Stories in the Hebrew Bible* (Louisville, KY: Westminster/John Knox, 1994), 74.

91. Ronson, *The Women of the Torah,* 23.

92. Lockyer, *All the Women of the Bible,* 62.

93. H. V. Morton, *Women of the Bible* (New York: Dodd, Mead, 1941), 24.

94. Morton, *Women of the Bible,* 25.

95. Peter Calvocoressi, *Who's Who in the Bible* (New York: Penguin Books, 1999), 165.

96. Sangster, *The Women of the Bible,* 53.

97. Morton, *Women of the Bible,* 24.

98. Currid, *Genesis,* 1:304.

99. Ephraim A. Speiser, *The Anchor Bible: Genesis* (New York: Doubleday, 1964), 118.

100. Alter, *Genesis: Translation and Commentary,* 68.

101. Rosenblatt and Horwitz, *Wrestling with Angels,* 143.

102. Gien Karssen, *Her Name Is Woman: Book Two* (Colorado Springs: NavPress, 1977), 23.

103. Francisco, "Genesis," 1:167.

104. Hartley, *New International Biblical Commentary: Genesis,* 165.

105. Hartley, *New International Biblical Commentary: Genesis,* 165.

106. Calvin, *Genesis,* 155.

107. Richards and Richards, *Every Woman in the Bible,* 41.

108. Owens, *Daughters of Eve,* 21.

109. Romans 4:16

110. Walter Wangerin, Jr., *The Book of God: The Bible as a Novel* (Grand Rapids: Zondervan, 1996), 20.

111. Francisco, "Genesis," 1:167.

112. Speiser, *The Anchor Bible: Genesis,* 118.

113. Marsha Pravder Mirkin, *The Women Who Danced by the Sea: Finding Ourselves in the Stories of Our Biblical Foremothers* (Rhinebeck, NY: Monkfish, 2004), 29.

114. Rosenblatt and Horwitz, *Wrestling with Angels,* 188.

115. Psalm 30:11

116. Psalm 37:3

117. Psalm 127:3, NLT

118. 2 Samuel 22:31

119. Ann Spangler and Jean E. Syswerda, *Women of the Bible* (Grand Rapids: Zondervan, 1999), 33.

Chapter Two: Hagar

1. Ann Spangler and Jean E. Syswerda, *Women of the Bible* (Grand Rapids: Zondervan, 1999), 35.

2. Frances Vander Velde, *Women of the Bible* (Grand Rapids: Kregel, 1985), 37.

3. Rose Sallberg Kam, *Their Stories, Our Stories: Women of the Bible* (New York: Continuum, 1995), 41.

4. Spangler and Syswerda, *Women of the Bible,* 33.

5. John E. Hartley, *New International Biblical Commentary: Genesis* (Peabody, MA: Hendrickson, 2000), 165.

6. Anne Roiphe, *Water from the Well: Sarah, Rebekah, Rachel, and Leah* (New York: William Morrow, 2006), 58.

7. Margaret E. Sangster, *The Women of the Bible: A Portrait Gallery* (New York: Christian Herald, 1911), 46.

8. Sangster, *The Women of the Bible,* 54.

9. Nora Ephron, *Heartburn* (Boston: G. K. Hall, 1983), 62.

10. Matthew Henry, *Matthew Henry's Commentary on the Whole Bible,* vol. 1, *Genesis to Deuteronomy* (1706; repr., Peabody, MA: Hendrickson, 1991), 86.

11. Julie-Allyson Ieron, *Names of Women of the Bible* (Chicago: Moody, 1998), 69.

12. C. F. Keil, *Commentary on the Old Testament,* vol. 1, *The Pentateuch* (1866–91; repr., Peabody, MA: Hendrickson, 1996), 140.

13. Ieron, *Names of Women of the Bible,* 672.

14. Carol Meyers, gen. ed., *Women in Scripture: A Dictionary of Named and Unnamed Women in the Hebrew Bible, the Apocryphal/Deuterocanonical Books and the New Testament* (New York: Houghton Mifflin, 2000), 86.

15. Herbert Lockyer, *All the Women of the Bible* (Grand Rapids: Zondervan, 1967), 62.

16. Carolyn Custis James, *Lost Women of the Bible: Finding Strength and Significance Through Their Stories* (Grand Rapids: Zondervan, 2005), 92.

17. William Mackintosh Mackay, *Bible Types of Modern Women* (New York: George H. Doran, 1922), 129.

18. Clyde Francisco, "Genesis," in *The Broadman Bible Commentary,* rev., gen. ed. Clifton J. Allen (Nashville: Broadman, 1969), 1:168.

19. Robert Alter, *Genesis: Translation and Commentary* (New York: W. W. Norton, 1996), 69.

20. Sue Richards and Larry Richards, *Every Woman in the Bible* (Nashville: Thomas Nelson, 1999), 39.

21. Henry, *Matthew Henry's Commentary,* 87.

22. Carolyn Nystrom, gen. ed., *The Bible for Today's Christian Woman, The Contemporary English Version* (Nashville: Thomas Nelson, 1998), 18.

23. Gerhard von Rad, *Genesis: A Commentary* (Philadelphia: Westminster Press, 1972), 194.

24. 1 Peter 2:18

25. 1 Peter 2:19, MSG

26. Von Rad, *Genesis: A Commentary,* 193.

27. James G. Murphy, *Barnes' Notes: Genesis* (1873; repr., Grand Rapids: Baker, 1998), 394.

28. Hartley, *New International Biblical Commentary: Genesis,* 166.

29. Marsha Pravder Mirkin, *The Women Who Danced by the Sea: Finding Ourselves in the Stories of Our Biblical Foremothers* (Rhinebeck, NY: Monkfish, 2004), 31.

30. Romans 11:33

31. John 3:16

32. Luke 1:31

33. Meyers, *Women in Scripture,* 87.

34. Von Rad, *Genesis: A Commentary,* 194.

35. Murphy, *Barnes' Notes: Genesis,* 394.
36. John H. Walton, Victor H. Matthews, and Mark W. Chavalas, *The IVP Bible Background Commentary: Old Testament* (Downers Grove, IL: InterVarsity, 2000), 49.
37. John Calvin, *Genesis,* in *The Crossway Classic Commentaries* (1554; repr., Wheaton, IL: Crossway, 2001), 158.
38. Exodus 33:20
39. Spangler and Syswerda, *Women of the Bible,* 33.
40. James, *Lost Women of the Bible,* 72.
41. Claus Westermann, *Genesis 12–36: A Continental Commentary,* trans. John J. Scullion (Minneapolis: Fortress Press, 1995), 339.
42. Nystrom, *The Bible for Today's Christian Woman, The Contemporary English Version,* 23.
43. Francisco, "Genesis," 1:184.
44. Roiphe, *Water from the Well,* 88.
45. Alice Ogden Bellis, *Helpmates, Harlots, and Heroes: Women's Stories in the Hebrew Bible* (Louisville, KY: Westminster/John Knox, 1994), 74.
46. Murphy, *Barnes' Notes: Genesis,* 332.
47. George Matheson, *The Representative Women of the Bible* (London: Hodder and Stoughton, 1908), 73.
48. Calvin, *Genesis,* 195.
49. Avivah Gottlieb Zornberg, *The Beginning of Desire: Reflections on Genesis* (New York: Doubleday, 1995), 135.
50. Westermann, *Genesis 12–36: A Continental Commentary,* 339.
51. Hartley, *New International Biblical Commentary: Genesis,* 199.
52. Jonathan Kirsch, *The Harlot by the Side of the Road: Forbidden Tales of the Bible* (New York: Ballantine, 1997), 50.
53. Francisco, "Genesis," 1:185.
54. Walter Brueggemann, *Genesis: A Bible Commentary for Teaching and Preaching* (Atlanta: John Knox, 1982), 183.
55. Brueggemann, *Genesis,* 183.
56. Calvin, *Genesis,* 196.
57. Calvin, *Genesis,* 197.
58. "Hagar," Single Parent Online Retreat, www.singleparent.org/hagar.htm.
59. Genesis 16:10
60. John D. Currid, *Genesis* (Darlington, England: Evangelical Press, 2003), 1:377.
61. Murphy, *Barnes' Notes: Genesis,* 333.
62. Keil, *The Pentateuch,* 156.
63. Revelation 19:6, KJV
64. Ephraim A. Speiser, *The Anchor Bible: Genesis* (New York: Doubleday, 1964), 156.

65. Genesis 25:16
66. Murphy, *Barnes' Notes: Genesis,* 334.
67. Keil, *The Pentateuch,* 157.
68. Genesis 1:2
69. Revelation 22:17
70. Christiana de Groot, "Genesis," in *The IVP Women's Bible Commentary,* ed. Catherine Clark Kroeger and Mary J. Evans (Downers Grove, IL: InterVarsity, 2002), 13.
71. Katharine Doob Sakenfeld, *Just Wives? Stories of Power and Survival in the Old Testament and Today* (Louisville, KY: Westminster John Knox, 2003), 23.
72. Genesis 21:16
73. Sangster, *The Women of the Bible,* 55.
74. Michael E. Williams, ed., *The Storyteller's Companion to the Bible,* vol. 4, *Old Testament Women* (Nashville: Abingdon, 1993), 23.
75. Edith Deen, *All the Women of the Bible* (New York: Harper & Row, 1955), 266.
76. Tad Szulc, "Abraham: Journey of Faith," *National Geographic,* December 2001, 122.
77. Meyers, *Women in Scripture,* 87.
78. "Links to Images of Hagar/Ishmael," The Text This Week, www.textweek.com/art/hagar_Ishmael.htm.
79. Jeremiah 2:6

Chapter Three: Sarah

1. 1 Kings 9:4
2. Genesis 17:3, NLT
3. Harold John Ockenga, *Women Who Made Bible History: Messages and Character Sketches Dealing with Familiar Bible Women* (Grand Rapids: Zondervan, 1962), 21.
4. Barbara L. Thaw Ronson, *The Women of the Torah: Commentaries from the Talmud, Midrash, and Kabbalah* (Jerusalem: Jason Aronson, 1999), 28.
5. Rose Sallberg Kam, *Their Stories, Our Stories: Women of the Bible* (New York: Continuum, 1995), 34–35.
6. Kam, *Their Stories, Our Stories,* 53.
7. Meredith G. Kline, "Genesis," in *The New Bible Commentary Revised* (Grand Rapids: Eerdmans, 1970), 97.
8. John H. Walton, Victor H. Matthews, and Mark W. Chavalas, *The IVP Bible Background Commentary: Old Testament* (Downers Grove, IL: InterVarsity, 2000), 50.
9. Walton, Matthews, Chavalas, *The IVP Bible Background Commentary: Old Testament,* 50.
10. Ephraim A. Speiser, *The Anchor Bible: Genesis* (New York: Doubleday, 1964), 130.
11. John D. Currid, *Genesis* (Darlington, England: Evangelical Press, 2003), 1:326.

12. John E. Hartley, *New International Biblical Commentary: Genesis* (Peabody, MA: Hendrickson, 2000), 178.

13. Hartley, *New International Biblical Commentary: Genesis,* 178.

14. Matthew Henry, *Matthew Henry's Commentary on the Whole Bible,* vol. 1, *Genesis to Deuteronomy* (1706; repr., Peabody, MA: Hendrickson, 1991), 94.

15. Romans 10:17

16. Sharon Pace Jeansonne, *The Women of Genesis: From Sarah to Potiphar's Wife* (Minneapolis: Fortress Press, 1990), 23.

17. Robert Alter, *Genesis: Translation and Commentary* (New York: W. W. Norton, 1996), 79.

18. Genesis 25:1–2, 6

19. Alter, *Genesis: Translation and Commentary,* 79; Virginia Stem Owens, *Daughters of Eve: Women of the Bible Speak to Women of Today* (Colorado Springs: NavPress, 1995), 22; Derek Kidner, *Genesis: An Introduction and Commentary* (Downers Grove, IL: Tyndale, 1967), 132; James G. Murphy, *Barnes' Notes: Genesis* (1873; repr., Grand Rapids: Baker, 1998), 316; Avivah Gottlieb Zornberg, *The Beginning of Desire: Reflections on Genesis* (New York: Doubleday, 1995), 113.

20. C. F. Keil, *Commentary on the Old Testament,* vol. 1, *The Pentateuch* (1866–91; repr., Peabody, MA: Hendrickson, 1996), 146.

21. Henry, *Matthew Henry's Commentary,* 94.

22. Vanessa Ochs, *Sarah Laughed: Modern Lessons from the Wisdom and Stories of Biblical Women* (New York: McGraw-Hill, 2005), 111.

23. Exodus 9:5

24. Isaiah 51:6

25. Psalm 33:20

26. Currid, *Genesis,* 1:327.

27. Alter, *Genesis: Translation and Commentary,* 79.

28. Gerhard von Rad, *Genesis: A Commentary* (Philadelphia: Westminster Press, 1972), 207.

29. LaJoyce Martin, *Mother Eve's Garden Club: No Halos Required* (Sisters, OR: Multnomah, 1993), 141.

30. Clyde Francisco, "Genesis," in *The Broadman Bible Commentary,* rev., gen. ed. Clifton J. Allen (Nashville: Broadman, 1969), 1:174.

31. Hartley, *New International Biblical Commentary: Genesis,* 179.

32. John Calvin, *Genesis,* in *The Crossway Classic Commentaries* (1554; repr., Wheaton, IL: Crossway, 2001), 175.

33. Calvin, *Genesis,* 175.

34. Luke 1:50

35. Anne Roiphe, *Water from the Well: Sarah, Rebekah, Rachel, and Leah* (New York: William Morrow, 2006), 79.

36. Ochs, *Sarah Laughed*, 114.
37. Kam, *Their Stories, Our Stories,* 35.
38. Alter, *Genesis: Translation and Commentary,* 97.
39. "Grandmother Gives Birth to Triplets," *Portsmouth Herald,* January 9, 2000, www.seacoastonline.com/2000news/1_9_w1.htm.
40. Roiphe, *Water from the Well,* 95.
41. Genesis 21:6, NCV
42. Genesis 12:4
43. Genesis 16:16
44. Genesis 21:5
45. Genesis 18:14
46. Carolyn Nabors Baker, *Caught in a Higher Love: Inspiring Stories of Women in the Bible* (Nashville: Broadman & Holman, 1998), 18.
47. Genesis 21:6, KJV
48. Kline, "Genesis," 7.
49. Janice Nunnally-Cox, *Foremothers: Women of the Bible* (New York: Seabury, 1981), 9.
50. Owens, *Daughters of Eve,* 25.
51. Romans 10:9

Chapter Four: Rebekah the Wife

1. Genesis 24:2, KJV
2. Genesis 24:6, NASB
3. Psalm 139:4
4. Rose Sallberg Kam, *Their Stories, Our Stories: Women of the Bible* (New York: Continuum, 1995), 52.
5. Anna Trimiew, *Bible Almanac* (Lincolnwood, IL: Publications International, 1997), 234.
6. John H. Walton, Victor H. Matthews, and Mark W. Chavalas, *The IVP Bible Background Commentary: Old Testament* (Downers Grove, IL: InterVarsity, 2000), 56.
7. Robert Alter, *Genesis: Translation and Commentary* (New York: W. W. Norton, 1996), 116.
8. Walton, Matthews, Chavalas, *The IVP Bible Background Commentary: Old Testament,* 56.
9. Walton, Matthews, Chavalas, *The IVP Bible Background Commentary: Old Testament,* 56.
10. Claus Westermann, *Genesis 12–36: A Continental Commentary,* trans. John J. Scullion (Minneapolis: Fortress Press, 1995), 387.
11. Alter, *Genesis: Translation and Commentary,* 120.
12. Walton, Matthews, Chavalas, *The IVP Bible Background Commentary: Old Testament,* 56.

13. Westermann, *Genesis 12–36: A Continental Commentary,* 388.

14. Dietrich Gruen, contrib. ed., *Who's Who in the Bible* (Lincolnwood, IL: Publications International, 1997), 336.

15. Ephraim A. Speiser, *The Anchor Bible: Genesis* (New York: Doubleday, 1964), 184.

16. Alter, *Genesis: Translation and Commentary,* 117.

17. George Arthur Buttrick, dictionary ed., *The Interpreter's Dictionary of the Bible* (New York: Abingdon Press, 1962), 3:51.

18. James 1:17

19. Ann Spangler and Jean E. Syswerda, *Women of the Bible* (Grand Rapids: Zondervan, 1999), 47.

20. Julie-Allyson Ieron, *Names of Women of the Bible* (Chicago: Moody, 1998), 76.

21. Sherrilyn Kenyon, *The Writer's Digest Character Naming Sourcebook* (Cincinnati: Writer's Digest, 1994), 154.

22. Westermann, *Genesis 12–36: A Continental Commentary,* 389.

23. Clyde Francisco, "Genesis," in *The Broadman Bible Commentary,* rev., gen. ed. Clifton J. Allen (Nashville: Broadman, 1969), 1:196.

24. Virginia Stem Owens, *Daughters of Eve: Women of the Bible Speak to Women of Today* (Colorado Springs: NavPress, 1995), 151.

25. Westermann, *Genesis 12–36: A Continental Commentary,* 389.

26. Walton, Matthews, Chavalas, *The IVP Bible Background Commentary: Old Testament,* 56.

27. Marsha Pravder Mirkin, *The Women Who Danced by the Sea: Finding Ourselves in the Stories of Our Biblical Foremothers* (Rhinebeck, NY: Monkfish, 2004), 55.

28. Anne Roiphe, *Water from the Well: Sarah, Rebekah, Rachel, and Leah* (New York: William Morrow, 2006), 118.

29. Mirkin, *The Women Who Danced by the Sea,* 55.

30. Genesis 35:8

31. Vanessa Ochs, *Sarah Laughed: Modern Lessons from the Wisdom and Stories of Biblical Women* (New York: McGraw-Hill, 2005), 126.

32. 1 Samuel 25:23

33. Alter, *Genesis: Translation and Commentary,* 122.

34. James M. Freeman, *Manners and Customs of the Bible* (New Kensington, PA: Whitaker House, 1996), 82.

35. Miki Raver, *Listen to Her Voice: Women of the Hebrew Bible* (San Francisco: Chronicle Books, 1998), 36.

36. James G. Murphy, *Barnes' Notes: Genesis* (1873; repr., Grand Rapids: Baker, 1998), 357.

37. Genesis 25:20

38. 1 John 4:19

39. George Matheson, *The Representative Women of the Bible* (London: Hodder and Stoughton, 1908), 87.

40. Genesis 25:20–21, CEV

41. John E. Hartley, *New International Biblical Commentary: Genesis* (Peabody, MA: Hendrickson, 2000), 235.

42. Genesis 22:14

43. Matthew Henry, *Matthew Henry's Commentary on the Whole Bible,* vol. 1, *Genesis to Deuteronomy* (1706; repr., Peabody, MA: Hendrickson, 1991), 124.

44. Francisco, "Genesis," 1:199.

45. Henry, *Matthew Henry's Commentary,* 124.

46. Speiser, *The Anchor Bible: Genesis,* 193.

47. Hartley, *New International Biblical Commentary: Genesis,* 235.

48. Genesis 3:16, AMP

49. Westermann, *Genesis 12–36: A Continental Commentary,* 413.

50. Francisco, "Genesis," 1:199–200.

51. Derek Kidner, *Genesis: An Introduction and Commentary* (Downers Grove, IL: Tyndale, 1967), 151.

52. Hartley, *New International Biblical Commentary: Genesis,* 235.

53. Kidner, *Genesis: An Introduction and Commentary,* 151.

54. Kidner, *Genesis: An Introduction and Commentary,* 151.

55. Genesis 4:4–5

56. Hartley, *New International Biblical Commentary: Genesis,* 236.

57. 2 Samuel 7:22

58. John Calvin, *Genesis,* in *The Crossway Classic Commentaries* (1554; repr., Wheaton, IL: Crossway, 2001), 224.

59. Kidner, *Genesis: An Introduction and Commentary,* 151.

60. Alter, *Genesis: Translation and Commentary,* 128.

61. Francisco, "Genesis," 1:200.

62. Henry, *Matthew Henry's Commentary,* 125.

63. Sarah Towne Smith Martyn, *Women of the Bible* (New York: American Tract Society, 1868), 9.

64. Kidner, *Genesis: An Introduction and Commentary,* 152.

65. Alice Ogden Bellis, *Helpmates, Harlots, and Heroes: Women's Stories in the Hebrew Bible* (Louisville, KY: Westminster/John Knox, 1994), 84.

66. Deuteronomy 21:17

67. Francisco, "Genesis," 1:201.

68. Murphy, *Barnes' Notes: Genesis,* 368.

69. Roiphe, *Water from the Well,* 140.

70. Hartley, *New International Biblical Commentary: Genesis,* 236.

71. Genesis 25:29

72. Genesis 25:33
73. Freeman, *Manners and Customs of the Bible,* 32–33.
74. Genesis 25:23
75. Francisco, "Genesis," 1:201.
76. Sylvia Charles, *Women in the Word* (South Plainfield, NJ: Bridge Publishing, 1984), 19.
77. H. V. Morton, *Women of the Bible* (New York: Dodd, Mead, 1941), 41.
78. Morton, *Women of the Bible,* 40.
79. Barbara J. Essex, *Bad Girls of the Bible: Exploring Women of Questionable Virtue* (Cleveland, OH: United Church Press, 1999), 29.
80. Henry T. Sell, *Studies of Famous Bible Women* (New York: Revell, 1925), 23.
81. LaJoyce Martin, *Mother Eve's Garden Club: No Halos Required* (Sisters, OR: Multnomah, 1993), 130.
82. Raver, *Listen to Her Voice,* 51.
83. Morton, *Women of the Bible,* 41.
84. Murphy, *Barnes' Notes: Genesis,* 367.

Chapter Five: Rebekah the Mother

1. John E. Hartley, *New International Biblical Commentary: Genesis* (Peabody, MA: Hendrickson, 2000), 246.
2. Hartley, *New International Biblical Commentary: Genesis,* 247.
3. Ephraim A. Speiser, *The Anchor Bible: Genesis* (New York: Doubleday, 1964), 212.
4. Deuteronomy 14:4–5
5. James M. Freeman, *Manners and Customs of the Bible* (New Kensington, PA: Whitaker House, 1996), 34.
6. Derek Kidner, *Genesis: An Introduction and Commentary* (Downers Grove, IL: Tyndale, 1967), 156.
7. Rose Sallberg Kam, *Their Stories, Our Stories: Women of the Bible* (New York: Continuum, 1995), 53.
8. Christiana de Groot, "Genesis," in *The IVP Women's Bible Commentary,* ed. Catherine Clark Kroeger and Mary J. Evans (Downers Grove, IL: InterVarsity, 2002), 17.
9. Frances Vander Velde, *Women of the Bible* (Grand Rapids: Kregel, 1985), 49.
10. Vander Velde, *Women of the Bible,* 49.
11. George Matheson, *The Representative Women of the Bible* (London: Hodder and Stoughton, 1908), 96.
12. Hartley, *New International Biblical Commentary: Genesis,* 248.
13. Justin Kaplan, ed., *Bartlett's Familiar Quotations: A Collection of Passages, Phrases, and Proverbs Traced to Their Sources in Ancient and Modern Literature,* 16th ed. (Boston: Little, Brown, 1992), 462.

14. Proverbs 25:21

15. Margaret E. Sangster, *The Women of the Bible: A Portrait Gallery* (New York: Christian Herald, 1911), 90.

16. Sarah Towne Smith Martyn, *Women of the Bible* (New York: American Tract Society, 1868), 9.

17. Warren W. Wiersbe, *Be Authentic: Genesis 25–50: Exhibiting Real Faith in the Real World* (Colorado Springs: Chariot Victor, 1997), 27.

18. Genesis 12:3

19. Anne Roiphe, *Water from the Well: Sarah, Rebekah, Rachel, and Leah* (New York: William Morrow, 2006), 162.

20. 1 John 4:10

21. Claus Westermann, *Genesis 12–36: A Continental Commentary,* trans. John J. Scullion (Minneapolis: Fortress Press, 1995), 439.

22. James G. Murphy, *Barnes' Notes: Genesis* (1873; repr., Grand Rapids: Baker, 1998), 382.

23. Westermann, *Genesis 12–36: A Continental Commentary,* 438.

24. Henry T. Sell, *Studies of Famous Bible Women* (New York: Revell, 1925), 22.

25. Gerhard von Rad, *Genesis: A Commentary* (Philadelphia: Westminster Press, 1972), 277.

26. Meredith G. Kline, "Genesis," in *The New Bible Commentary Revised* (Grand Rapids: Eerdmans, 1970), 102.

27. Clyde Francisco, "Genesis," in *The Broadman Bible Commentary,* rev., gen. ed. Clifton J. Allen (Nashville: Broadman, 1969), 1:206.

28. Matthew Henry, *Matthew Henry's Commentary on the Whole Bible,* vol. 1, *Genesis to Deuteronomy* (1706; repr., Peabody, MA: Hendrickson, 1991), 133.

29. Hartley, *New International Biblical Commentary: Genesis,* 250–51.

30. Francisco, "Genesis," 1:207.

31. Hartley, *New International Biblical Commentary: Genesis,* 251.

32. Speiser, *The Anchor Bible: Genesis,* 207.

33. Von Rad, *Genesis: A Commentary,* 279.

34. Francisco, "Genesis," 1:207.

35. Hartley, *New International Biblical Commentary: Genesis,* 252.

36. Deuteronomy 19:21

37. Westermann, *Genesis 12–36: A Continental Commentary,* 443.

38. Hartley, *New International Biblical Commentary: Genesis,* 252.

39. Kidner, *Genesis: An Introduction and Commentary,* 157.

40. Genesis 26:35

41. Genesis 26:34

42. Genesis 25:22, MSG

43. Francisco, "Genesis," 1:206.

44. Sangster, *The Women of the Bible,* 90.
45. Martyn, *Women of the Bible,* 9.
46. Barbara J. Essex, *Bad Girls of the Bible: Exploring Women of Questionable Virtue* (Cleveland, OH: United Church Press, 1999), 28.
47. John Calvin, *Genesis,* in *The Crossway Classic Commentaries* (1554; repr., Wheaton, IL: Crossway, 2001), 238.
48. Sell, *Studies of Famous Bible Women,* 23.
49. Norma Rosen, *Biblical Women Unbound: Counter-Tales* (Philadelphia: Jewish Publication Society, 1996), 66.
50. Essex, *Bad Girls of the Bible,* 28.
51. Westermann, *Genesis 12–36: A Continental Commentary,* 438.
52. Roiphe, *Water from the Well,* 169.
53. Henry, *Matthew Henry's Commentary,* 131.
54. Job 12:16
55. Edith Deen, *Wisdom from Women in the Bible* (New York: HarperCollins, 2003), 15.
56. Ephesians 6:10
57. Isaiah 8:17
58. Galatians 3:9
59. Hebrews 12:17

Chapter Six: Leah the Unseen
1. Acts 9:15
2. 2 Corinthians 9:15
3. Genesis 48:3
4. John E. Hartley, *New International Biblical Commentary: Genesis* (Peabody, MA: Hendrickson, 2000), 256.
5. Matthew 28:20
6. Matthew Henry, *Matthew Henry's Commentary on the Whole Bible,* vol. 1, *Genesis to Deuteronomy* (1706; repr., Peabody, MA: Hendrickson, 1991), 138.
7. Barbara L. Thaw Ronson, *The Women of the Torah: Commentaries from the Talmud, Midrash, and Kabbalah* (Jerusalem: Jason Aronson, 1999), 113.
8. George Arthur Buttrick, dictionary ed., *The Interpreter's Dictionary of the Bible* (New York: Abingdon Press, 1962), 4:317.
9. Derek Kidner, *Genesis: An Introduction and Commentary* (Downers Grove, IL: Tyndale, 1967), 159.
10. Warren W. Wiersbe, *Be Authentic: Genesis 25–50: Exhibiting Real Faith in the Real World* (Colorado Springs: Chariot Victor, 1997), 34.
11. James G. Murphy, *Barnes' Notes: Genesis* (1873; repr., Grand Rapids: Baker, 1998), 387.

12. Clyde Francisco, "Genesis," in *The Broadman Bible Commentary*, rev., gen. ed. Clifton J. Allen (Nashville: Broadman, 1969), 1:212.

13. Edith Deen, *All the Women of the Bible* (New York: Harper & Row, 1955), 29.

14. Murphy, *Barnes' Notes: Genesis*, 391.

15. Ephraim A. Speiser, *The Anchor Bible: Genesis* (New York: Doubleday, 1964), 222.

16. Rose Sallberg Kam, *Their Stories, Our Stories: Women of the Bible* (New York: Continuum, 1995), 62.

17. Dorothy Kelley Patterson, gen. ed., *The Woman's Study Bible, The New King James Version* (Nashville: Thomas Nelson, 1995), 57.

18. Irene Nowell, *Women in the Old Testament* (Collegeville, MN: Liturgical Press, 1997), 30.

19. Henry, *Matthew Henry's Commentary*, 140.

20. Michael E. Williams, ed., *The Storyteller's Companion to the Bible*, vol. 4, *Old Testament Women* (Nashville: Abingdon, 1993), 146.

21. Kam, *Their Stories, Our Stories*, 62.

22. Sharon Pace Jeansonne, *The Women of Genesis: From Sarah to Potiphar's Wife* (Minneapolis: Fortress Press, 1990), 71.

23. Meredith G. Kline, "Genesis," in *The New Bible Commentary Revised* (Grand Rapids: Eerdmans, 1970), 103.

24. Harold John Ockenga, *Women Who Made Bible History: Messages and Character Sketches Dealing with Familiar Bible Women* (Grand Rapids: Zondervan, 1962), 37.

25. Kathy Collard Miller, *Women of the Bible* (Lancaster, PA: Starburst, 1999), 69.

26. Carol Meyers, gen. ed., *Women in Scripture: A Dictionary of Named and Unnamed Women in the Hebrew Bible, the Apocryphal/Deuterocanonical Books and the New Testament* (New York: Houghton Mifflin, 2000), 139.

27. Speiser, *The Anchor Bible: Genesis*, 222.

28. Ronson, *The Women of the Torah*, 120.

29. Speiser, *The Anchor Bible: Genesis*, 222.

30. William P. Barker, *Everyone in the Bible* (Old Tappan, NJ: Revell, 1966), 157.

31. Ronson, *The Women of the Torah*, 120.

32. Leonard J. Swidler, *Biblical Affirmations of Woman* (Philadelphia: Westminster Press, 1979), 141.

33. Williams, *Old Testament Women*, 146.

34. Williams, *Old Testament Women*, 146.

35. Meyers, *Women in Scripture*, 109.

36. Gerhard von Rad, *Genesis: A Commentary* (Philadelphia: Westminster Press, 1972), 291.

37. James M. Freeman, *Manners and Customs of the Bible* (New Kensington, PA: Whitaker House, 1996), 37.

38. Eugenia Price, *God Speaks to Women Today* (Grand Rapids: Zondervan, 1964), 62.

39. Julie-Allyson Ieron, *Names of Women of the Bible* (Chicago: Moody, 1998), 81.

40. Norma Rosen, *Biblical Women Unbound: Counter-Tales* (Philadelphia: Jewish Publication Society, 1996), 79.

41. Francis Brown, *The New Brown-Driver-Briggs-Gensenius Hebrew and English Lexicon* (Lafayette, IN: Associated Publishers and Authors, 1980), 940.

42. Sue Richards and Larry Richards, *Every Woman in the Bible* (Nashville: Thomas Nelson, 1999), 46.

43. Ronson, *The Women of the Torah*, 123.

44. Matthew 6:22

45. Ieron, *Names of Women of the Bible*, 85.

46. Alice Ogden Bellis, *Helpmates, Harlots, and Heroes: Women's Stories in the Hebrew Bible* (Louisville, KY: Westminster/John Knox, 1994), 85.

47. Deen, *All the Women of the Bible*, 31.

48. H. V. Morton, *Women of the Bible* (New York: Dodd, Mead, 1941), 46.

49. Miki Raver, *Listen to Her Voice: Women of the Hebrew Bible* (San Francisco: Chronicle Books, 1998), 63.

50. Genesis 28:2

51. Ronson, *The Women of the Torah*, 124.

52. Morton, *Women of the Bible*, 44.

53. Miller, *Women of the Bible*, 71.

54. Paul C. Brownlow, *A Shepherd's Heart* (Fort Worth, TX: Brownlow, 1997), 22.

55. Ronson, *The Women of the Torah*, 124.

56. Francisco, "Genesis," 1:213.

57. Morton Bryan Wharton, *Famous Women of the Old Testament: A Series of Popular Lectures Delivered in the First Baptist Church, Montgomery, Alabama* (Chicago: W. P. Blessing, 1889), 71.

58. Ronson, *The Women of the Torah*, 125.

59. Robert Alter, *Genesis: Translation and Commentary* (New York: W. W. Norton, 1996), 154.

60. Jeansonne, *The Women of Genesis*, note 8, 134.

61. Raver, *Listen to Her Voice*, 63.

62. George Matheson, *The Representative Women of the Bible* (London: Hodder and Stoughton, 1908), 113.

63. Freeman, *Manners and Customs of the Bible*, 32.

64. Kam, *Their Stories, Our Stories*, 59.

65. Margaret E. Sangster, *The Women of the Bible: A Portrait Gallery* (New York: Christian Herald, 1911), 67.

66. Von Rad, *Genesis: A Commentary*, 291.

67. Psalm 94:1, NASB

68. Patterson, *The Woman's Study Bible, The New King James Version*, 61.
69. Jill Briscoe, *Running on Empty* (Wheaton, IL: Harold Shaw, 1995), 30.
70. Frances Vander Velde, *Women of the Bible* (Grand Rapids: Kregel, 1985), 60.
71. Von Rad, *Genesis: A Commentary*, 292.
72. Vander Velde, *Women of the Bible*, 61.
73. Revelation 4:11, KJV
74. Matheson, *The Representative Women of the Bible*, 114.
75. Bellis, *Helpmates, Harlots, and Heroes*, 85.
76. James 4:17

Chapter Seven: Leah the Unloved

1. Carolyn Nabors Baker, *Caught in a Higher Love: Inspiring Stories of Women in the Bible* (Nashville: Broadman & Holman, 1998), 68.
2. Matthew Henry, *Matthew Henry's Commentary on the Whole Bible*, vol. 1, *Genesis to Deuteronomy* (1706; repr., Peabody, MA: Hendrickson, 1991), 141.
3. Henry, *Matthew Henry's Commentary*, 141.
4. Gien Karssen, *Her Name Is Woman: Book Two* (Colorado Springs: NavPress, 1977), 49.
5. Frances Vander Velde, *Women of the Bible* (Grand Rapids: Kregel, 1985), 61.
6. James M. Freeman, *Manners and Customs of the Bible* (New Kensington, PA: Whitaker House, 1996), 37.
7. Henry, *Matthew Henry's Commentary*, 141.
8. John H. Walton, Victor H. Matthews, and Mark W. Chavalas, *The IVP Bible Background Commentary: Old Testament* (Downers Grove, IL: InterVarsity, 2000), 62.
9. John Calvin, *Genesis*, in *The Crossway Classic Commentaries* (1554; repr., Wheaton, IL: Crossway, 2001), 254.
10. Henry, *Matthew Henry's Commentary*, 141.
11. Ethel Clark Lewis, *Portraits of Bible Women* (New York: Vantage Press, 1956), 72.
12. Eugenia Price, *God Speaks to Women Today* (Grand Rapids: Zondervan, 1964), 68.
13. Genesis 2:24
14. George Arthur Buttrick, dictionary ed., *The Interpreter's Dictionary of the Bible* (New York: Abingdon Press, 1962), 3:280.
15. Leviticus 18:18
16. Anne Roiphe, *Water from the Well: Sarah, Rebekah, Rachel, and Leah* (New York: William Morrow, 2006), 198.
17. Kathy Collard Miller, *Women of the Bible* (Lancaster, PA: Starburst, 1999), 75.
18. Job 34:21
19. Warren W. Wiersbe, *Be Authentic: Genesis 25–50: Exhibiting Real Faith in the Real World* (Colorado Springs: Chariot Victor, 1997), 42.

20. James Faulkner, *Romances and Intrigues of the Women of the Bible* (New York: Vantage Press, 1957), 32.

21. Henry, *Matthew Henry's Commentary,* 141.

22. Robert Alter, *Genesis: Translation and Commentary* (New York: W. W. Norton, 1996), 155.

23. Deuteronomy 21:15, 17

24. Proverbs 30:21

25. Proverbs 30:23

26. Genesis 29:31

27. Jill Briscoe, *Running on Empty* (Wheaton, IL: Harold Shaw, 1995), 32.

28. 2 Chronicles 16:9

29. Sharon Pace Jeansonne, *The Women of Genesis: From Sarah to Potiphar's Wife* (Minneapolis: Fortress Press, 1990), 75.

30. Exodus 33:19

31. Henry, *Matthew Henry's Commentary,* 142.

32. Alter, *Genesis: Translation and Commentary,* 199.

33. *The Holy Bible, New Living Translation* (Wheaton, IL: Tyndale, 1996), note on Genesis 29:32.

34. Ephraim A. Speiser, *The Anchor Bible: Genesis* (New York: Doubleday, 1964), 228.

35. Alter, *Genesis: Translation and Commentary,* 156.

36. Psalm 127:4

37. *The Holy Bible, New Living Translation,* note on Genesis 29:33.

38. Vanessa Ochs, *Sarah Laughed: Modern Lessons from the Wisdom and Stories of Biblical Women* (New York: McGraw-Hill, 2005), 180.

39. Roiphe, *Water from the Well,* 207.

40. Julia Staton, *What the Bible Says About Women* (Joplin, MO: College Press, 1980), 153.

41. Staton, *What the Bible Says About Women,* 152.

42. Briscoe, *Running on Empty,* 31.

43. Karssen, *Her Name Is Woman,* 40–41.

44. Speiser, *The Anchor Bible: Genesis,* 228.

45. Dorothy Kelley Patterson, gen. ed., *The Woman's Study Bible, The New King James Version* (Nashville: Thomas Nelson, 1995), 61.

46. Ochs, *Sarah Laughed,* 180.

47. *The Holy Bible, New Living Translation,* note on Genesis 29:35.

48. Isaiah 61:3

49. Alter, *Genesis: Translation and Commentary,* 157.

50. Genesis 49:31

51. Ralph H. Elliott, *The Message of Genesis* (St. Louis, MO: Abbot Books, 1962), 168.

52. Hebrews 7:14

53. Henry, *Matthew Henry's Commentary*, 142.

54. Matthew 1:1–2

55. John E. Hartley, *New International Biblical Commentary: Genesis* (Peabody, MA: Hendrickson, 2000), 262.

56. Psalm 113:9, ICB

57. Staton, *What the Bible Says About Women*, 195.

58. Romans 12:12

59. Ochs, *Sarah Laughed*, 180.

60. "Popular Baby Names," Social Security Administration, www.ssa.gov/OACT/babynames.

61. Herbert Lockyer, *All the Women of the Bible* (Grand Rapids: Zondervan, 1967), 83.

62. Roiphe, *Water from the Well*, 250.

63. Charles Henry Mackintosh, *Genesis to Deuteronomy: Notes on the Pentateuch* (1880; repr., Neptune, NJ: Loizeaux Brothers, 1972), 114.

64. Margaret E. Sangster, *The Women of the Bible: A Portrait Gallery* (New York: Christian Herald, 1911), 71.

65. Baker, *Caught in a Higher Love*, 71.

66. Henry, *Matthew Henry's Commentary*, 141.

67. Patterson, *The Woman's Study Bible, The New King James Version*, 61.

Chapter Eight: Rachel

1. Frederick Buechner, *The Son of Laughter: A Novel* (New York: HarperSan Francisco, 1994), 124.

2. Frederick Drimmer, *Daughters of Eve: Women in the Bible* (Norwalk, CT: C. R. Gibson, 1975), 61.

3. Song of Songs 8:6, KJV

4. Norman J. Cohen, *Self, Struggle and Change: Family Conflict Stories in Genesis and Their Healing Insights for Our Lives* (Woodstock, VT: Jewish Lights, 1995), 137.

5. Edith Deen, *All the Women of the Bible* (New York: Harper & Row, 1955), 31.

6. H. V. Morton, *Women of the Bible* (New York: Dodd, Mead, 1941), 47.

7. Genesis 29:21

8. Genesis 25:30, NLT

9. Avivah Gottlieb Zornberg, *The Beginning of Desire: Reflections on Genesis* (New York: Doubleday, 1995), 210.

10. Robert Alter, *Genesis: Translation and Commentary* (New York: W. W. Norton, 1996), 158.

11. Barbara L. Thaw Ronson, *The Women of the Torah: Commentaries from the Talmud, Midrash, and Kabbalah* (Jerusalem: Jason Aronson, 1999), 136.

12. Alter, *Genesis: Translation and Commentary*, 158.

13. Jill Briscoe, *Running on Empty* (Wheaton, IL: Harold Shaw, 1995), 35.

14. Alter, *Genesis: Translation and Commentary*, 159.

15. Clyde Francisco, "Genesis," in *The Broadman Bible Commentary*, rev., gen. ed. Clifton J. Allen (Nashville: Broadman, 1969), 1:215.

16. Briscoe, *Running on Empty*, 35.

17. Genesis 35:22

18. Naomi H. Rosenblatt and Joshua Horwitz, *Wrestling with Angels: What Genesis Teaches Us About Our Spiritual Identity, Sexuality, and Personal Relationships* (New York: Delta/Dell, 1995), 275.

19. John Calvin, *Genesis,* in *The Crossway Classic Commentaries* (1554; repr., Wheaton, IL: Crossway, 2001), 258.

20. Calvin, *Genesis,* 258.

21. Kyle M. Yates Sr., "Genesis," in *The Wycliffe Bible Commentary*, ed. Charles F. Pfeiffer and Everett F. Harrison (Chicago: Moody Bible Institute, 1962), 33.

22. Alter, *Genesis: Translation and Commentary*, 159.

23. Francisco, "Genesis," 1:215.

24. Anne Roiphe, *Water from the Well: Sarah, Rebekah, Rachel, and Leah* (New York: William Morrow, 2006), 214.

25. Roiphe, *Water from the Well*, 215.

26. Eugenia Price, *God Speaks to Women Today* (Grand Rapids: Zondervan, 1964), 61.

27. Calvin, *Genesis,* 258.

28. Francisco, "Genesis," 1:216.

29. George Arthur Buttrick, dictionary ed., *The Interpreter's Dictionary of the Bible* (New York: Abingdon Press, 1962), 1:438.

30. Buttrick, *The Interpreter's Dictionary of the Bible,* 4:958.

31. Julia Staton, *What the Bible Says About Women* (Joplin, MO: College Press, 1980), 194.

32. Sharon Pace Jeansonne, *The Women of Genesis: From Sarah to Potiphar's Wife* (Minneapolis: Fortress Press, 1990), 77.

33. John E. Hartley, *New International Biblical Commentary: Genesis* (Peabody, MA: Hendrickson, 2000), 267.

34. Rose Sallberg Kam, *Their Stories, Our Stories: Women of the Bible* (New York: Continuum, 1995), 59.

35. Roiphe, *Water from the Well*, 217.

36. Claus Westermann, *Genesis 12–36: A Continental Commentary*, trans. John J. Scullion (Minneapolis: Fortress Press, 1995), 475.

37. Genesis 25:30

38. Cohen, *Self, Struggle and Change*, 142.

39. Jeansonne, *The Women of Genesis*, 77.

40. Janice Nunnally-Cox, *Foremothers: Women of the Bible* (New York: Seabury, 1981), 20.

41. Rosenblatt and Horwitz, *Wrestling with Angels,* 275.

42. Francisco, "Genesis," 1:216.

43. Cohen, *Self, Struggle and Change,* 142.

44. Alter, *Genesis: Translation and Commentary,* 160.

45. Roiphe, *Water from the Well,* 222.

46. Genesis 27:43

47. Genesis 29:28

48. Hartley, *New International Biblical Commentary: Genesis,* 266.

49. Francisco, "Genesis," 1:216.

50. Briscoe, *Running on Empty,* 37.

51. Derek Kidner, *Genesis: An Introduction and Commentary* (Downers Grove, IL: Tyndale, 1967), 162.

52. Kam, *Their Stories, Our Stories,* 61.

53. Herbert Lockyer, *All the Women of the Bible* (Grand Rapids: Zondervan, 1967), 45.

54. Ronson, *The Women of the Torah,* 140.

55. Walter Brueggemann, *Genesis: A Bible Commentary for Teaching and Preaching* (Atlanta: John Knox, 1982), 255.

56. Psalm 25:7

57. Luke 23:42

58. Ephraim A. Speiser, *The Anchor Bible: Genesis* (New York: Doubleday, 1964), 230.

59. Roiphe, *Water from the Well,* 228.

60. Frederick E. Greenspahn, *When Brothers Dwell Together: The Preeminence of Younger Siblings in the Hebrew Bible* (Oxford: Oxford University Press, 1994), 94.

61. Clarence Edward Macartney, *Great Women of the Bible* (New York: Abingdon-Cokesbury, 1942), 143.

62. Hartley, *New International Biblical Commentary: Genesis,* 267.

63. Genesis 30:26

64. Genesis 30:28

65. Genesis 30:36

66. Yates, "Genesis," 34.

67. Genesis 30:43

68. Genesis 31:2

69. Sherrill G. Stevens, *Layman's Bible Book Commentary,* vol. 1, *Genesis* (Nashville: Broadman, 1978), 102.

70. Genesis 31:7

71. Genesis 31:13

72. Jeansonne, *The Women of Genesis,* 80.

73. Alice Ogden Bellis, *Helpmates, Harlots, and Heroes: Women's Stories in the Hebrew Bible* (Louisville, KY: Westminster/John Knox, 1994), 85.

74. Speiser, *The Anchor Bible: Genesis,* 241.

75. Alter, *Genesis: Translation and Commentary,* 168.
76. Jeansonne, *The Women of Genesis,* 81.
77. Speiser, *The Anchor Bible: Genesis,* 245.
78. Christiana de Groot, "Genesis," in *The IVP Women's Bible Commentary,* ed. Catherine Clark Kroeger and Mary J. Evans (Downers Grove, IL: InterVarsity, 2002), 22–23.
79. Francisco, "Genesis," 1:219.
80. Yates, "Genesis," 34.
81. Warren W. Wiersbe, *Be Authentic: Genesis 25–50: Exhibiting Real Faith in the Real World* (Colorado Springs: Chariot Victor, 1997), 47.
82. Genesis 31:19
83. Exodus 20:3
84. Exodus 20:4
85. Exodus 20:12
86. Exodus 20:15
87. Miki Raver, *Listen to Her Voice: Women of the Hebrew Bible* (San Francisco: Chronicle Books, 1998), 56.
88. James G. Murphy, *Barnes' Notes: Genesis* (1873; repr., Grand Rapids: Baker, 1998), 406.
89. Yates, "Genesis," 34.
90. Hartley, *New International Biblical Commentary: Genesis,* 273.
91. Calvin, *Genesis,* 266.
92. Yates, "Genesis," 34.
93. Ronson, *The Women of the Torah,* 147.
94. Genesis 31:20, MSG
95. Genesis 31:23
96. Genesis 31:26
97. Hartley, *New International Biblical Commentary: Genesis,* 274.
98. Genesis 31:29
99. Hartley, *New International Biblical Commentary: Genesis,* 274.
100. Genesis 31:29
101. Genesis 31:30
102. Genesis 31:32
103. Gerhard von Rad, *Genesis: A Commentary* (Philadelphia: Westminster Press, 1972), 309.
104. Kidner, *Genesis: An Introduction and Commentary,* 166.
105. Genesis 31:33
106. Alter, *Genesis: Translation and Commentary,* 172.
107. Meredith G. Kline, "Genesis," in *The New Bible Commentary Revised* (Grand Rapids: Eerdmans, 1970), 104.

108. Von Rad, *Genesis: A Commentary*, 310.
109. Genesis 31:49, KJV
110. Genesis 31:55
111. Morton, *Women of the Bible*, 48.
112. Matthew Henry, *Matthew Henry's Commentary on the Whole Bible*, vol. 1, *Genesis to Deuteronomy* (1706; repr., Peabody, MA: Hendrickson, 1991), 164.
113. Speiser, *The Anchor Bible: Genesis*, 272.
114. Calvin, *Genesis*, 277.
115. Kidner, *Genesis: An Introduction and Commentary*, 176.
116. Macartney, *Great Women of the Bible*, 148.
117. Morton, *Women of the Bible*, 47–48.
118. Ruth 4:11
119. Roiphe, *Water from the Well*, 255.
120. Roiphe, *Water from the Well*, 260.
121. Morton, *Women of the Bible*, 46.
122. Sylvia Charles, *Women in the Word* (South Plainfield, NJ: Bridge Publishing, 1984), 73.
123. Quotations Book, www.quotationsbook.com.
124. Isaiah 25:8

Conclusion: Endless Life

1. Romans 7:24
2. Psalm 22:6
3. Genesis 32:10
4. Job 42:6
5. Romans 4:18
6. Romans 4:16
7. Cornelius Vanderwaal, *Search the Scriptures*, vol. 1, *Genesis-Exodus* (St. Catherines, Ontario, Canada: Paideia Press, 1978), 88.
8. Romans 9:10–12
9. Romans 9:11–12, MSG
10. Romans 9:13
11. Romans 9:14
12. Romans 9:14
13. Romans 9:15, MSG
14. Romans 9:16
15. John 15:5
16. Romans 3:24, MSG
17. Titus 3:7, MSG
18. Titus 3:7, MSG

Acknowledgments

Alas, I was *more* than a Slightly Bad Girl, delivering this manuscript to my publisher waaaay past deadline. A heartfelt hug to those who waited so patiently and offered such fine editorial direction: Sara Fortenberry, Jeanette Thomason, Laura Barker, Carol Bartley, Glenna Salsbury, Lisa Guest, and my own dear son, Matt Higgs. May God bless you many times over for your generous efforts.

To all my supportive friends at WaterBrook Press—Steve Cobb, Dudley Delffs, Ginia Hairston, Carie Freimuth, Lori Addicott, Leah McMahan, Mark Ford, Kristopher Orr, and so many others—thank you for the creativity and generosity you've bestowed on this grateful author again and again.

Finally, to my one and only husband, Bill Higgs: you are the wisest home and office manager, the finest chef, the best father, and the dearest man I have ever known. I'm so glad we said, "I do."

A Chat with Liz

For the fourth entry in her Bad Girls of the Bible series, best-selling author Liz Curtis Higgs shares the lessons she's learned from five women who've lived in her writing study since the turn of this century. Sarah, Hagar, Rebekah, Leah, and Rachel follow in the footsteps of the Bad Girls, Really Bad Girls, and Not-So-Bad Girl before them, captured in a series of books, workbooks, and videos that have already helped more than one million women around the world experience God's grace anew.

Here, Liz gives us a closer look at how *Slightly Bad Girls of the Bible* came to be and the discoveries she made while spending so many years immersed in the lives of these biblical women. Readers often ask for more details about Liz's spiritual journey, so you'll find her testimony here as well as helpful suggestions for using *Slightly Bad Girls of the Bible* in a group study.

Now let's join Liz Curtis Higgs for a sister-to-sister chat…

How did you come to see these five women as Slightly Bad rather than the Good Girls we often picture them to be?

Many of us first learned about Sarah, Rebekah, and Rachel when we were children. Sunday school teachers, using flannelboard figures, simplified and sanitized the biblical stories, leaving out the scandalous details, hoping these seemingly virtuous women would inspire young girls to go and do likewise. No wonder we mistakenly pictured the matriarchs as Ultra Good Girls! Hagar and Leah, meanwhile, seldom made it to the flannelboard. They lived in the margins, unnoticed, when in truth they both played major roles in the patriarchal stories.

Now that we've studied the Genesis account firsthand and discovered the truth for ourselves—sorting out good from bad, fact from myth—we can see Sarah and company for who they really were. Frankly, I find that reality *more* encouraging than if they'd turned out to be paragons of virtue. Since

I'm far from perfect, I need to know how God can work through strong-willed, impatient women.

Which category do most biblical women fall under: Bad, Really Bad, Slightly Bad, or Good Girl? What about modern women?

Jesus clearly stated, "No one is good—except God alone" (Mark 10:18), meaning all the women of the Bible actually qualify as Bad Girls. And so do we. We're all sinners in need of a Savior. *All* of us, then and now. Even those apparent Good Girls of the Bible—Ruth, Abigail, Esther, Anna, and Elizabeth, for example—must have had flaws, the details of which the Lord chose not to include in his Word. No need to imagine what those imperfections were, yet we can be sure they had them just as we do.

Because human nature (including mine) revels in categorizing and comparing, we often think of good, better, best; bad, worse, worst. Or, in my case, Slightly Bad, Not-So-Bad, just plain Bad, and Really Bad! Yet Paul reminds us, "There is no one righteous, not even one" (Romans 3:10). So, biblical or modern, we must confess we're all bad—and the Lord is all good. The categories I chose simply gave us a place to begin our discussion of these women with whom we so closely identify, no matter which Bad Girls badge they're wearing.

What discoveries did you make while researching and writing *Slightly Bad Girls of the Bible*?

I was intrigued by all the threads of commonality among the Hebrew women. Barrenness. Feistiness. Impatience. An eagerness to take matters into their own hands. A willingness to deceive even those they loved. A relationship with God, however tenuous it might appear to us. Until I studied them all in a row, I'd not seen the strong family resemblance. Soon I discovered some of those same threads running through my own life, not because we're related by blood, but because we're related by spiritual birth—as you and I are. We're God's women: chosen by God, blessed by God, loved by God.

Yet it was Hagar who took my breath away. Before I examined her story in Genesis, she was a shadowy figure for me; I knew little beyond her status as an Egyptian slave. Then here she came strolling across the page, a head-strong woman, happy to stand up to her mistress and proud to be pregnant by her master. Well! She was sought out by the Lord *twice* in the wilderness; she was spoken to, provided for, and watched over. Hagar has no small claim to fame; clearly God honored her and the seed in her womb.

I'm still grappling with God's promises to Hagar, his involvement in Ishmael's future, and how that relates to today's tensions in the Middle East. I am neither a historian nor a politician, but I know there is something to be grasped here, some truth much bigger than my mind can comprehend. I rest in knowing "the plans of the LORD stand firm forever, the purposes of his heart through all generations" (Psalm 33:11).

What preconceived notions potentially stand in the way of our learning new and vital truths from these matriarchs of faith?
Some of the Bad Girls we've studied in books past—Athaliah, Michal, Herodias—were unfamiliar names to many of us, so we came to their stories with blank slates and fresh chalk. But our church nurseries are filled with Sarahs, Rebekahs, and Rachels. We think we know these women and certainly consider them positive role models, or we wouldn't name our daughters after them. (No Jezebels in most nurseries, I've noticed!)

In order to glean something fresh from their stories and apply those truths to our lives, we have to resist the urge to protest, "But I thought she…" and "Wasn't she the one who…" and simply read each verse anew, especially the verses that tell us things we don't want to know. These matriarchs were sometimes sharp tongued and short tempered; they laughed at God, tried to be God, ignored God; they ordered their husbands around.

Who knew? Now we do.

You've spent years with Leah and Rachel, both for this book and for your Scottish historical novels. What do you find most compelling about these sisters and their entangled lives?
I love stories brimming with genuine conflict. Two women sharing one hus-band definitely qualifies. Yet theirs was not a typical love triangle: Leah

wanted Jacob, Jacob wanted Rachel, and Rachel wanted children like Leah had. The fact that they were sisters, though very different in appearance and temperament, and that Jacob was their cousin, only heightened the drama. They were family before anyone said, "I do."

And oh, the wedding night! We have sufficient action to paint a vivid scene, yet many crucial details remain unaccounted for: Rachel's location and Leah's motivation, Laban's duplicity and Jacob's stupidity.

Then the birth of each son revealed the spiritual condition of his mother's heart, a plot device only the Lord could have conceived. Despite their mutual heartache, all three characters grew throughout the lengthy Genesis narrative, which makes for an engaging story in any century.

Sarah, Rebekah, and Rachel are described as beautiful and loved; Hagar and Leah are not. How can we come to a place of peace about our appearance and our relationships—two aspects of our lives that often overshadow the rest?

As we seek deeper meaning in our lives, those among us who are beautiful (by the world's standards; all women are beautiful to God) might look for beauty in others and resist the temptation to compare. For the less than beautiful (again, only by the world's measure), we can take a page from Leah's book and turn our poor-me pining into praise, reminding ourselves that beauty is fleeting and relationships, though a blessing, are temporal. Peace comes in realizing the beauty that matters most is "the unfading beauty of a gentle and quiet spirit" (1 Peter 3:4). And the love that truly satisfies comes from above, "so we know and rely on the love God has for us" (1 John 4:16).

Do I believe this stuff, or am I just spouting Christian platitudes? Girlfriend, I believe it with all my heart. I've spent the past twenty-five years learning to celebrate my abundant body, my thinning hair, my nearsighted eyes, and everything else God blessed me with. When we see our appearance as the Lord's gift to us and not a curse, we can get on with our lives, focusing on others rather than ourselves. And though I am one loved woman (only Bill knows why!), I also spent years celebrating my singleness, and I continue to encourage my sisters to let God's love fill all the neglected corners, all the empty spaces.

Beautiful or plain, loved or unloved, our flawed Slightly Bad Girls discovered the same eternal truth: "The LORD is faithful to all his promises and loving toward all he has made" (Psalm 145:13).

Many of us grew up hearing about biblical women as our role models for virtuous behavior. Where did you get the idea to look more closely at the women of the Bible from this unusual perspective?

Years ago, when I began traveling and speaking, biblical sisters were my favorite topic. I covered the usual Good Girls—Jochebed and Miriam, Ruth and Naomi, Mary and Elizabeth—then tossed in Jezebel for a little zing, sharing my testimony and confessing my own bulldozer approach to life. When women sidled up to me after my presentations and murmured, "I'm like Jezebel too," I realized I might not be the only one (no kidding, Liz!). And so I began collecting ideas for a book project with Jezebel as the centerpiece, letting the notion simmer while I stayed busy writing picture books and raising two dear children to read them.

Fast-forward to June 1998, when I shared the platform at a women's conference in Michigan with a gifted Bible teacher, Elizabeth George. After she was introduced, Elizabeth told the audience she was writing a book about women of the Bible, then added with a smile, "Only the good ones, of course."

Troublemaker that I am, when it was my turn to speak, I jumped up and announced, "Then I'm going to write a book called *Bad Girls of the Bible*." When a thousand women exploded with laughter—including dear Elizabeth—I glanced heavenward in astonishment. *Lord, is that you?* Not just Jezebel, but *lots* of Bad Girls? Within weeks, I'd written a sample chapter (Potiphar's wife) and faxed it to WaterBrook Press, asking if they'd be willing to publish a book with such an outrageous title. They were; they did; and here we are.

Your obvious love for God's Word shines through every page of this series. What do you see as the value of Bible study for women, given how busy our lives are these days?

I truly understand the too-busy-for-Bible-study challenge. But I also know that when we carve out time to gather with a group or study on our own, God richly rewards our willingness to open his Word and dive in. Scripture changes us at the cellular level. It touches our hearts, renews our minds, and ultimately transforms our behavior. "The word is very near you; it is in your mouth and in your heart so you may obey it" (Deuteronomy 30:14). That's the value of Bible study: we're made new, from the inside out.

I brought home my first Bible in February 1982, the month I awakened to the reality of Christ as the Living Word of God. I'd always seen the Bible as a dry, boring collection of archaic rules. Imagine my surprise when I discovered it was a life-changing book filled with wisdom, grace, and incredible stories. Talk about a page-turner!

Each translation has something to offer: King James for the beauty of its language; New American Standard for its fine rendering of the Greek (it's also my favorite for memorization); the New Living Translation for a contemporary take; and the New International Version, a solid standard. For twenty-first-century application, it's hard to beat Eugene Peterson's brilliant paraphrase, *The Message*. Whichever translation helps you grasp the power of God's truth is the right one to use.

If you're particularly pressed for time, try digesting the Word in small bites. One short psalm. Ten verses from Proverbs. A single parable from the Gospels. Even one verse, memorized and meditated upon each day, can restore and strengthen our faith. None of us are too busy for a verse a day. Once you get a taste, you'll want a plateful, I promise.

Why do you think so many women are drawn to the idea of studying the Bad Girls of the Bible?

Let's face it, we've *done* the Good Girls, over and over. They inspire us, yes, but they also intimidate and even discourage us, especially when we compare their virtues to our failures, their courage to our cowardice. The lives of these two dozen Bad Girls, on the other hand, create a more colorful and varied tapestry for us to examine. We're encouraged by those whose lives are redeemed. *There's hope for me.* Others offer us cautionary tales. *I'm not going there!* And some give us much to consider. *Would I do the same?*

There's another reason women have been responsive to this series: Good or Bad, Girls just wanna have *fun.* Oh, the photos I've received of dear Christian women draped in filmy veils and sporting thick, black eyeliner! One Bible study leader described the Bad Girls series as "a refreshing, funny, thought-provoking, wonderful look at these women in the Bible we can *so* relate to." I'm ever in debt to my sisters who got the concept from the get-go.

Have you seen any differences between how Good Girls and Bad Girls respond to the truths they encounter in the lives of these biblical women?

Only the Lord knows our hearts, so I'm careful not to judge a sister by her words or her actions. But if we're talking about those of us who've spent a lifetime walking the straight and narrow versus sisters who've wandered down some dark alleys, then yes, such women may respond differently, yet they often take away the same truths.

One sister wrote, "I've done Bible study all my life. However, your study took me to places I've never been. It brought me face to face with my humanness and showed me just how much God loves and forgives me." Though we'd consider her a Good Girl, this woman wisely embraced God's grace afresh. A self-described Bad Girl also shared her story: "This has been the hardest year of my life. In a jail cell with forty-eight other women, I gave my life to Christ and was baptized shortly thereafter. Now I want to be obedient and faithful. I want to be a godly woman and a mentor to others."

Isn't God amazing? He doesn't see us as Good Girls or Bad Girls; he simply sees us as *his:* "For I have redeemed you; I have summoned you by name; you are mine" (Isaiah 43:1).

Can you share a few highlights from women who have expressed to you how God has touched their hearts through this series?

Believe me, God alone deserves the credit for encouraging words like these…

- "I was really worried about being forgiven. Now I know that through God's love anything can happen."
- "The cumulative effect of reading a bit and saying 'That is me' has inspired me to look at my past as a Bad Girl and to look to the future as a Not-So-Bad Girl."
- "Your reinforcement throughout your books of how much God loves us made me weep!"
- "I'd been wrestling with feeling unworthy, feeling I'd let down my heavenly Father. Thanks to your wonderful book, I have found answers, been enlightened, and truly blessed."

As you connect with women through your books and speaking engagements, what need seems to weigh heaviest on their hearts?

One woman's question says it all: "Can I know for sure that God has forgiven me, even if I can't forgive myself?" Forgiveness and the peace it produces elude us. Without them, we remain perpetually stuck, going through the motions on Sundays but not moving forward in our faith.

The answer to the first part is, of course, *yes*. God has forgiven us completely: "as far as the east is from the west, so far has he removed our transgressions from us" (Psalm 103:12). Never doubt the cross. Our sins have been paid in full. All of them, for all time. Before we even got here, grace was in place: "This grace was given us in Christ Jesus before the beginning of time" (2 Timothy 1:9).

As to the second part of her question, I have surprising news: the concept of "forgiving yourself" isn't in the Bible. Honest. Not in there. Instead, God says, "My grace is sufficient for you" (2 Corinthians 12:9). Calvary was enough, dear sister. Truly *enough*. We can't add to his grace, nor can we subtract from it. It's a finished work.

The ongoing questions I've received on this topic are what prompted me to write *Embrace Grace,* offering further encouragement for any sister struggling to believe that she is truly loved and utterly forgiven.

You often describe yourself as a Former Bad Girl. What's the story behind that?

A lengthy and sordid tale, I'm afraid; what follows is the Cliffs Notes version.

Not much happened before 1970. At least, not in my life. I was the quintessential Good Girl: honor roll, church choir, Girl Scouts, yada yada. But then I turned sixteen, got my driver's license, and strapped on my Bad Girl shoes. My rebel's heart quickened when I rode in fast cars with fast boys. I didn't feel very pretty, so if a guy told me I looked good, I was his, if only for the night. Half the night. An hour.

Marijuana made me laugh (and eat), speed kept me awake, whiskey made me feel sexy, and cocaine made me feel like having more cocaine. For me the 1970s were a blur of sex, drugs, and rock'n'roll. Like I said, sordid.

By 1981 I'd found my way to Kentucky (by way of Pennsylvania, Indiana, and Michigan), having traveled up and down the dial as a radio personality. A husband-and-wife morning team joined our station, and we soon became friends, though I could see we lived very different lives. They were *so* straight! They talked about God. They read the Bible. They were weird.

They also hugged me regularly. And loved me unconditionally.

Little by little my heart softened toward God. Could he possibly forgive me, after all I'd done? He'd loved me as a child; could he love me still?

Early in January 1982 I showed up at their church, determined to see if there were any other people like those two: funny, loving, nonjudgmental, Bible-toting Christians. There were whole pews full of them.

Then I heard God's Word. And I knew why I'd come.

When I gave my heart to Christ, he gave it right back to me, good as new. The first verse I memorized will always be my favorite: "Therefore, if anyone is in Christ, he is a new creation; the old has gone, the new has come!" (2 Corinthians 5:17). Or as we say at the Higgs house, "Ta-da!"

So are you always a Good Girl now?

Not even close.

Granted, the days of my flashy, splashy sins are behind me: I didn't smoke a joint in the church parking lot last Wednesday night, I don't carry a small flask of Southern Comfort in my purse, and I haven't checked out the sound guy at church and thought, "Oh baby."

But I still sin. You might not always notice, but I do. God notices too. Unkind thoughts about another writer's work. Unkind words to my dear husband. Unkind actions toward my rolling suitcase when it won't roll. (My suitcase doesn't care, but the people hanging around baggage claim didn't ask for a PDA: Public Display of Aggravation.)

So I'll stick with being a Former Bad Girl. Kinda like our redeemed Rahab, who even in the New Testament is still called "Rahab the prostitute" (James 2:25). Once an FBG, always an FBG, and that's okay by me. George Santayana said, "Those who cannot remember the past are condemned to repeat it." I remember, sis. The only kind of repetition I want is going back to the Lord and to his Word, day in and day out.

What's behind your decision to first look at each story from a contemporary, fictional perspective? Why not jump right into the Bible study—or just keep the stories grounded in a biblical time period?

Both those options make so much sense and would have shortened my writing time considerably! But I wanted to try something different. Something unexpected, even a tad risky. By introducing each biblical character through contemporary fiction I hoped readers might see them as living, breathing people, just like us. It also keeps us from dismissing these ancient stories with the excuse of "That was then, this is now." The struggles of these women are as relevant and timely as ever, and I pray the opening stories demonstrate that.

Plus, I love writing fiction as much as I love teaching the Bible. (Oh! Did she say that?) Yes, I did. And for good reason. Story was born in the heart of

God. He is *the* Storyteller, the author of our faith (Hebrews 12:2) and the author of life (Acts 3:15).

Story moves us like nothing else. It sneaks past our defenses and makes a beeline to the heart. You can resist rhetoric, but it's harder to fight narrative. Story draws you in; setting helps you feel at home; characters make you care what happens. Without realizing it, you're turning pages, no longer aware of the chair you're sitting in or the weather outside your window. Story has taken you somewhere else—a place where God can transform you.

What steps do you take to be sure your "girlfriend theology" is biblically accurate?

I love books. Love buying them, reading them, shelving them, pulling them back out again. The Internet is fine for some projects, but for biblical studies I like printed and bound resources that have passed muster with an editorial board and been published by a reputable house.

I read classic commentaries by John Calvin from the sixteenth century and Matthew Henry from the early eighteenth century because of the timelessness of their insights. And contemporary writers like Carolyn Nabors Baker *(Caught in a Higher Love)*, Virginia Stem Owens *(Daughters of Eve)*, and Rose Sallberg Kam *(Their Stories, Our Stories)* keep me grounded in the needs of women here and now. Then there are all the great nineteenth-century writers, their evangelical zeal still burning from the Great Awakening. And many Jewish writers who offer a unique perspective on the stories from the Hebrew Bible.

When I'm working in Genesis (all those Slightly Bad Girls lived there, plus Eve, Lot's wife, Potiphar's wife, and Tamar), I drag out the big guns in biblical scholarship: Gerhard von Rad, Walter Brueggemann, Derek Kidner, Claus Westermann, Ephraim A. Speiser, and others. The four-volume *Interpreter's Dictionary of the Bible* is within easy reach too, as are more than a dozen translations of the Bible.

Last, but truly not least, I turn to my husband. Before we married, Bill earned a PhD in Old Testament Languages and so serves as my final reader before the book heads to the printer. Bill wisely insists I do all my own research, all my own writing, and all my own interpreting, but it *is* a blessing (and a relief) to know my pages pass through his hands before my readers see them.

Even though you obviously take God's Word seriously, you don't take yourself too seriously. Why do we find a thread of humor running through your Bad Girls of the Bible series?

You can blame my family for that. As the youngest of six kids, I grew up surrounded by people who loved to laugh. Humor was currency in our home, highly valued by my parents and siblings. At the Higgs house we also delight in pointing out funny stuff and laughing together. Humor puts things in perspective and keeps the hard times from wearing us down.

In my writing, I don't really *try* to be funny, but the occasional amusing phrase does seem to find its way onto the page. My hope is that the humorous moments don't detract from the serious ones. As a speaker and Bible teacher, I use humor to put an audience at ease and to help them stay engaged through the meatier passages. That's my goal with the Bad Girls series as well, using a touch of humor to keep us involved with the story and the study. When one reader admits, "Your books crack me up," and the next one says, "I learned so much," then I know I'm on the right track.

Can you explain more about your writing process for this series, including your approach to research and how you decide where to set each fictional retelling?

I begin with Scripture, the only words that truly matter. Fourteen translations and dozens of commentaries and research books later, these Bad Girls begin to live and breathe in my writing study. Because I travel, I need all my research at my fingertips, so into the computer the words go—first the biblical text, then relevant comments from scholars to help me understand each verse. That research process takes about three months for each book.

Next I write the nonfiction portion, trying to strike a balance between something that's enjoyable and easily read yet something that has enough meat to feed readers looking for substance. All that takes another three or four months.

Finally, I get to write the fictional openings. (Like saving a brownie for dessert.) By that point, I *know* that Bad Girl. Know her story, know her heart, and know what she wants us to observe about her, close up. I choose a contemporary name that approximates the biblical one or is symbolic of the character's journey, pick a city that suits her style and her story, and off we go. Those opening scenes come quickly.

Once I send the manuscript off to my editor, I rent the two dozen movies that came out while I was writing and see if I have any friends left who want to go to lunch.

What's the greatest personal insight you've gained from writing this series?

In studying the Old Testament stories, I was amazed by God's patience. He could have pushed the *smite* button many times, yet he didn't. In exploring the New Testament stories, I delighted in watching Jesus interact with women, hearing the kindness in his words, imagining the warmth of his expression, seeing again and again how he cared for people and didn't judge them. I love the Pauline epistles, yet it was grand to be immersed in the Gospel accounts and spend time with Jesus as he traveled from town to town.

An even bigger surprise came when my books found their way into readers' hands. Letters and e-mails poured in, more personal than any prompted by my earlier works. When letters began, "I've never told anyone this but…," I knew the words that followed would be sacred, painful. I also knew the courage it took to put them on paper, to send them on their way, to wait for a reply. That gift of trust from my readers was the biggest blessing of all.

How would you recommend using the Bad Girls series in a group setting?

All four **books** in the series follow the same basic format—contemporary fiction, nonfiction teaching, summary lessons, and discussion questions—yet each book covers different women in Scripture. Feel free to read the books in any order that suits. *Bad Girls of the Bible* has ten chapters, *Really Bad Girls of the Bible* and *Slightly Bad Girls of the Bible* both have eight, and there are six chapters in *Unveiling Mary Magdalene* (previously released as *Mad Mary*). The questions included at the end of each chapter are designed for personal reflection or for small group discussion. Using their own notebooks, women can jot down their answers and share them each week. At the very end of each book you'll find supportive scriptures for each of those questions.

The **workbooks** are designed to go *with* the books. If you enjoy daily preparation and digging deeper into the Bible, then the workbooks are of great value. Each of the discussion questions from the book is significantly expanded, directing you back to Scripture to examine the story itself more closely, as well as pointing you elsewhere in the Bible to reveal the bigger picture. But do keep in mind that they're not designed to stand alone, nor do they parallel the DVDs. So many workbook questions direct readers back to the original book that not having it in hand might yield more frustration than insight. If, for budgetary reasons, each member can afford a book but not a workbook, I'd suggest investing in at least one copy of the workbook for the teacher/group leader to use in lesson preparation.

The four **videos** on DVD are each one hour long and completely different in content. They capture on film live presentations in which I cover material from the book of the same title. In the case of *Bad Girls of the Bible*, *Really Bad Girls of the Bible*, and *Slightly Bad Girls of the Bible*, the biblical women are introduced in short, thumbnail sketches, so any of those three videos works best for the *first* hour your group meets. Women will hear my heart for the subject matter, discover a bit of my testimony, and (I hope) be enthusiastic as you distribute their books for the study to come. Because *Unveiling Mary Magdalene* focuses on one woman, I'd recommend showing that video for the *last* session of the study, reinforcing the lessons learned and sending women out the door joyfully shouting with Mary Magdalene, "I have seen the Lord!" (John 20:18).

About the Author

An award-winning speaker, LIZ CURTIS HIGGS has addressed audiences from more than fifteen hundred platforms in all fifty states and in eight foreign countries. She is the author of twenty-six books, with more than three million copies in print, including her best-selling nonfiction books, *Bad Girls of the Bible* and *Really Bad Girls of the Bible,* and her best-selling historical fiction, *Thorn in My Heart; Fair Is the Rose; Whence Came a Prince,* a Christy Award winner; and *Grace in Thine Eyes,* listed in the Top Five Christian Fiction books for 2006 by *Library Journal.*

Liz is delighted to hear from readers and enjoys keeping in touch once a year through her free printed newsletter, *The Graceful Heart.* For the latest issue, please write to her:

Liz Curtis Higgs
P.O. Box 43577
Louisville, KY 40253-0577

Or visit her Web site:
www.LizCurtisHiggs.com

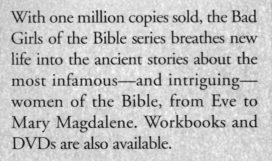